Lawrence Ferlinghetti

POET-AT-LARGE

Larry Smith

SOUTHERN ILLINOIS UNIVERSITY PRESS

Carbondale and Edwardsville

Printed in the United States of America
Designed by Guy Fleming
Production supervised by John DeBacher

Library of Congress Cataloging in Publication Data
Smith, Larry
Lawrence Ferlinghetti, poet-at-large.
Bibliography: p.
Includes index.
1. Ferlinghetti, Lawrence. 2. Poets, American—20th century—Biography. I. Title.
PS3511.E557Z88 1983 811'.54 82-10835
ISBN 0-8093-1101-1

FRONTISPIECE, Lawrence Ferlinghetti, 1973.
Photograph by Ilka Hartmann
Courtesy of New Directions Publishing Corp.

CONTENTS

ILLUSTRATIONS

PREFACE

COMING to the writing of Lawrence Ferlinghetti presents various obstacles, problems which later reflect obvious strengths in the art. Ferlinghetti is a multi-artist—poet, dramatist, film writer, novelist, painter—adept in various approaches—realist, surrealist, abstract-expressionist, absurdist—who further dares to violate the American "specialist" syndrome by becoming an equal literary force as an editor and publisher. Defying classification as either an academic poet or a brawling street poet, combining a doctorate from the Sorbonne with a street-wise experience of life, Ferlinghetti is intellectually aware as well as humanistically involved. Add to this his direct socio-political engagement and his broad popularity and you have a writer who goes far beyond the limits of the typical. In fact, what Ferlinghetti presents in his work and his life is the embodiment of the contemporary poet-hero broken out of his traditional insularity and forged by experience into a model of the engaged spokesman of our times.

One more paradox. While Ferlinghetti is distinctly tied to America, and to San Francisco in particular, he is best understood as an international artist. While his image of the poet as public-prophet is derived in part from the example of Walt Whitman and Henry David Thoreau and supported by the later examples of Ezra Pound, William Carlos Williams, and E. E. Cummings, his role is more truly in character with the international figure of the artist as revolutionary truthsayer, the see-er and seer model of Arthur Rimbaud and Guillaume Apollinaire. Embracing Rimbaud's sense of the radical immediacy of the poetic act in desperate times, Ferlinghetti is equally at one with Apollinaire's expansive vision of "The New Spirit and the Poets." Apollinaire's call is for a writing to emblazon "perspectives on the universe and on the soul of man, and the sense of duty which lays bare our feelings and limits or rather contains their manifestations. It strives further to inherit from the romantics a curiosity which will incite it to explore all the domains suitable for furnishing literary subject matter which will permit life to be exalted in whatever form it occurs. To explore truth, to search for it, as much in the ethnic domain, for example as in that of the imagination—those are the principal characteristics of the new spirit."[1] Like Apollinaire, Ferlinghetti seeks to fully connect and expand the life-art relationship by respecting no artificial limits and by boldly seeking the intellectual and emotional truth, wherever it leads—in the authentic act of the poet. Like Apollinaire, he dares to live his art. Ferlinghetti's more immediate models of the engaged artist are France's Jean-Paul Sartre and Albert Camus, America's Kenneth Patchen, Kenneth Rexroth, and Allen Ginsberg.

What all of this points to is the absolute necessity of adjusting our critical perspectives to those of the poet and his work. Ferlinghetti's writing does follow a tradition, but it is the expansive and dangerous tradition of the poet who boldly seeks Rimbaud's goal "to change life" through his art. By approaching Lawrence Ferlinghetti as the contemporary poet-prophet of engagement and wonder we can more truly understand both his methods and his multi-achievement as: oral poet, poet of the streets, super-realist, actualist of the public nightmare, political poet, poetry-and-jazz poet, bohemian poet, painter-poet, absurd expressionist dramatist, avant-garde novelist, anti-Art poet, and, finally, visionary poet of consciousness. The engaged poetics of his works, integral with his stance as poet-at-large, will be explored closely in chapter two and then applied to his various art forms—poetry, drama, and prose—in the succeeding chapters. Stance and art are mutually revealed by virtue of Ferlinghetti's authentic commitment, for his self-declared goal remains clear—to be the poet as "*agent provocateur*—subversive, anarchistic, and prophetic."[2]

We begin with a biographical basis. Ferlinghetti follows the surrealists in their disdain for history as opposed to the immediacy and necessity of the poetic act, and has for years eschewed those who overvalued the factual sense of reality through personal biography. He has been notoriously evasive of biographers until recently when he consented to cooperate with Neeli Cherkovski in his *Ferlinghetti: A Biography* (Doubleday, 1979). His maturing respect for historical perspective is also evidenced in his most recent chronicle of *Literary San Francisco: A Pictorial History* (Harper & Row and City Lights, 1980), which he coauthored with his City Lights coeditor Nancy Joyce Peters. Recognizing that biographical facts are secondary to the creation and consideration of the writing, this study places them before the reader as a means of seeing the life and art in their relationship. More than an interesting story of a noted American writer, editor, and political activist, the biographical facts provide a means of comprehending and connecting Ferlinghetti's basic motives with the resultant diversity of contents and forms he achieved—the cohesive core of the personality form. By engaging the person of the poet more fully here we perceive the resonating framework of his life and work, we understand the nature, forces, and form of that personality which shapes his work and which makes him the contemporary model of the engaged poet-at-large.

There is no attempt here at a critical summing up, only a trust in a truer opening of the work through a long overdue, full critical consideration. The chronology which follows sets out the historical facts of Lawrence Ferlinghetti's life, writing, and publishing in their time relationship. It is indebted to the author's cooperation and to the groundwork done by Neeli Cherkovski, whose study suggests the strong sense of Ferlinghetti's search for self which underlies the writing—motive and fact—of Ferlinghetti's entire career. This theme and the essential cohesiveness of Ferlinghetti's life and art will be treated in the biographical portrait which follows the chronology.

This study ends with some conclusions concerning a reassessment of Ferlinghetti's quarter century of achievement and with an annotated bibliography which is offered as a starting point for future study. The intent throughout is not to sum up but rather to open up the truly deserving body of Ferlinghetti's work.

Bowling Green State University
Firelands College
Huron, Ohio
May 18, 1982

LARRY SMITH

ACKNOWLEDGMENTS

I wish to express my appreciation for the initial advice and encouragement of J. H. Matthews, Stephen Smigocki, Franklin Rosemont, Robert Hawley, and John Tytell. They knew such a book was necessary.

I was assisted in my research by Nancy Joyce Peters, Miriam Patchen, and, of course, Lawrence Ferlinghetti who patiently answered questions and opened his library and manuscripts to me. More than anything else, this book is an acknowledgment of the lasting work of Lawrence Ferlinghetti.

I am grateful for the research support of the Firelands College Library and Bowling Green State University. Mary Jane Hahler assisted me in translations from the Spanish and French; Denni Horan provided technical help.

And to my wife, Ann, and my family I owe thanks for their encouragement and understanding.

In particular, I express gratitude to New Directions Publishing Corporation for permission to quote from and to reproduce copyrighted material from:

Lawrence Ferlinghetti, *Who Are We Now?*
Copyright © 1976 by Lawrence Ferlinghetti.

Lawrence Ferlinghetti, *Landscapes of Living & Dying*.
Copyright © 1979 by Lawrence Ferlinghetti.

Lawrence Ferlinghetti, *Endless Life*.
Copyright © 1981 by Lawrence Ferlinghetti.

Lawrence Ferlinghetti, *The Mexican Night*.
Copyright © 1970 by Lawrence Ferlinghetti.

Lawrence Ferlinghetti, *Her*.
Copyright © 1960 by Lawrence Ferlinghetti.

And for selected photographs as indicated in the text.

I am also endebted to City Lights Books for permission to quote from and to reproduce copyrighted material from:

City Lights Journal # 3. Copyright © 1966 by Lawrence Ferlinghetti.
Lawrence Ferlinghetti, *Northwest Ecolog*.
Copyright © 1978 by Lawrence Ferlinghetti.

Lawrence Ferlinghetti, *Pictures of the Gone World*.
Copyright © 1955 by Lawrence Ferlinghetti.

And for selected photographs as indicated in the text from The Ferlinghetti Collection.

I am endebted to Elsa Dorfman and the Witkin Gallery, Inc., for permission to reproduce a photographic image of "Lawrence Ferlinghetti at the Walker Evans Show." Copyright © 1979 Elsa Dorfman and The Whitkin Gallery, Inc.

Lawrence Ferlinghetti

CHRONOLOGY

1919 Born Mar. 24, Yonkers, New York, to Clemence Mendes-Monsanto (French and Portuguese Sephardic Jew) and Charles Ferling (Italian immigrant); youngest of five brothers. Father dies seven months before his birth; mother is committed to State Hospital in Poughkeepsie, New York, shortly after Lawrence's birth (for five years).

1920 Lawrence is given to Emily Mendes-Monsanto (great-aunt) who leaves her husband and takes infant Ferlinghetti to France to live at the Alsatian capital of Strasbourg. First five years he speaks French.

1924 Emily ("French mother") returns with young Ferlinghetti to New York where she is reconciled with husband Ludwig, who in turn teaches the child English.

1925 Emily takes Lawrence to live with wealthy Bisland family in exclusive Bronxville, New York, where she tutors the children of Presley and Anna Lawrence Bisland. One day Emily disappears forever, leaving him to live with the Bisland family.

1927 Attends Riverside Country School, a boarding school near Bronxville. He begins to write poetry.

1929–33 Attends Bronxville Public School, boarding with Zilla Larned Wilson family; adolescence—becomes Eagle Scout, delivers newspapers, plays basketball, enjoys printshop courses; becomes a member of the "Parkway Road Pirates" street gang and is arrested for petty stealing.

1933 Sally Bisland gives him a copy of Baudelair poems (French and English), stirs an interest in literature.

1933–37 Attends Mount Hermon, private high school near Greenfield, Mass. He encounters the writings of Thomas Wolfe and Henry David Thoreau. Graduates June 1937.

1937–41 Attends University of North Carolina at Chapel Hill; reads James T. Farrell, John Dos Passos, Hemingway, Faulkner; begins to write novel inspired by *Look Homeward, Angel.*

1939 Summer, travels with two college friends to Mexico via freight train and hitchhiking; reads populist writers—Carl Sandburg, Edgar Lee Masters, Vachel Lindsay.

1940 Begins keeping notebooks of his writing; influenced by professor Phillips Russell.

1941 Graduates from Chapel Hill with a degree in journalism; spends summer on Little Whaleboat Island, Maine.

1941–45 U.S. Navy service, stationed in New York, Mid-Atlantic Ocean, England, Norfolk, Virginia, at Normandy in subchaser during landing of Allied forces, France. Achieves rank of lieutenant commander. During stays in New York City, befriends Laura Lou Lyons, a Swarthmore College student who involves him in Greenwich Village radical political perspectives. Reads T. S. Eliot and Ezra Pound.

1944 Discovers Jacques Prévert poem on paper tablecloth in Brittany. Ship returns to U.S., then to Panama, Pacific Islands, Midway, Japan—visits Nagasaki six weeks after the dropping of A-Bomb—discharged in Portland, Oregon, with rank of lieutenant commander.

1945 Bronxville, New York—begins work in *Time* magazine mailroom (eight months). Greenwich Village apartment; begins writing stories.

1947 Attends Columbia University, taking courses from Lionel Trilling, Mark Van Doren, William York Tindall; reads William Carlos Williams, Marianne Moore, E. E. Cummings, Kenneth Patchen, Dylan Thomas, Henry Miller, James Joyce, Gertrude Stein, William Butler Yeats, Eliot's *Four Quartets*. Columbia M.A. thesis is a study of the influence of John Ruskin's writing on painter J. M. W. Turner.
Leaves for France to attend Sorbonne on G.I. Bill.

1948 Paris, living with French Letellier family while attending Sorbonne and art school; working on Thomas Wolfe-type novel "The Way of Dispossession" (unpublished). Befriends George Whitman (fellow American on G.I. Bill, who later founds Mistral Bookshop in Paris); travels throughout France, to Provence. Reads René Char and H. D. Moves to basement apartment, 89 Rue de Vaugirard in Montparnasse, where he rooms for a while with Ivan Cousins; working on dissertation. Begins first version of novel, *Her*; begins series of poems after Pound's *Cantos*—"Palimpsest" (unpublished).

1949	Returns to New York for final visit with Mrs. Bisland; on return voyage to Europe meets Selden Kirby-Smith, a graduate of Swarthmore and Columbia; has shipboard romance. Completes dissertation on "The City as a Symbol in Modern Poetry: In Search of a Metropolitan Tradition" (in French) on urban writings of Whitman, Crane, Eliot, Mayakovsky, Francis Thompson, and Verhaeren. Working on *Her*.
1950	Visits Spain and Puerto de Andraitx, Majorca; Kirby-Smith visits him there. Working on "Palimpsest" poems. Dec., returns to U.S.; visits brothers and mother in New York with Kirby-Smith, engaged to be married. Travels by train across the U.S. for first visit to San Francisco, where he decides to live.
1951	April 10, Ferlinghetti and Kirby-Smith marry in Jacksonville, Florida. May, San Francisco, living in apartment rented by Parisian woman Gertrude Schmidt; teaches French in adult education classes and writes art reviews for *Art Digest* (New York); rents artist studio on San Francisco waterfront (9 Mission Street).
1952	339 Chestnut St. apartments in San Francisco, teachers summer term at University of San Francisco; writes book reviews for *San Francisco Chronicle*; becomes involved in political squabble over murals of Anton Refregier (Communist) during McCarthy era.
1952	Meets Kenneth Patchen, Kenneth Rexroth (focal figure for West Coast poets, artists, political activists), Robert Duncan, and Berkeley poets—Thomas Parkinson, Philip Lamantia, and James Broughton. Meets Peter Martin of *City Lights* magazine. They plan bookshop (popular culture, film, literature, political).
1953	June, City Lights Bookstore opens at 261 Columbus Ave., San Francisco; Shigeyoski Murao is hired to help run the store.
1955	Takes over ownership of *City Lights* magazine and bookstore, all paperback publications. Aug. 10, City Lights Books publications begin. Meets Allen Ginsberg in City Lights Bookstore. Six Gallery Reading in San Francisco (Ginsberg, McClure, Lamantia, Snyder) launches Beat movement.

Begins working on "painter-poems"; five Prévert poem translations appear in *City Lights* magazine; eight Prévert translations and original poem "Brother, Brother" appear in *Inferno* magazine (San Francisco). Two Prévert translations appear in *The California Quarterly* (Los Angeles).

Completes book of poems, *Pictures of the Gone World*.

Pictures of the Gone World (City Lights Pocket Poets Series), no. 1; Kenneth Rexroth's *30 Spanish Poems of Love and Exile*, no. 2; Kenneth Patchen's *Poems of Humor and Protest*, no. 3.

Early poems appear in *New Directions 16*.

1957 Mar. 25, *Howl* is seized by U.S. Customs officials (printed in England by Villiers).
Apr. 3, American Civil Liberties Union protests the seizure of *Howl*; during first week of June Ferlinghetti and Shig Murao are arrested by San Francisco police; ACLU posts bail.
Summer trial of *Howl* presided over by Judge Clayton Horn; chief defense attorney Jake Ehrlich, chief prosecutor Ralph McIntosh; expert witness testimony brought in Oct. 3. Judge Horn rules for Ferlinghetti.

1957 *Evergreen Review*, no. 2 draws attention to San Francisco poets (pictures, article, poetry).
Begins doing poetry-and-jazz sessions with Kenneth Rexroth at the Cellar Club in San Francisco's North Beach area.

1958 Moves to Victorian home on Potrero Hill, San Francisco; Ferlinghetti and Ginsberg are being investigated by the F.B.I.

1959 Meets Bob Kaufman. Jan., attends South American Conference with Allen Ginsberg and Kirby—University of Concepcion in Chile; he and Kirby tour Latin America—Bolivia, Peru, Mexico City—during Cuban Revolution.

1960 Buys small land parcel at Bixby Canyon, near Big Sur. Nov., trip to Caribbean tracing family roots of Mendes-Monsanto, then to Chapel Hill, Puerto Rico, Haiti. Dec., arrives in Cuba to report on revolution; meets Pablo Neruda and young Cuban poets. Befriends Chilean poet Nicanor Parra.

1961 Reads "One Thousand Fearful Words for Fidel Castro" at Fair Play for Cuba Committee Rally in San Francisco.

1962 Daughter Julie is born. Cuban Crisis.
June, play "The Alligation" performed at San Francisco Poetry Festival; Nov.–Dec. performed at Hamlet, Houston, Texas.

Poems from *Coney* appear in *The Nation, Evergreen Review, The Miscellaneous Man.* May 19, Ferlinghetti article in *San Francisco Chronicle* in defense of *Howl.*	Allen Ginsberg's *Howl,* no. 4; City Lights publishes a photo offset edition in U.S.; May 29, seized copies of *Howl* are released.
"Horn on HOWL" article appears in *Evergreen Review,* no. 4. *Have You Sold Your Dozen Roses?* (filmscript) produced at California School of Fine Arts Film Workshop, shown at Edinburgh International Film Festival.	Marie Ponsot's *True Minds,* no. 5; Denise Levertov's *Here and Now,* no. 6; Norman Mailer's "The White Negro" (pamphlet).
A Coney Island of the Mind (New York: New Directions). *Tentative Description of a Dinner to Impeach President Eisenhower* (broadside); first read at Poets' Follies 1958.	William Carlos Williams's *Kora in Hell,* no. 7; Gregory Corso's *Gasoline,* no. 8. (Ferlinghetti rejects Jack Kerouac's *On the Road* and William S. Burrough's *Naked Lunch.*)
Recordings: *Poetry Reading at the Cellar* (Fantasy Records) and *"Tentative Description of a Dinner Given to Promote the Impeachment of President Eisenhower" and Other Poems* (Fantasy). Revising *Her* for publication. *Her* (New York: New Directions).	Jacques Prévert's *Paroles,* trans. Ferlinghetti, no. 9. Bob Kaufman broadsides, "Second April" and "The Abomunist Manifesto."
Edits *Beatitude* (mimeographed magazine) with Bob Kaufman, John Kelley, William J. Margolis, and Allen Ginsberg. *One Thousand Fearful Words for Fidel Castro* (City Lights, broadside).	Nicanor Parra's *Anti-Poems;* Lord Buckley's *Hiporama of the Classics; Beatitude Anthology.*
Coedits *Journal for the Protection of All Beings* with David Meltzer and Michael McClure (first issue, City Lights). *Starting from San Francisco* (New York: New Directions).	Kenneth Patchen's *Love Poems,* no. 13; Ginsberg's *Kaddish,* no. 14; Jack Kerouac's *Book of Dreams,* no. 15; Edward Dahlberg's *Bottom Dogs; Red Cats,* no. 16 (Russian poets Voznesensky, Yevtushenko, Kirsanov); Paul Bowles' *A Hundred Camels in the Courtyard;* Malcolm Lowry's *Selected Poems,* no. 17; Ginsberg's *Reality Sandwiches,* no. 18.

1963 Son Lorenzo is born. May 30, returns to Paris alone, then to Spain.

1964

1965 Family travels to Nerja, Spain, for four-month stay.
May, reads at Spoleto Festival of Two Worlds in Italy, then returns to France.
June 11, Royal Albert Hall, London Reading (Ferlinghetti, Corso, Ginsberg, Voznesensky, Ernst Jandl, Alexander Trocchi) made into book and film *Wholly Communion*, Peter Whitehead.

1966 Does anti-Vietnam War readings during mid-sixties, often touring with Robert Bly in Pacific Southwest.

1967 Germany, at Berlin Literary Colloquium with Voznesensky, reads "After the Cries of the Birds" and prose "Genesis" of the poem.
Feb., trip to Russia; visits Writers' Union in Moscow; seven day trans-Siberian train trip, "I damn near died . . ."
First LSD drug experience, recounted in "Mock Confessional" (*Open Eye, Open Heart*); City Lights Publishing moves to new offices at Upper Grant Ave.; summer, Human Be-In at Golden Gate Park (Ferlinghetti, Ginsberg, and McClure read).
Dec. 9, arrested at Oakland Army Induction Center for demonstrating against the draft (with Kay Boyle and Joan Baez); sentenced to 19 days in Santa Rita prison.

1968 June 8, mass reading at Nourse Auditorium, reads "Assassination Raga."

1969

Writing	*Publications (City Lights)*
Edits *City Lights Journal*, no. 1; *Unfair Arguments with Existence* (plays) (New York: New Directions).	William S. Burroughs' *Yage Letters*.
Routines (New York: New Directions, plays); edits *City Lights Journal*, no. 2.	Daniel Moore's *Dawn Visions;* Frank O'Hara's *Lunch Poems*, no. 19;
Where Is Vietnam? (City Lights, broadside); writes "The Free Spirit Turning Thru Spain" long anti-Franco poem (unpublished).	*Artaud Anthology*, ed. Jack Hirschman.
To Fuck Is to Love Again (New York: Fuck You Pr., pamphlet).	
Edits *City Lights Journal*, no. 3; writing long play "Uncle Ahab" (unpublished).	Charles Olson's *Call Me Ishmael;* Carl Solomon's *Mishaps, Perhaps*.
An Eye on the World: Selected Poems (MacGibbon and Kee: London); *After the Cries of the Birds* (San Francisco: Hasselwood Books).	Philip Lamantia's *Selected Poems*, no. 20; Bob Kaufman's *Golden Sardines*, no. 21.
Moscow in the Wilderness, Segovia in the Snow (San Francisco: Beach Books, broadside).	Rene Daumal's *Mount Analogue;* Janine Pommy-Vega's *Poems to Fernando*, no. 22.
Mar. "Santa Rita Journal" is published in *Ramparts*.	Ginsberg's *Planet News*, no. 23; Charles Upton's *Panic Grass*, no. 24.
Edits *Journal for the Protection of All Beings*, 3 ("Green Flag" issue from works on People's Park protest, May 1969).	Pablo Picasso's *Hunk of Skin*, no. 25. trans. Paul Blackburn.

1970 Nancy Joyce Peters becomes Ferlinghetti's assistant editor at City Lights Publishing.

1971

1972 Experiencing marital difficulties, moves to apartment over City Lights Publishing on Grant Ave.; travels with son and Allen Ginsberg to Australia; readings at Adelaide Festival, Melbourne, and Sydney; joined by Voznesensky.
Nancy Joyce Peters becomes Coeditor of City Lights Books.

1973 Fishing trip to Hawaii with son; launches Poets' Theatre through City Lights; reading for Greek Resistance Movement, reads "Forty Odd Questions for the Greek Regime and One Cry for Freedom." Meets J. Krishnamurti and becomes involved in San Francisco Zen Center.

1974 Involved during the seventies with United Farm Workers of America, antinuclear power protests, and ecological concerns such as the Greenpeace antiwhaling campaign.

1975 Issues "The Populist Manifesto" (Berkeley radio, Walt Whitman Day at Rutgers Univ., small and big press publications); refuses to read poetry at the Library of Congress.

1976 Divorce from Kirby-Smith; children come to live with him and Paula Lillevand; relaxes at Bixby Canyon; Shig Murao is hospitalized and leaves City Lights over argument. Ferlinghetti is outspoken against small press publications and authors taking federally funded grants.
Trip to Mexico, readings.

1977 San Francisco Art Commission honors Ferlinghetti at Civil Art Festival; display of his photographs and paintings at Capricorn Asunder Gallery, San Francisco.

Writing	*Publications (City Lights)*
The Mexican Night (New York: New Directions, journal).	Timothy Leary's *Eagle Brief* (prison writings); Robert Bly's *The Teeth Mother Naked at Last*, no. 26; Diane DiPrima's *Revolutionary Letters*, no. 27; Jack Kerouac's *Scattered Poems*, no. 28; Walt Whitman's *An American Primer*.
Love Is No Stone on the Moon (Berkeley, ARIF, pamphlet); Edits Neal Cassady's writings. *Back Roads to Far Places* (New York: New Directions).	Neal Cassady's *The First Third*.
Tape of readings for *Contemporary American Poets*. *Open Eye* (Melbourne: Sun Books), bound with Ginsberg's *Open Head*.	Charles Bukowski's *Erections, Ejaculations, Exhibitions, and General Tales of Ordinary Madness*; Voznesensky's *Dogalypse*, no. 29, trans. Ferlinghetti; Ginsberg's *The Fall of America: Poems of These States*, no. 30.
Open Eye, Open Heart (New York: New Directions).	
	Pete Winslow's *A Daisy in the Memory of a Shark*, no. 31; Harold Norse's *Hotel Nirvana*, no. 32; Ann Waldman's *Fast Speaking Woman*, no. 33.
Edits *City Lights Anthology* (large section of the Surrealist movement in the U.S.).	Jack Hirschman's *Lyripol*, no. 34.
A Political Pamphlet; (San Francisco: Anarchist Resistance Press); *Who Are We Now?* (New York: New Directions).	
White on White (City Lights, broadside).	Ginsberg's *Mind Breaths*, no. 35; Karl Marx's *Love Poems*, trans. Richard Lettau and Ferlinghetti.

1978

1979 Daughter living with Ferlinghetti at 250 Francisco Street, San Francisco, while son lives with mother at Bolinas, California. Italy, reads at First International Festival of Poetry outside Rome (Ginsberg, Orlovsky, Ted Berrigan, Ann Waldman, and Leroi Jones).

1980 Participates in Conference on Urban Literature at Rutgers Univ.; France, reads at "Polyphonix 2," Paris celebration of City Lights Books' 25th year. Developing new journal, "Free Spirit," to consolidate surrealism, anarchism, socialism with themes from popular culture, active in "Group 80," San Francisco writers collective.

1981 *Lawrence Ferlinghetti: A Descriptive Bibliography* by Bill Morgan (New York: Garland Publishing)
June, participates in Big Mountain Navajo-Hopi Poetry Benefit Reading with Lamantia, McClure, Kaye McDonough, Miriam Patchen, Nancy Joyce Peters, and Stephen Schwartz, San Francisco.

Writing	*Publications (City Lights)*
Edits *City Lights Journal*, no. 4; "Adieu à Charlot: Second Populist Manifesto"; *Northwest Ecolog* (City Lights, journal and poems).	Stefan Brecht's *Poems*, no. 36; James Laughlin's *In Another Country*.
Landscape of the Living and Dying: (New York: New Directions); *The Sea and Ourselves at Cape Ann* (Madison, Wis.: Red Ozier, pamphlet).	Peter Orlovsky's *Clean Asshole Poems*, no. 37. *Lord Buckley Hiparama of the Classics*.
"Modern Poetry Is Prose (But It Is Saying Plenty): Third Populist Manifesto"; film of "The Old Italians Dying," poet Ferlinghetti and filmmaker Herman Barlandt, premiers at San Francisco Fourth International Poetry Festival; *A Trip to Italy and France* (New York: New Directions, poems); *Literary San Francisco: A Pictorial History*, no. 39; (City Lights and Harper & Row) edited and text by Ferlinghetti and Nancy Joyce Peters; *Her Too*, Excerpt from Work-in-Progress (New York: Nadja Pr.).	*Antler: Factory*, no. 38. Philip Lamantia's *Becoming Visible*, no. 39; *Unamerican Activities: The Campaign Against the Underground Press*.
Endless Life: Selected Poems (New Directions), text selected by the author; *Populist Manifestoes* (San Francisco: Grey Fox).	Allen Ginsberg's *Poetic Odes*, no. 40.

Lawrence Ferlinghetti

1

Biographic Portrait

And there are days
when I see all too clearly
And there are days
When I am everyone I meet.

("All Too Clearly")

SINCE the 1955 publication of Lawrence Ferlinghetti's *Pictures of the Gone World*, which launched his writing career as well as his City Lights Books, he has produced eighteen books of poetry, drama, and prose, numerous poem broadsides, and has translated the works of Jacques Prévert, Andrei Voznesensky, and Karl Marx. He has pioneered the poetry-and-jazz experiments and captured his readings on film and recordings. When he reads publicly, it is an engaging encounter between poet and audience, the word and the world. Beyond his editorial work on the countless books of international avant-garde writing done at City Lights, he has personally edited the *City Lights Journal*, *City Lights Anthology*, and conspired in the editorship of *The Journal for the Protection of All Beings* and *Beatitude*. He is widely anthologized and authentically popular, warranting Leslie A. Fiedler's acclaim as "the nearest thing to a best-selling poet we have."[1] Ferlinghetti is a key figure in the development of the San Francisco Renaissance in poetry and the West Coast beat movement as well as being America's most vital spokesman for activist and avant-garde writing. Poet William Everson justly concludes that "of all the American poets emergent in the Fifties Ferlinghetti is the most genuinely popular, entering the literary awareness of the youth of this time more palpably even than Ginsberg."[2] His is a distinctly contemporaneous and authentic voice engaged in a populist and artistic reforging of life. Critic Karl Malkoff describes well the basic thrust of Ferlinghetti's work: "It is evident that he has for himself replaced his meaningless surroundings with what is for him a living tradition, drawing from it the energy to create and possibly to revitalize his world."[3]

One feels compelled to remember all this when confronting the blank face of the critical reaction that has met his work. Scattered reviews of a mixed nature and a few chapters in the books of fellow poet-critics are all that exist. No longer can this embarrassing lapse be excused under the guise of a reaction to the leftist attitudes or the experimental nature of the works nor as a result of the blatant academic defiance of Ferlinghetti's stance. The symbolic abandoning of him to the masses has only prolonged and aggravated the need to come to terms with his essential art. This study proposes to begin the necessary critical appreciation by first exposing the biographical basis which provides the basic motive and cohesive personality core for the work; then by recognizing the author's radically engaged stance toward life and art as the basis of his functional aesthetics, both experimental and rhetorical in design; and, finally, by treating the work itself, rather than the author's fame or notoriety. We begin with the life story of the poet's consciousness.

With poet Lawrence Ferlinghetti we knew so little for so long, yet we knew much more than we thought. When we examine the factual details of his life we learn that the image of the poet which Ferlinghetti sought to live was derived from the international models of Blake, Apollinaire, Prévert, Sartre, and from Thoreau, Whitman, Thomas Wolfe, and Charlie Chaplin. In his relentless quest for the authentic in himself and in the world, realist and idealist combine in search of a new mold of life and art. We come to understand the Ferlinghetti poem, like the person, as issuing from an authentic voice—personal, immediate, expressive and oral, existentially alive to the humor of survival. As Ferlinghetti seeks to discover and create his life through molding inner and outer realities into art, he is alive to his role as experiencing consciousness. He adopts wholeheartedly the role of author-narrator-hero, the poet-at-large, recording and revealing life. For Ferlinghetti, consciousness is all, and what we failed to see for so long was the personal and biographic nature of that consciousness.

Ferlinghetti has lately emerged through his quarter century of writing as the good gray poet whose vitality has not forsaken the suffering and absurdity of the human condition, but rather grown through it to a more personal and universal understanding. He is still in the San Francisco streets of America, his blue eyes sparkling with innocence and wit. His own image of the creative and concerned artist has remained that lone yet universal figure of the compassionate comic, Charlie Chaplin:

> Chaplin is dead but I'd wear his bowler
> having outlived all our myths but his
> the myth of the pure and subjective
> the collective subjective
> the Little Man in each of us.[4]
>
> ("Adieu à Charlot: Second Populist Manifesto")

What emerges from a consideration of the life of Lawrence Ferlinghetti is the overriding sense of this persistent struggle to know himself and his world. From his personal sense of abandonment at birth has emerged his long and genuine quest to integrate himself with existence. It has resulted in much of the profound sense of loss that haunts his life yet has provided much of the creative tension and direction of his writing career. A writer who dares to live his art is rewarded with an art inextricably bound to life. As we have come to know, the tragic-comic "Little Man" which underlies his work:

a little charleychaplin man
who may or may not catch

her fair eternal form
spreadeagled in the empty air
of existence[5]

is authentically his and ultimately our own collective recognition of self.

STARTING FROM LOSS

FEW writers have begun life with such a deep sense of loss or searched as hard to regain a sense of identity with the world. His father's death several months before his birth, his mother's being committed to a mental hospital shortly thereafter, his being whisked off alone at infancy by his great-aunt Emily, who carried him to France for the first five years of his life, his stay in a New York orphanage followed by a sudden rise to a life of wealth and isolation with the Bisland family in exclusive Bronxville, New York—all this engendered in the young Lawrence Ferlinghetti the sense of a life yet to be discovered and written. Close parallels exist in the lives and careers of two men who perhaps most profoundly affected his own—Guillaume Apollinaire and Charlie Chaplin. Indeed, the sense of melodrama that plays about Ferlinghetti's youth is intensely factual. His struggle to rise above the loss and to convert it into strength manifests itself chiefly in his frank and authentic search for a subjectively integrated reality. It provides the tension, the wit, the loneliness, and the directness of his writing. Life was not a given; it was to be discovered and created.

I lawrence ferlinghetti
wrought from the dark in my mother long ago
born in a small back bedroom—
. . . .
Someone squeezed my heart
to make it go

I cried and sprang up
Open eye open heart where
do I wander
I cried and ran off
into the heart of the world[6]

It took Ferlinghetti more than fifty years to deliver this "True Confessional," though he admits elsewhere to having searched in vain for a priest who would accept it. This mythic view of his own life is pronounced in Ferlinghetti, and this recent personal self-portrait provides a telling comparison with the "beat" and outspoken poet of the 1958 "Autobiography":

I am leading a quiet life
in Mike's Place every day
contemplating my navel.
I am a part
of the body's long madness.
I have wandered in various nightwoods.
I have leaned in drunken doorways.
I have written wild stories
without punctuation.
I am the man.
I was there.

(*Coney*, 64–65)

These lines, which were originally taken to be part of a "hip" character projection, are now shown in the light of Neeli Cherkovski's *Ferlinghetti: A Biography* to be all too autobiographically true. And yet, the Ferlinghetti of "Autobiography," who remembers, "I had an unhappy childhood. / I saw Lindberg land. / I looked homeward / and saw no angel" (*Coney*, 60), is very much the contemporary man of the streets who expresses his Everyman's life as a cultural mirror. His writing demonstrates an enduring conviction to recognizing and expressing "the Little Man in each of us," that subjective and collective path to understanding. His sense of life-reporting as seen in his notebooks and journals which grow into his poems and prose books establish the primary autobiographic source and mode of his art. In Ferlinghetti's work you deal with what you are, and what you are is out there in the busy world each day recognizing and recording it.

Who has not imagined the moment of his/her own conception, that lucky and irrational act of love? Ferlinghetti sets his on a sunny riverbank in Ossining, New York, where a beautiful French and Sephardic Jew named Clemence Mendes-Monsanto and her Italian immigrant husband Charles Ferling conceive their last of five sons (*Open*, 3). Charles Ferling (as the name was adapted in America) had come from the Northern Lombardy region of Italy in the 1890s to settle in New York's Yonkers area, where he worked in real estate and as an auctioneer. A well educated man, he first drew the attention of Clemence Mendes-Monsanto through his fluency in English, Italian, and French. Though born in this country, she was the daughter of a French woman, Clemence Carrin, and a Jew from the Sephardic (Spanish-Portuguese) region, Herman Mendes-Monsanto. Herman's family had emigrated to the Netherlands and Virgin Islands, eventually to the island of Saint Thomas, then to New York. Ferlinghetti's maternal grandfather had been educated in a European university, and he later taught at the Naval Academy at Annapolis and at a small New York City college. He authored a successful Spanish grammar text which later helped to support Ferlinghetti's mother.[7]

Into this literate, multilingual, turn-of-the-century immigrant family walked the familiar visitors—poverty and tragedy. The death of Ferlinghetti's father before his birth forced his mother to move from one house to another, slipping further into poverty and despair. Finally, after an emotional collapse, Clemence Ferlinghetti was committed to the State Hospital in Poughkeepsie, New York. The four older brothers were sent to a boarding home in Ossining, New York, and the infant Lawrence was taken by Emily Mendes-Monsanto, his mother's aunt. This tall, slender, intelligent and aggressive woman then left her husband Ludwig and took the child to France. She became the "French mother" of Ferlinghetti's preschool years in the Alsatian capital of Strasbourg, France.

Here he spoke and lived as a French child, never knowing of his American family. When Emily returned to her estranged husband Ludwig in New York, they promptly went into debt, forcing Emily to temporarily place young Lawrence in a Chappaqua, New York orphanage—ironically near his lost family. Seven lonely months passed for young Lawrence whose sense of displacement sharpened in the harsh system of routine. "I am my son, my mother, my father, / I am born of myself / my own flesh sucked" (*Open*, 4) becomes the cry of this orphan.

Rescued once more by the enterprising Emily, who had secured a position as French tutor to the daughter of Presley and Anna Lawrence Bisland, Ferlinghetti moves to Plashbourne, the gabled stone mansion of the wealthy Bisland family. In exclusive Bronxville, New York, Ferlinghetti is to make this ivy covered castle, so uncharacteristic of the public Ferlinghetti of Greenwich Village and San Francisco days, his home for the remainder of his childhood. One day, months after beginning her work there, Emily, the closest person in his life, suddenly disappears forever, leaving him with the Bislands who welcome him as their own son. The Bislands had lost a son Lawrence in childbirth.

Life with the Bislands can be characterized as limited isolation. Both Presley and Anna Bisland were older, well-read, and kind, but sharply limited in their ability to provide the affection the young Lawrence craved. Ferlinghetti retains the kindest of feelings toward them for their years as "parents emeritus." It was, however, one more experience with abandon and isolation, and one which unfortunately taught the young Ferlinghetti to guard himself by withdrawing. He began to close the doors of his identity and of his need for affection to the world. He paints this portrait of his early school years:

> And I began to go
> through my number
> I was a wind-up toy
> someone had dropped wound-up

into a world already
running down.

(*Open*, 4)

For two years Ferlinghetti attended Riverside Country School, a boarding school near Bronxville. Then the Bislands placed him with the Zilla Larned Wilson family where he could attend the public schools of Bronxville. It was a solidifying experience for Ferlinghetti, who welcomed the human contact and the freedom which the Wilson family engendered. Though there was no father in the family, the older boy Bill served as a heroic big brother to adolescent Ferlinghetti. It was a time when he could earn his own money as a paperboy—"I still can hear the paper thump / on lost porches" (*Coney*, 60)—and experience the athletic comradeship of basketball. He could pursue such diverse interests as printing press courses, boy scouting, and street gang rebellion. His comic line from "Autobiography," "I got caught stealing pencils / from the Five and Ten Cent Store / the same month I made Eagle Scout" (*Coney*, 60) is ironic but true. Yet it exhibits his brave venturing into realms of personal and social experience. He writes his first poems in these years.

Ironically, in 1929 his mother, Clemence, and his brothers appear one day at the Bisland home and ask to see him. Ferlinghetti, who had heard but not believed in the existence of this family, is confronted with their reality and an almost impossible choice. The Bislands and his mother agree to allow him to decide which family he wishes to live with. At ten years of age he chooses the only family he has known, the Bislands, but the decision is like all the experiences of abandonment which will haunt him most of his life.

As Neeli Cherkovski, Ferlinghetti's biographer, points out, Lawrence Ferlinghetti had turned to the books in the Bisland library as a strange sort of second parent. They were so much like him, closed yet full of secret hidden doors.[8] It is a fascination that grows and becomes a permanent identification for Ferlinghetti, from his grade-school days of working in the print shop to his years of keeping journals, and his writing, bookstore, and international publishing career. When Sally Bisland gives him a French-English copy of Baudelaire in 1933 he sees a further connection in his life with writing and literature. One can understand the pull that writing had upon him as a means of exploring, freeing, and controlling his own life. It offered the long sought means of growing close to life, as he testifies in "True Confession":

> I had only to close my eyes
> for another world to appear
> too near and too dear
> to be anything but myself
> my inside self
> where everything real
> was to happen.
>
> (*Open*, 4–5)

Ferlinghetti had found the way inward through words, something he was to develop further in his four years (1933–37) at Mount Hermon private high school near Greenfield, Massachusetts. The private school with its strict religious code was in part a measure the Bislands took to correct the rebellious values he had picked up in the Parkway Road Pirates street gang. Despite the disciplined and sanctimonious school atmosphere, he learned to relate to the other boys as friends, and it was here that he discovered the Romantic writings of Thomas Wolfe and Henry David Thoreau. These writers and thinkers permanently impressed Ferlinghetti with the values of American romanticism wherever they might be found. This period of adolescent questing and discovery is recorded with touching accuracy in this early poem:

> The pennycandystore beyond the El
> is where I first
>   fell in love
>   with unreality
> Jellybeans in the semi-gloom
> of that september afternoon

Into this impressionistic New York portrait of time and place, colored by the youthful pleasures of "licorice sticks / and tootsie rolls / and Oh Boy Gum," comes the dawning awareness of impending love and loss:

> Outside the leaves were falling as they died
>
> A wind had blown away the sun
>
> A girl ran in
> Her hair was rainy
> Her breasts were breathless in the little room
>
> Outside the leaves were falling
> and they cried
> Too soon! Too soon!
> (*Coney*, 35)

Ferlinghetti writes here through the emotional memory so characteristic of Thomas Wolfe's modern romanticism. He isolates the images of candy, leaves, and girl in the recorded moment of consciousness, then spirals them all together (the ambiguous "they cried") in the rendering of falling—into awareness. It is a personal and telling image of a life brought from innocent childhood onto the emotional seas which lay ahead. The epiphanous moment is now colored by the ambiguity of adolescence. Yet the integrated moment of the poem, like Ferlinghetti's own life, has moved progressively toward involvement, expression, and the imaginative release of writing.

CASTING OUT LINES

A stronger and more determined Lawrence Ferlinghetti followed his love for the writings of Thomas Wolfe to their mythic source in Ashville, North Carolina. From

1937–41 he studied English and journalism at the University of North Carolina; Chapel Hill provided a scenic yet liberal atmosphere for his college years. He worked on both the college newspaper and Thomas Wolfe's old *Carolina* magazine, and he read the novels of James T. Farrell, John Dos Passos, Ernest Hemingway, and William Faulkner under the tutelage of Professor Phillips Russell. It was Russell who broke down the academic rigidity for him and introduced him to the populists—Carl Sandburg, Edgar Lee Masters, Vachel Lindsay—whom Ferlinghetti admired for "the way these writers communicated directly. None of them was obscure."[9] He began writing his own short stories and started his own novel modeled after *Look Homeward, Angel*. His poetry followed the pattern of most young writers—prolific and derivative.

During the summer of 1939 he began his pattern of journey taking when he and two college friends rode freight trains and hitchhiked across the South to Mexico City, a city that retained a permanent attraction for him. The political situation in Mexico drew his journalistic eye, and his self-assurance blossomed from this early "on the road" experience. One incident from the journey is recorded in his *Tyrannus Nix?*; it comes in a directive to then President Richard Nixon:

> I've hitched back and forth across the face of America looking for a face I once rode a freight from Joplin to Chattanooga and saw your face on a siding   It was the face of the Yard Dick busting the sterno bums   I was a college kid and thought it was fun   The whole world a fraternity razing   But now I remember the face in the dark by the tracks the dark jowls and the hard eyes like yours oh American Dick[10]

Ferlinghetti records here the uneven development of his sensory, emotional and moral consciousness. At Chapel Hill he had begun another lifelong pattern of keeping a notebook of his thinking and writings. The college years had fostered in him a combined stance of journalist and poet—he was emerging as the true observer as well as the plunger of inner depths.

After his graduation in 1941 he spent a carefree and reflective summer on Little Whaleboat Island, Maine, and dove into the fervor of World War II by enlisting in the Navy just prior to Pearl Harbor. His four-year naval experience (1941–45) fulfilled the promise of showing him the world while it also fostered his self-reliance. He was stationed in New York, the Mid-Atlantic, England, Norfolk, Virginia, France, (where he discovered the writing of Jacques Prévert scribbled on a restaurant tablecloth) and even participated in the landing at Normandy by commanding an offshore subchaser. In 1944 he did a tour of the Pacific which brought another kind of awareness. After touring Panama, the Pacific Islands, and Midway, his crew landed at Japan where they witnessed the unforgivable landscape of bombed-out Nagasaki. Ferlinghetti remembers, "You'd see hands sticking out of the mud . . . all kinds of broken teacups . . . hair sticking out of the road—a quagmire—people don't realize how total the destruction was."[11] The young lieutenant commander received his discharge papers days later from Portland, Oregon, but the vision of war's senseless destruction had been permanently etched on the consciousness of this contemporary pacifist.

His social and political awareness had also experienced a growth during his Navy years when he would use his New York leave to visit a group of Swarthmore College students living in Greenwich Village. Laura Lou Lyons and her brother were active liberals of those times who acquainted him with radical pacifist thinking as well as leftist political theory. Ferlinghetti recalls, "I had never run into this. I saw copies of *Nation* on their coffee tables, and I had never seen such a publication. The *Nation* and the *New Republic* were the leading journals of the day. *Partisan Review* was a big number. I had never run into this at Chapel Hill, and it was the first inkling that there was anything such as an anti-war position. In the Navy I had never heard of such a thing; I was completely politically illiterate."[12] This was in 1941, and in the fifties the Swarthmore College faculty would become prime targets for the McCarthy investigations, while Laura Lou Lyons would go on to become one of the first women graduates from Columbia Law School and a member of the American Arbitration Association.

After the war, Ferlinghetti returned to Bronxville and the Bisland family, with whom he had maintained warm relationships throughout the war. He took a job in the mailroom of *Time* magazine for an eight-month period; but soon determined to use his G.I. Bill to gain further education at Columbia. He moved into a Greenwich Village apartment and began another period of self-seeking. Here was the spawning ground for young writers and artists. E. E. Cummings and Kenneth Patchen, two writers of profound influence on Ferlinghetti, were living in the village, and others whom he had read—William Carlos Williams, Marianne Moore, even Dylan Thomas—were frequent visitors. He responded to their outspoken writing: "They were . . . like a political education to me."[13]

Columbia University provided a literary mecca of the moderns for the quiet and studious Ferlinghetti. In courses from Lionel Trilling, Mark Van Doren, William York Tindall, and Joseph Wood Krutch he read the works of James Joyce, Gertrude Stein, Henry Miller, T. S. Eliot, and William Butler Yeats (having discovered an abandoned copy of Yeats on the Third Avenue elevated train). Though he had read both Ezra Pound and T. S. Eliot much earlier, this is the period of Eliot's *Four Quartets*, a book that has had a lifelong philosophical and artistic influence on Ferlinghetti. "It's the greatest modern prose, the most beautiful modern prose there is, I think. It's called poetry, but it's essentially prose. It's beautiful; it's the greatest work Eliot wrote, I think,"[14] Ferlinghetti still exclaims today.

The culmination of his Columbia experience was a masters degree thesis on the influence of the writing of John Ruskin on the painting of J. M. W. Turner. These artists of mid-nineteenth century England attracted Ferlinghetti's own interest in the relationship between writing and painting. It was a most important connection for Ferlinghetti, who has pursued dual expression in writing and painting, who later reviewed the art being done in San Francisco for *Art Digest*, and whose first book, *Pictures of the Gone World* (1955) (as well as many other poems throughout the years) deals with the relationship of word to painted images. Art and artists in relationship to life is one of Ferlinghetti's most consistent sources and themes.

In 1947 he decided to pursue his own artistic identity abroad, and left for Paris to study at the Sorbonne. He confesses the personal paralysis of this Columbia-Greenwich Village period: "I grew and did not renew myself but grew sad and wrinkled as I was my son and I was my father not known and not forgotten, and then I was grown out of school at last in a Brooklyn spring."[15] Anna Bisland, whose husband Presley had died that year, was kind enough to pick up Ferlinghetti's degree from Columbia, for he was already sailing fresh and deeper waters toward a new and fuller sense of self.

With the deliberation of a graduate student who privately wants to be a writer-artist, Ferlinghetti sought the broader cultural experience of Europe. It was also a symbolic return to his youth in France. It must, however, be pointed out that Ferlinghetti was still the humble student pursuing experience and knowledge as initiation. He clarifies, "I didn't know any literary people at all when I was living in France in those days, and I didn't know any Americans who were there writing."[16] As warm and direct as his writing is, it is somewhat of a surprise to find that Ferlinghetti is typically introverted and reticent in unfamiliar situations. "I have travelled among men. . . . I have wandered lonely / as a crowd," (*Coney*, 60) he confesses in "Autobiography." In Paris he immersed himself dually in the common life and in the international academic world of modern literature. "I went to the Sorbonne once a month to sign this book and otherwise I didn't have anything to do with any literary scene."[17] He remained the young man living and searching inside himself, yet needing self-expression.

He was living with the French Letellier family, on Place Voltaire, the workers' part of town. The father was an old communist who taught classical music, and Ferlinghetti practiced his French with the family around the breakfast table. He also completed his first version of the Thomas Wolfe-type novel "The Way of Dispossession" which was subsequently rejected by Doubleday and Simon and Shuster, and never published. Readings in modern international poetry which focused on the city, the area of his dissertation, took him into a wide area of European and American avant-garde writing, including H. D., Andre Breton's *Nadja*, Djuna Barnes's *Nightwood*, and the urban poetry of Mayakovsky and Verhaeren.

In Paris he befriended a fellow American living abroad on the G.I. Bill, George Whitman, who later founded the international Mistral Bookshop in Paris. The two young men shared interests and outlooks. Ferlinghetti soon travelled throughout France, in particular to Provence where he came across the writings of Rene Char. At the time, Ferlinghetti was working on his own book of poetry concerning his life, the "Palimpsest" poems which he has never published, perhaps because these poems are so heavily influenced by Pound's *Cantos*.

After a year with the Letellier family, Ferlinghetti reluctantly sought cheaper living quarters and found them at 89 Rue de Vaugirard in Montparnasse, a dark and damp basement apartment complete with rats. It was, nevertheless, a place where he did much solid work—completing his dissertation and a first draft of the novel *Her*—and one which retained a fond place in his memory. The larger significance of the apartment, which is not immediately apparent, is that it provided an atmosphere for much of the semi-autobiographical and surrealistic *Her* which was written in 1949 and 1950. Ferlinghetti's own description is most important here: "It was a cellar with two rooms and a little tiny air-shaft kitchen with a sink hollowed out of solid stone, which must have been there since the Middle Ages, and a front room that had a French window on a courtyard. That was the only window in the two rooms. The middle room had no windows at all. It was very damp in there. And it was dark. There was only light from this front window."[18] This cavelike dwelling in the midst of bohemian Paris not only provides images and tone for the novel *Her*, but its symbolic and expressionistic atmosphere stressing dampness and light is a setting for many of Ferlinghetti's experimental dramas. Ferlinghetti lived here for almost three years, sharing the tight quarters his first year with his old Navy friend Ivan Cousins.

For his dissertation Ferlinghetti had chosen a topic that would later prove to be particularly suited to his role as international publisher and populist poet of the streets—"La Cité: Symbole dans la poesie moderne: A la recherche d'un Tradition Metropolitaine" (The City as a Symbol in Modern Poetry: In Search of a Metropolitan Tradition). The study centered on T. S. Eliot's *The Waste Land*, Hart Crane's *The Bridge*, Walt Whitman's *Leaves of Grass, Federico Garcia Lorca's The Poet in New York*, Francis Thompson's *City of Dreadful Night*, Mayakovsky's poem on "Brooklyn Bridge," and *The Tentacular City* by French-Belgian poet Verhaeren. His readings took him far beyond these basic works into diverse writings by an international avant-garde. This foundation in European literature, particularly with the French and Spanish surrealists, is a crucial recognition in coming to terms with his own conception of a new, functional, and public art. He too was in search of a tradition. His defense of his dissertation received a sound approval, accented by his quick-witted defense of a liberal translation of Eliot, "A translation is like a woman. When she is beautiful, she is not faithful. When she is faithful, she is not beautiful."[19]

He returned to New York for a brief and final visit with Anna Bisland in 1949 and encountered on his return voyage to Europe a chance companion who would remain with him for the next twenty-five years. A bright and talkative young woman with dark hair and slender figure, Selden Kirby-Smith (Kirby), soon became his shipboard companion. She was a Swarthmore and Columbia graduate with an M.A. on D. H. Lawrence, and she remembered, though he could not, watching admiringly the intense young Ferlinghetti in the classes they shared at Columbia. They continued seeing each other in Paris, Ferlinghetti introducing her to the Left Bank while he continued to work on his novel and his painting. He had walked off the street into an art school one day with his easel and remained a gratis student. Just as he had taken a brief respite after taking his Columbia and Chapel Hill degrees, so here he travelled to Madrid and to a small fishing village in Majorca, Puerto de Andraitx, where Kirby later joined him. It was here that he completed the "Palimpsest" poems, and, after taking stock, decided to head back to the states with Kirby for a new encounter with himself on native grounds.

San Francisco Rebirth

The 1950s marked a time of regenerated life through increased commitment, both for Lawrence Ferlinghetti and for the cultural and political climate of San Francisco. He had found a ripe and open atmosphere where he could move from the shy observer, "leading a quiet life on East Broadway" into the engaged poet-prophet who "may cause the lips / of those who are asleep / to speak" (*Coney*, 60, 66). However, this change did not happen at once and certainly not in isolation.

Fresh from Paris in 1950, Ferlinghetti had a long train trip across the states to his destination of San Francisco where he recognized an affinity with its more open and European culture. He returned to the East Coast long enough to marry Kirby-Smith and to honeymoon in a fishing lodge at Lake Geneva, Florida. Then they headed west. Their first home in San Francisco was a small apartment rented from a Parisian woman, Gertrude Schmidt. Ferlinghetti began a series of short jobs. He taught French in adult education classes, then began to write reviews of San Francisco art exhibits for the New York based *Art Digest*. Ferlinghetti was doing his own painting at 9 Mission Street, an art studio on the San Francisco waterfront. As an artist he was drawn to the abstract expressionists whom he reviewed and was carrying out the influence of Franz Kline, who experimented with bold canvases of black and white. Surprisingly, Ferlinghetti was giving serious thought to becoming a critic at this time. His Notebook for 1951–52 includes an essay on "Subjective Realism" treating Jean Cocteau and the surrealists and the March 1952 declaration that "The function of the critic is insight. If the critic has not intuition he has nothing," and the final lament, "If I could find a J. M. W. Turner to champion, I might become a great art critic."

His literary concerns in 1952 led him to a summer teaching job at the University of San Francisco. That summer term at the conservative Catholic college marked one of the shortest academic teaching careers ever. Fortunately Ferlinghetti recognized a larger audience and a closer alliance with a public outside the classroom. He was working on his translations of the poems of Jacques Prévert and Guillaume Apollinaire as well as revising his novel *Her*. His book reviews for the *San Francisco Chronicle* (1951–55) helped establish him in the writing climate of the area, and he and Kirby soon moved to the North Beach area, to an apartment at 339 Chestnut Street where he began to write the poems for *Pictures of the Gone World*.

Ferlinghetti had entered and become a small part of the writing atmosphere that would ferment into the San Francisco Renaissance in poetry. He reviewed poetry readings, including one at the San Francisco Museum of Art by Kenneth Patchen, a writer he had admired all through the 1940s for his bold and independent stance toward politics, war, and art. He met Patchen through a mutual friend, Holly Beye, later in 1952 and subsequently published his *Poems of Humor and Protest* and *Love Poems* when City Lights began. He started to attend the evenings at Kenneth Rexroth's home where Rexroth acted as a focal point and spiritual father of many poets, artists, and political activists. Rexroth had come to San Francisco from Chicago in 1927 and had soon become active in the anarchist wave of the place, joining and leading a John Reed Club, an Anarchist Club, and an

Artists and Writers' Union in the thirties.[20] Though Ferlinghetti was originally a shy participant at the meetings, he and Rexroth launched there a lifelong friendship. Included in the circle of poetic ferment of the San Francisco Renaissance were Robert Duncan and the San Francisco-Berkeley poets Thomas Parkinson, Philip Lamantia, and James Broughton. Others, such as Gary Snyder, Lew Welch, Philip Whalen, Michael McClure, Jack Spicer, and Brother Antoninus were working individually, yet stood united in their anti-establishment attitude. Ferlinghetti had his Prévert translations published in the little magazines *Inferno* and *City Lights* and was working on the painter poems of *Pictures*. The climate was right; there remained a few key events to precipitate the renaissance movement, and Ferlinghetti, the emerging artist-poet-publisher, would play a most critical role.

In 1952 Ferlinghetti met the man who had published his Prévert translations. Peter Martin, a young sociology instructor at San Francisco State College, was publishing a small magazine focusing mainly on popular culture and cinema. His *City Lights*, titled after Charlie Chaplin's celebrated film, proved an avenue for interests he shared with Ferlinghetti. They complemented each other in a wide coverage of the cultural scene, and so became business partners in a venture to keep the magazine alive. Ferlinghetti had been struck by the barren commercial values and the elitist nature of American book publishing and sales. "When I first came to town in the early fifties, there was no book store to walk into to browse, no place to talk to people, to just hang out. I remember going into downtown bookstores and immediately being approached by clerks who wanted to know exactly what I was looking for."[21] Paperback book sales, he noted, were limited to drug store racks of indiscriminate popular taste. To fill this gap in San Francisco, Martin and Ferlinghetti invested $500 each and in June 1953 launched one of this country's most famous and successful book stores, City Lights Bookstore. Ferlinghetti remembers, "One of the original ideas of the store was for it not to be an uptight place, but a center for the intellectual community, to be non-affiliated, not tied up with, not belonging to any official organization. . . . We were open seven days a week till midnight, and we literally could not shut the doors at closing time. We seemed to be responding to a deeply felt need."[22] Martin and Ferlinghetti were committed to keeping the magazine going by this sales venture, but they were also deliberate about establishing the bookstore as a cultural center. They sought to represent a wide perspective on political and popular culture, and avant-garde writing. A further catalyst was added in the person of Shigeyoshi Murao (Shig) who at first volunteered to work in the bookstore, then stayed on to manage it for more than twenty years. *City Lights* was headquartered above the tiny triangular bookstore, and it continued to publish a total of five issues until Martin decided to move back to New York in 1955, selling his interest in the store to Ferlinghetti.

Having established the bookstore as a ready source of income, Ferlinghetti was soon able to realize several enduring ambitions. On August 10, 1955, City Lights Books began publishing with Ferlinghetti's own collection of poems, *Pictures of the Gone World*. Besides launching his first book and press, he initiated his now famous Pocket Poets Series. Modeled after the European pattern of publishing small, inexpensive editions, he set an American precedent as a strictly paperback press. Unlike many small presses that sought to print fine, expensive, and limited editions of avant-garde writing, City Lights produced books that were compact, clear, and ready for mass consumption at seventy-five cents to one dollar. His description of the preparation for that first book is revealing: "The first one was done by hand. David Ruff, and Holly Beye and Kirby and myself and Mimi Orr pasted on covers and gathered it by hand, like any other little press. The first printing was a thousand copies."[23] This symbolic birth of poet and publisher was further reinforced by Ferlinghetti's reclaiming his father's original name. He emerged from the private Lawrence Ferling to the public figure of Lawrence Ferlinghetti.

In *Pictures of the Gone World* he was revealed as a lyric yet laconic poet of common language yet broad cultural awareness. He had found a cohesive expression for his diverse influences and experiences. His comic-sad voice projected his self into a realm of public significance, as in this characteristic poem:

26
Reading Yeats I do not think
of Ireland
but of midsummer New York
and of myself back then
reading that copy I found
on the Thirdavenue El

the El
with its flying fans
and its signs reading
SPITTING IS FORBIDDEN

Ferlinghetti is out there in a world made real by its trail of gritty little lives held in balance for him against the world which Yeats and art would suggest, a balance which is clearly and finally broken by the weight of common humanity:

Reading Yeats I do not think
of Arcady
and of its woods which Yeats thought dead
I think instead
of all the gone faces
getting off at midtown places
with their hats and their jobs.[24]

This poem marks clearly the character and direction of Ferlinghetti's poetry and personality. He declares his allegiance as a poet of the people, of all the strange gone faces which demand a stronger, more vital caring. From the start his engagement in humanity and in the making of a new art to service them requires him to venture into the public realm with all his skills as a populist poet-at-large.

Two other books by his most admired contemporaries soon followed in the Pocket Poets Series: Kenneth Rexroth's

30 Spanish Poems of Love and Exile, number 2, and a collection of Kenneth Patchen's *Poems of Humor and Protest*, number 3. The combined cultural meeting place and radically new publishing press of City Lights added impetus to the emergence of the San Francisco Renaissance in poetry, yet other more stunning events lay just around the corner for Ferlinghetti, events that would place City Lights Books in the forefront of this literary revolution of the 1950s.

In 1955 a young Allen Ginsberg walked into City Lights Bookstore and introduced himself to Lawrence Ferlinghetti, who was by now well established in the San Francisco scene. He showed Ferlinghetti a collection of his poems and told him of another long work capturing the spirit of these times. Ferlinghetti was impressed, yet temporarily lacked the funds to do a book for Ginsberg. However, these two young writers began an important and lasting alliance. Their shared respect for such older writers as Walt Whitman, William Carlos Williams, Rexroth, and Patchen helped them to mutually support a new literary tradition against the mainstream of American letters. All too soon they would become public figures stimulating an unrestrained creativity from their fellow contemporaries. The San Francisco Renaissance and the beat movement merged in Ferlinghetti and Ginsberg.

At the historic old Six Gallery Reading in San Francisco poets Philip Lamantia, Michael McClure, Gary Snyder, Philip Whalen, and Allen Ginsberg read while others, including Kenneth Rexroth and Jack Kerouac, provided introductions and boisterous support. Somehow the audience sensed the energy and importance of this monumental confluence of poetry and outlook, a feeling that was certainly brought home by the feverish intensity with which Ginsberg delivered his masterpiece, *Howl*. Ferlinghetti himself was awed by the power demonstrated that night, and, after he and Kirby returned home, that evening, he sent off to Ginsberg a short and sweet telegram echoing Emerson's to Whitman: "I greet you at the beginning of a great career. When do I get the manuscript?"[25] Thus the story of *Howl*, Pocket Poets Book number 4 began.

By 1956 Ferlinghetti had begun another long and fruitful alliance when *New Directions 16* published his first poems from the "Coney Island of the Mind" series. James Laughlin, editor and publisher of New Directions, was impressed with Ferlinghetti's open and direct writing, and he and Ferlinghetti planned a collection of his writings along the pattern of the Pocket Poets Series. It was to include the writings of "A Coney Island of the Mind" and to be expanded by sections from *Pictures of the Gone World* and by 1958, when it went to press, with the "Oral Messages" Ferlinghetti was doing with poetry-and-jazz. This book, *A Coney Island of the Mind* (1958), which Laughlin accepted as an unsolicited manuscript lacking even an introductory note, has become one of the most popular and best-selling books of contemporary poetry (selling close to a million copies by 1980), rivaled only by Ginsberg's *Howl*. James Laughlin provided that crucial encouragement and support which a young writer so needs. In his sincere response to Ferlinghetti's first poems, ("I don't know when I have felt so drawn to a new poet") he offered acceptance and recognition of Ferlinghetti's international writing: "I think you could have here the kind of success that Prévert has had in France."[26] Laughlin continues to be Ferlinghetti's chief publisher and, in many ways, they act as East and West Coast counterparts in their publishing of avant-garde writing.

The first printing of *Howl and Other Poems* hit the streets early in 1957. Fifteen hundred copies had been printed by Villiers of Great Britain, and they were eagerly anticipated by a literate public. It was the second printing of three thousand copies that ran into trouble with the U.S. Customs office in San Francisco. On March 25, 1957, Chester McPhee, Collector of Customs, seized five hundred copies of *Howl* with the declaration: "The words and the sense of the writing is obscene. You wouldn't want your children to come across it."[27] Thus began one of the most celebrated cases of censorship in the United States since the 1933 trial of the ban on James Joyce's *Ulysses*. In anticipation of such problems, Ferlinghetti had already submitted a copy of *Howl* to the American Civil Liberties Union which promptly informed McPhee that it was prepared to fight the seizure. Further, Ferlinghetti met the publishing delay with a simultaneous photo offset edition of *Howl* done in San Francisco. However, the struggle with the censorship move proved to be the focus of international attention and the book's greatest test.

On May 19, Ferlinghetti made a public declaration in the pages of the *San Francisco Chronicle*, whose book editor William Hogan had been supportive of his case. Ferlinghetti claimed *Howl* was "the most significant single long poem to be published in this country since World War II, perhaps since T. S. Eliot's *Four Quartets*."[28] He challenged critics to name another work "since the War which is as significant of its time and place and generation."[29] Boldly suggesting that Collector McPhee be given a medal for rendering the book famous, he went on to focus clearly on the book's intent: "It is not the poet but what he observes which is revealed as obscene. The great obscene wastes of *Howl* are the sad wastes of the mechanized world, lost among atom bombs and insane nationalisms."[30] The book was released on May 29, setting the stage for the second round of confrontation.

During the first week of June, Ferlinghetti and Shig Muroa were arrested and booked by Captain William Hanrahan of the San Francisco Police Department. The ACLU posted bail and the summer-long court case was begun. The Deputy Attorney, Ralph McIntosh, was met by some of the ablest defence attorneys the ACLU could provide—Jake Ehrlich, Lawrence Speiser, and Albert Bendich. Other critical support poured in from editors, poets, educators, and critics, including Henry Rago (editor of *Poetry*), Robert Duncan and Ruth Witt-Diamant (of the San Francisco State College Poetry Center), Thomas Parkinson (of the University of California at Berkeley), James Laughlin, Kenneth Patchen, and others. Barney Rosset and Donald Allen, editors of *Evergreen Review*, published an important section in their second issue featuring the San Francisco writers as a collective movement and printed Ginsberg's poem *Howl*. Their explanation was characteristic of the support for the work: "We believe that it is a significant modern poem, and that Allen Ginsberg's intention was to sincerely and honestly present a portion of his own experience of the life of this generation. . . . Our final considered opinion was that Allen Ginsberg's *Howl* is an achieved poem."[31]

Ferlinghetti did not testify at the trial, and Ginsberg was out of the country. It was, however, a period of intense public attention which Ferlinghetti as a young publisher and spokesman for art and free speech welcomed as a personal test. Ferlinghetti's defense was based on the testimony of expert witnesses: Walter Van Tilburg Clark, Herbert Blau, Arthur Foff, Mark Linenthal (all of San Francisco State College), Kenneth Rexroth, Vincent McHugh, Luther Nichols (book editor of the *San Francisco Examiner*) and Leo Lowenthal. Perhaps the strongest defense came from critic-educator Mark Schorer who as the first witness aptly summed up the work's intent and method. Schorer explained clearly the thematic structure of the work around the elements of materialism, conformity, mechanization, and war as seen through a personal reflective consciousness which has confronted the madness. As to the question of language, and the trial was increasingly becoming one of freedom of speech, he stated concisely, "To write in the language of the streets really meant not to write in the language of poetry; this is the language narrowly determined by critics to be the proper language for poetry. One must always be in rebellion. Each person had to determine his or her own language—from the level of their own mind and their own body."[32] This, in particular, had been and continues to be Ferlinghetti's and City Lights' bold approach to language as a functional and vital reflection of the times and the personal consciousness. He had a lot at stake in the outcome of the trial, and, despite the weak accusations of two local, offended teachers for the prosecution, he was generally relieved and personally exultant over the final verdict of Judge Clayton Horn. Not only did the conservative judge rule that "I do not believe that *Howl* is without even the slightest redeeming social importance," but he also affirmed the book's underlying intent, "It ends in a plea for holy living" and closed with an admonition that had ramifications for future cases of censorship, "Honni soit qui mal y pense (evil to him who thinks evil)."[33]

The importance of this court case to the life and career of Ferlinghetti, as well as to the whole blossoming of the San Francisco Renaissance in poetry and the West Coast beat movement, is difficult to overestimate. Ferlinghetti and Ginsberg became national, if not international, public figures spearheading a revolution in thinking as well as in writing. The case solidified the poetry into a movement with definite principles yet an openness of form. It made poetry a public matter. City Lights Books was catapulted from its tentative successes into broad public attention. By the end of the trial 10,000 copies of *Howl*, a seminal work of the beat movement, had been printed. Having established a precedent, City Lights was followed by other radical small presses such as White Rabbit, Jargon, Auerhahn, and Totem, and as David Kherdian records, "an explosion of little magazines followed both in New York and in San Francisco—'Beatitude,' 'Origin,' 'Semina,' 'Ark II/Moby I,' 'Yugen,' 'Kulchur,' 'Floating Bear,' 'Now,' 'Evergreen Review,' 'Foot,' and 'Measure.'"[34] The dramatic act of defiance and declaration of principles symbolized in the publication and defense of *Howl* had brought the energy of the East Coast Beat Movement to the rich tradition of freedom and experimentation with ideas and expression indigenous to the San Francisco Renaissance. Ferlinghetti's role was vital, and the maturing struggle fostered a release of his inner self while confirming his own outer directedness.

In some other interesting ways Ferlinghetti became a public figure during these years, 1957–59. He and Kenneth Rexroth had been experimenting with combining the brother arts of poetry and jazz in an effort to widen the audience and expand the forms of each. Ferlinghetti was explicit about his motives: "The poets today are talking to themselves, they have no other audience. The competition with the mass media is too much . . . We're trying to capture an audience. . . . The jazz comes in as part of an attempt to get the audience back."[35] Rexroth had invited Ferlinghetti to perform with him and The Cellar Jazz Quintet at San Francisco's The Cellar club. Rexroth provides a portrait of the Ferlinghetti of those days: "He is a lazy-looking, good-natured man with the canny cocky eye of an old-time vaudeville tenor."[36] Kenneth Patchen, who had a long interest in jazz, soon began to perform his own brand of poetry-and-jazz at the Blackhawk Club. Patchen went the furthest with the form in terms of developing a truly new form—poetry-jazz—and in terms of propagating the art, performing at Los Angeles' Jazz Concert Hall (for two months in 1959), over television and on college campuses along the West Coast, then in Vancouver, Canada's jazz center, and at New York's celebrated Five Spot Cafe. The whole poetry-and-jazz scene had received national attention in a *Time* magazine article (Dec. 2, 1957), and some fine performances were recorded by Ferlinghetti, Rexroth, Patchen, Jack Kerouac, and Philip Whalen.[37] Though Ferlinghetti continued to use various types of music in his popular readings—single concerts with the rock music groups Jefferson Airplane and The Band, and more persuasively with his own autoharp accompaniment—he soon grew disillusioned with the poetry-and-jazz form as it was soon supplanted by cheap imitations in little coffee houses throughout the states. Reflecting on that period of poetry-and-jazz experimentation, Ferlinghetti today concludes, "Well, it was an interesting experiment, but generally it wasn't very successful. The musicians generally . . . well, their attitude was usually, 'Like, go ahead and read your poetry, but we got to blow.' And you ended up sounding like you were hawking fish on the street corner trying to be heard above the din. . . . It was a good device for getting a larger audience for poetry, but generally it was murder on the poetry."[38] Nevertheless, Ferlinghetti's development of various forms culminating in the seven-poem "Oral Messages" section of *A Coney Island of the Mind,* particularly the fugue-type poem "Autobiography," demonstrates clearly that the oral poet was developing as he sought larger ways of making poetry a vital and popular form. The practical perspective of publisher combined with the visionary role of poet to engender a more coherent and essential art.

He and Kirby had also found an ideal Victorian home on Potrero Hill in San Francisco which they renovated together. Working on the house and writing in his upstairs office overlooking the bay provided Ferlinghetti with a secure sense of place and a larger perspective on the frantic activities of those days. His energy and commitment during the 1950s was phenomenal. He had found himself and his element in San Francisco. Three more books in the Pocket Poets Series were issued: William Carlos Williams' *Kora in Hell: Improvisations*, number 7, Gregory Corso's *Gasoline*, number 8, and his own translations of Jacques Prévert's *Paroles*, number 9. Not wishing to tie his press too exclusively to the Beat Movement, and recognizing its limits in terms of doing a "big" American novel, Ferlinghetti turned down two important books, Kerouac's *On the Road* and William S. Burroughs' *Naked Lunch*. Though he probably regreted his decision later, he did go on to publish other works by Kerouac, Burroughs, and Neal Cassady.

Ferlinghetti's relationship with Jack Kerouac is a revealing story in itself. Though Ferlinghetti eventually published two of Kerouac's books—*The Book of Dreams*, number 15, edited by Philip Whalen and *Scattered Poems*, number 28, posthumously edited by Ann Charters—as well as a broadside on Rimbaud, it was a demanding relationship on Ferlinghetti as a publisher and a friend. Politically at opposite poles, Kerouac would later refer to both Ferlinghetti and Gregory Corso as communists, while Ferlinghetti marked Kerouac as a rightist reactionary. Yet, in the summer of 1960, Ferlinghetti generously offered Kerouac the use of his Bixby Canyon cabin as a place to dry out, pull himself together, and write. Ferlinghetti had to literally lead Kerouac to the cabin with provisions and leave him in the solitude, hoping that Kerouac would find the inner strength in isolation to finish his work on *Book of Dreams*. Kerouac was not in a solitary mood, and his nightmarish month at Bixby Canyon resulted in the fictionalized *Big Sur* novel which portrayed Ferlinghetti as "Lorenzo Monsanto." Though Kerouac had appreciated Ferlinghetti's kindness and support, nicknaming him "The Smiler," his jealousy and perversity caused him to portray Ferlinghetti as a cordial businessman in *Big Sur*, to which Ferlinghetti has reacted, "I don't particularly feel like a genial businessman."[39] Nevertheless, Ferlinghetti has remained a loyal supporter of Kerouac's writing genius, as evidenced in his recent "Look Homeward, Jack: Two Correspondences." In particular, the parallel is drawn between Kerouac and Thomas Wolfe as mythic writers of America: "Wolfe's place, said Maxwell Perkins, was all America—So with Jack—Kerouac's vision a car vision, seen from windows of old autos speeding cross-country . . . Wolfe and Jack writing together now in eternity . . . omniverous insatiable consumers of life, which consumed them both too early."[40] In this affectionate joint tribute Ferlinghetti offers a final toast to the heartbreaking genius of Kerouac and Wolfe.

Before the 1950s came to a close, Ferlinghetti made one further venture, this time into the realm of political activism. Following the example of Prévert's political verse, he had written a long poem on the Eisenhower administration, which he appropriately titled, "Tentative Description of a Dinner Given to Promote the Impeachment of President Eisenhower." He read the poem first at the 1959 Poets' Follies in San Francisco, then in Berkeley, and at a convention of the American Library Association. He was struck by the reticence of his audiences and by the offense most of them seemed to take. He clarified on the covernotes of the recording of his reading that he was not attacking the person of President Eisenhower, but the incompetence and misguided values of his administration, as the poem demonstrates:

> And after it became obvious that the President was doing everything in his power to make the world safe for nationalism his brilliant military mind never having realized that nationalism itself was the idiotic superstition which would blow up the world.[41]

What is important here is that Ferlinghetti is developing a poetry of direct personal and social involvement. That the public could find this social and political criticism not in keeping with the image of poetry was a mark of American nonchalance toward the mission of both writing and government. Ferlinghetti entered the political arena in 1958 and has been in it ever since, writing a poem to or about each of the succeeding presidential administrations and issuing broadsides on the social and political issues of our times. As has later been disclosed under the Freedom of Information Act, this also marks the period in which Ferlinghetti and Ginsberg were under investigation by the Federal Bureau of Investigation. Labelling their work as "trash . . . responsible in some measure to demoralization in America" the F.B.I. branded the writers as unstable subversives.[42] This official testimony to national fear and repression makes clear the essential nature of Ferlinghetti's outspoken work.

This development toward more and larger realms of involvement is made clear in a statement which Ferlinghetti felt compelled to publish several times in 1958. It is a declaration of his values as well as a clarification of his stance toward the Beat nihilism or "cool" aloofness of the "hipsters" which he so totally rejected:

> William Seward Burroughs said, "Only the dead and the junkie don't care—they are inscrutable." I'm neither. Man. And this is where all the tall droopy corn about the Beat Generation and its being "Existentialist" is as phoney as a four-dollar piece of lettuce. Because Jeal-Paul Sartre cares and has always hollered that the writer especially should be committed. *Engagement* is one of his favorite dirty words. He would give the horse laugh to the idea of Disengagement and the Art of the Beat Generation. Me too. And that Abominable Snowman of modern poetry, Allen Ginsberg, would probably say the same. Only the dead are disengaged.[43]

This frank declaration of engagement is most crucial in any understanding of Ferlinghetti's writing and life. It colors his view of writing as a vital populist act integral with the artist's life and sets the stage for his fuller development and commitment in the 1960s.

Larger Realms of Involvement

Ferlinghetti began a period of progressive involvement in global affairs in January of 1959 when he, Kirby, and Allen Ginsberg traveled to a fifteen-nation writers' conference at the University of Concepción in Chile. They encountered there a gathering made up almost exclusively of doctrinaire communists whose writing sought a very real revolution, while Ginsberg and Ferlinghetti were better characterized as socio-political rebels. His stay in Chile, followed by a tour of Bolivia, Peru, and Mexico, awakened him to the striking levels of illiteracy and poverty, and the primitive labor conditions. Having visited the undersea coal mines at Lota (near Concepción) where the miners emerged from ten-hour work days and one-dollar-an-hour wages in their primitive elevator cages, Ferlinghetti was deeply moved by their plight. At the close of the conference, he completed the twenty-five question literary survey ("What strikes you as the most important thing you've seen in Chile? What is the most important poetry that you've seen in Chile? Who were the most important literary personages in Chile?") with the single repeated response: "The faces of the miners in their cages at Lota." His long poem, "Hidden Door," which depicts the mythic good and evil of mankind, was based on this Latin American experience. While in Chile, he also became friendly with the Chilean poet, Nicanor Parra, whose poems he published in the City Lights *Anti-Poems* volume.

Ferlinghetti's own experimental novel, *Her*, was published by New Directions in 1960. It was a book he had labored on since the 1948 writing during his student days in Paris, a book which he himself characterized as "a surreal semi-autobiographical blackbook record of a semi-mad period in my life."[44] It was truly an experimental and complex novel which received much more attention in Europe with its more open acceptance of both surrealism and the anti-novel. This point continues to trouble Ferlinghetti, indicating both his belief in the form and his personal attachment with the work. In April of 1960 Ferlinghetti also set off an East Coast controversy when he read the beat crucifixion poem "Sometime during eternity" at Oyster Bay College. It was heralded and decried in the *New York Post*, *Newsday*, and the *New York Times*.

The early 1960s was also a time of consolidation and personal growth for Ferlinghetti. His need for a retreat from his growing involvements was met with the purchase of a small parcel of coastal land at Bixby Canyon near Big Sur. In the small and simple cabin which he and Kirby fixed he found a place for the needed solitude and reflection of his writing. The success of City Lights Books and Bookstore allowed the Ferlinghettis to begin a family which provided a source of solidarity when his two children Julie and Lorenzo were born in 1961 and 1962. Against the background of his own sense of family loss he sought to give his children the time and care they needed. This desire for a sense of family was further answered in November of 1960 when he and Kirby traced his family roots back to the Caribbean. He followed the Mendes-Monsanto family back to Puerto Rico, Haiti, and most importantly to Saint Thomas in the Virgin Islands where he discovered his mother's sister Gladys Woods. She provided them with a place to stay and with many missing family details. She also revealed that another aunt, Mrs. Jean McGrath, was living only a short distance from the Ferlinghettis in Bolinas, California. Perhaps this sense of family and past which he had discovered helped him to venture more securely into involvements with world affairs as well as into personal revelations in his writing.

In December, after a brief stay at Chapel Hill, the Ferlinghettis flew to Castro's Cuba in order to report on the revolution there. Ferlinghetti had become involved in the Fair Play for Cuba Committee, which sought meaningful dialogue between the United States and Cuba to counter the prevailing U.S. attitude that the revolution was merely a communist conspiracy. He was immediately struck by the freedom and cohesiveness of the Cuban people, noting in his journal, "All I've seen so far indicates Havana, and Cuba in general, are much, much better off economically than all other Caribbean countries, even British Jamaica, U.S. Puerto Rico (which is considered a U.S. imperialist colony here), and U.S. St. Thomas."[45] He noticed the absence of middle-class attire, that all were dressed as workers, and when he walked into the streets he met a solitary guard seated beneath a sign at the newspaper office of *Revolucion*—the sign read, "PRENSA LIBRE."[46] Before leaving Cuba, the Ferlinghettis made the acquaintance of many young Cuban poets and befriended the Chilean poet Pablo Neruda, who read one night at the Assembly Hall. Ferlinghetti returned to San Francisco with a favorable report to a country which was plotting the demise of the Cuban leader, and he delivered it at the January Fair Play for Cuba Committee rally. In "One Thousand Fearful Words for Fidel Castro" (one of the first City Lights broadsides), Ferlinghetti gauged the American perspective by setting his poem in Mike's Place, North Beach, allowing a telling contrast in the lifestyles of the two countries. The tone is a mixture of laconic reporting and elegiac lament in anticipation of Castro's death at American hands:

> I was sitting in Mike's place, Fidel
> waiting for someone else to act
> like a good Liberal
> I hadn't quite finished reading Camus' *Rebel*
> so I couldn't quite recognize you, Fidel
> walking up and down your island
> when they came for you, Fidel
>
> (*Starting*, 51)

And yet the most daring assertion of the poem statement is the analogy drawn between Fidel Castro and Abraham Lincoln, "one of your boyhood heroes" as each are methodically murdered "in the course of human events" (*Starting*, 52). This bold declaration, against the American grain, which suggests Ferlinghetti's growing acceptance of a humanitarian socialism as the best form of government, earned him the rancor of a great many American political and literary critics as well as the renewed attention of the F.B.I.

Ferlinghetti was just as active in the field of editing and publishing during this period of the early sixties, using the international attention which City Lights had earned to promote some of the best writing that was both radically experimental and socio-politically engaged. In 1960 he coedited *Beatitude*, a mimeographed West Coast beat magazine, with Bob Kaufman, John Kelley, William S. Marjolis, and Allen Ginsberg. The following year he, David Meltzer, and Michael McClure edited the first issue of *Journal for the Protection of All Beings* on the theme of "A Visionary Revolutionary Review." In 1963 *City Lights Journal* was launched, establishing a format of featuring avant-garde work by Kerouac, Burroughs, Ed Sanders, and Ted Joans from the East Coast and Daniel Moore and Richard Brautigan from the West. A special international section featured the writing of India and was edited by Gary Snyder and Allen Ginsberg. *City Lights* number 2 appeared in 1964 and broadened the perspective to include Bengali poets, work by Czechoslovakian poet Miroslav Holub, French novelist Louis-Ferdinand Celine, and New York's Frank O'Hara and San Francisco's Julian Beck. In the political realm there was a controversial interview with Ezra Pound and an appeal for public support in the Paris censorship case of Olympia Press's editor Maurice Girodias. The magazine is a very accurate reflection of Ferlinghetti's own international perspective on the issues and writing of the times; it is integral with the man.

In the Pocket Poets Series Ferlinghetti added two by Ginsberg, *Kaddish*, number 14, and *Reality Sandwiches*, number 18, as well as Patchen's collected *Love Poems*, number 13, Kerouac's *Book of Dreams*, number 15, Malcolm Lowry's *Selected Poems*, number 17, and Frank O'Hara's *Lunch Poems*, number 13. Ferlinghetti also put together the works of three Russian poets, Andrei Voznesensky, Yevgeny Yevtushenko, and Simyon Kirsanov, in *Red Cats*, number 16, translated by

Anselm Hollo. Other books appeared by Paul Bowles, William S. Burroughs, Daniel Moore, and a collection of Antonin Artaud, *Artaud Anthology*, edited by Jack Hirschman.

In the midst of this prolific output, Ferlinghetti's third collection of poems *Starting from San Francisco* (New Directions, 1961) was released. Included with the book was a small recording of Ferlinghetti readings from the poems. The longer poems of this work reflected his increased global travels and revolutionary visions, as he himself described them: "These poems represent to me a kind of a halfway house in the ascent of a mountain I hardly knew existed until I stopped and looked back at the flatlands below" (*Starting*, covernotes). The cover photo for that volume was the symbolic lost Inca city of Machu Picchu, located in Peru near the Chilean border, and it depicts well the book's mode of looking backwards while journeying ahead.

In another arena entirely, Ferlinghetti published two books of short experimental dramas, *Unfair Arguments with Existence* (1963) and *Routines* (1964), both with New Directions. He documents the evolution of these new works: "These rough drafts of plays for a new theatre, or for one that barely exists, these beat-up little dramas taken from Real Life, these unfair arguments with existence (groping toward some tentative mystique) were written in little over a year, dreaming in the back of the Caffe Trieste San Francisco or elsewhere nowhere near a stage."[47] These terse little dramatic happenings which he describes as "routine happenstances that *turn out to be* crises, catharses, epiphanies, confrontations, manifestations, moments of truth, fatal instances,"[48] disclose his longstanding interest in the expressionist and absurdist theatre of Brecht, Artaud, Ionesco, and Beckett. Written in the crowded little Caffe Trieste in North Beach, they are, nevertheless, full of political references, surrealist images, and existential allusions. Though most were never designed to be performed, many have been produced, yet most exist as a new type of theatre of the mind.

Though Ferlinghetti's international direction often finds him in transit to other parts of the globe, in 1965 he began a particularly important period of travel and exploration. In January the entire family flew to Spain where they spent four months in the tiny coastal town of Nerja. Here Ferlinghetti was struck by the control of the Franco regime and wrote a long and as yet unpublished anti-Franco poem, "The Free Spirit Turning Thru Spain." With the family settled back in the United States, Ferlinghetti continued on to Spoleto, Italy, in May. He had been invited to read at the Spoleto Festival of Two Worlds with a truly international cast of poets: Charles Olson, Ingeborg Bachman, Rafael Alberti, Barbara Guest, and, most importantly, Ezra Pound. Though Ferlinghetti was a little uncertain of his relationship with Pound, having published the controversial interview in *City Lights Journal,* it was clearly a momentous meeting with a man who had profoundly influenced Ferlinghetti's early development and shaped his view of poetry as a vital art of the times. His response to Pound's reading was recorded in the beautiful prose poem portrait "Pound at Spoleto" which first appeared in the 1966 *City Lights Journal* number 3. A segment from "Pound at Spoleto" provides a moving portrayal of both the aged poet and Ferlinghetti's own deep attachment:

> The applause was prolonged and Pound tried to rise from his armchair. A microphone was partly in the way. He grasped the arms of the chair with his boney hands and tried to rise. He could not and he tried again and could not. His old friend did not try to help him. Finally she put a poem in his hand and after at least a minute his voice came out. First the jaw moved and then the voice came out, inaudible. . . . The hall had gone silent at a stroke. The voice knocked me down, so soft, so thin, so frail, so stubborn still. I put my head on my arms on the velvet sill of the box. I was surprised to see a single tear drop on my knee. The thin, indomitable voice went on. Come to this! I went blind from the box, through the back door of it into the empty upper corridor and out into the sunlight, weeping.

Having internalized the presence of this living figure of modern poetry's spiritual revolt and commitment, the poet finds the world around him transformed: "Mute birds flew in the valley below, far off, the sun shone on the chestnut trees, and the leaves turned in the sun, and turned and turned, and would continue turning. His voice went on, and on, through the leaves."[49] What begins as a piece of journalistic reporting evolves through personal attention to the moment and its detail into the final clear Imagist poem. Ferlinghetti is indicating far more than his emotional reaction here; he has written a portrait that works through Pound's lessons and achieves a new bond between life and art. In a later version printed in *Open Eye, Open Heart* Ferlinghetti adapts the open-form spacing engendered through Pound to the final lines of tribute.

Back in Paris, Ferlinghetti received word of a grand poetry event to be held in London. On June 11, 1965, the International Poetry Reading happened at London's Royal Albert Hall amidst criticism and acclaim. English novelist Alexander Troochi served as master of ceremonies for the four hour happening which played to a crowd of seven thousand. Among the gregarious and revolutionary poets who read were Ferlinghetti's old and new friends: Allen Ginsberg, Gregory Corso, Adrian Mitchell, Michael Horovitz, German Ernst Jandl (who did concrete sound poetry), and Russian Andrei Voznesensky. Ferlinghetti read a controversial political poem which seemed to unite the crowd in a visionary spirit of anarchy and love, "To Fuck Is to Love Again / Kyrie Eleison Kerista / or / The Situation in the West, followed by a Holy Proposal." Beginning in his San Francisco "Dreaming of utopias / where everyone's a lover" the poet goes on to catalogue the absurdities of commerce and war and affronts the governmental waste of life with a more positive vision of sexual and compassionate energy directed toward a blessedness of life. It closes with the Eastern chant:

> *hosanna pulchrissima*
> *kyrie kyrie kyrie hallelujah*!
> we'll all still have the sun
> in which to recognize ourselves at last across the world
> over the obscene boundaries!
>
> (*Starting*, 64)

The poem demonstrates the full emergence of Ferlinghetti as a public and political spokesman seeking a Blakean and Eastern vision of oneness that defies nationalistic or artistic limits. The event was recorded in the film by Peter Whitehead and in the book *Wholly Communion* (Grove, 1965). The Eastern references testify to this period of Buddhist influence in Ferlinghetti's development.

When Ferlinghetti returned to San Francisco, he followed his involvements into the arena of protest at home. Together with poet Robert Bly, he began a series of protest readings throughout the United States against the Vietnam War. His broadside poem "Where Is Vietnam?" which confronts then President Lyndon Johnson (Colonel Cornpone) and an ignorant American public with the real and dark vision of death and destruction in Vietnam, was a well-suited parallel for Bly's own powerful "The Teeth Mother Naked at Last."

With new vigor Ferlinghetti turned to publishing and produced *City Lights Journal* number 3, Charles Olson's critical work on Melville, *Call Me Ishmael*, and Carl Solomon's *Mishaps, Perhaps* in 1966. His own selected poems appeared in a 1967 British collection, *An Eye on the World* (London: McGibbon and Kee). The works of American surrealists Philip Lamantia, *Selected Poems*, number 20, and Bob Kaufman, *Golden Sardines*, number 21, were added to the Pocket Poets Series bringing City Lights combined output to almost fifty publications.

David Kherdian provides a rare and interesting personal portrait of the man, Lawrence Ferlinghetti, during this period. Interviewing Ferlinghetti at his home on Portreto Hill, Kherdian records the upstairs office with its view of the bay and its files of City Lights correspondence surrounding the large desk and composing typewriter. Ferlinghetti's faithful dog, Homer, lies sleeping by his side as he fulfills his morning-to-noon writing routine. Much of this detail is also recorded in *U.S.A. Poets: Allen Ginsberg and Lawrence Ferlinghetti*, a film made by National Educational Television. Though he appears quite jocular before the cameras as he types behind a golden persona mask and walks the streets of San Francisco with his dog, there is the sense of personal distance about him which Kherdian's account also records:

> Ferlinghetti, now 47 and sprouting a closely cropped salt and pepper beard, is tall and lean, and takes the long silent strides of a much younger man. . . . His speech comes from a mind that seems intentionally halved: one being the banal words he speaks, the other the thoughtful words he considers. The cool distance he keeps from outsiders makes him seem phlegmatic, even churlish. . . . It's as if he'd willed all his energy to be mental, but without changing the look of impenetrable innocence and inscrutability on his face, or without even becoming cerebral—but thoughtful, observant, concerned with the minutest detail;—finding in such minutiae a universal disposition.[50]

Kherdian's portrait, though certainly a subjective impression, captures well the complex yet direct sensibility of the poet. Ferlinghetti's mixture of concrete factual detail and deep subconscious images is characteristic of his approach, and his intensity and intuition as a publisher are renowned. While he easily projects an extroverted self, he maintains an experienced guard on his private self. Yet, he is an adept engineer and advocate of lively discourse.

He next journeyed to Berlin where he read with Andrei Voznesensky at the Berlin Literary Colloquium in February, 1967. The work which he read, "After the Cries of the Birds," was an attempt to bring his personal and public sense together in an apocalyptic vision of mankind. As he records in the prose account of this writing, "Genesis of *After the Cries of the Birds*," the poem had its origins in diverse outer and inner experiences—"Beginning in Rock & Roll folk dances at Fillmore Auditorium Fall 1965 ... mixed with trips to my cabin Bixby Canyon Big Sur and its wild beach of white sand rock & kelp ... having withheld a 'symbolic portion' of my Federal Income taxes in unheard protest against Vietrock War ... lost in self and distracted age 45 body passed somnambule through cauchemar Paradise Lost Londons inperveable New York, to haven San Francisco 1951 family sprung up with love

... yet I still self-distracted & wandering after some still voice of the fourth person singular mislaid in the function of the orgasm ... a poet against my will, no other life-alternative, nothing else possible, poetry the only self-solution, the last and only resort."[31] Ferlinghetti's own characterization of the phases of his life and his poetic motivation are revealing and integral to the long evolution of this particular poem which received a further visionary impetus that summer: "After a definite break, a break-through, my first trip on LSD, one fine clear blue shining summer morning on Bixby Beach ... the light become an inutterable brightness ... Time is history ... Like the sea, the level of consciousness rises, lapping ... Ah! Light out of light!"[52] This first experience with the drug LSD projected him into a "Feeling of total loneliness, in the universe, a part of it, yet apart, lonely in the cave with my body, after the cries of the birds ... Only silence remains."[53] The vision is both negative and positive, subjective and universal, as an apocalypse turns chaos into silence and then opens to the infinitely possible. He concludes, "In the end there is no way to go but In. Into ourselves ... Pause & begin again."[54] This remarkable prose document of his writing and life, which he documents as having been written New Year's Day 1967, characterizes both his development and his direction as he seeks that further union of private and public self. The poem itself closes on this open stance, "The seas come in to cover us / Agape we are & agape we'll be."[55]

Ferlinghetti's Russian friend, poet Andrei Voznesensky, arranged a trip for him through Russia in February of 1967, on which he was able to note the discrepancies between communist ideals and realities, to visit the Writers' Union in Moscow, and to record many images for future writing in his Russian journals. One poem that came immediately from the experience was the broadside poem "Moscow in the Wilderness, Segovia in the Snow," the result of a seven-day trans-Siberian train trip inspired by the French writer Blaise Cendrars. Ferlinghetti recalls the severe cold which he caught on the trip, and notes that he "damn near died." The poem, however, captures the haunting ironies of the Russian people and landscape where Segovia, speaking through Ferlinghetti, wonders "Is Lenin listening / after fifty Octobers" and "Where is joy where is ecstasy / stretched out in the snow / where only the birds are at home." He records, instead, "There's a huge emptiness here / that stares from all the faces / All that is lost must be / looked for once more" (*Secret*, 43, 45). This poem and most of the other poems of travel and world reflection from this period soon appeared together in *The Secret Meaning of Things* (New York: New Directions, 1968), his fourth collection of poetry.

Back in his San Francisco haven, Ferlinghetti prepared himself for another round of confrontation at home. In the summer of 1967, he, Allen Ginsberg, and Michael McClure joined with the young "hippie" culture that was emerging in San Francisco for the first Human Be-In at Golden Gate Park. They were recognized as older voices who had sought all along a culture of freedom and peace. Then in a demonstration against the military draft at Oakland Army Induction Center on December 9, Ferlinghetti was arrested along with writer Kay Boyle and folk singer Joan Baez. Despite Ferlinghetti's plea that the demonstration's sole "purpose was to block the entrance to war. The motives of the demonstrators were pure and the action was totally nonviolent,"[56] they were sentenced to nineteen days in the Santa Rita county prison. Here Ferlinghetti worked in the laundry stencilling pants; he also kept a journal which was smuggled out and published in *Ramparts* magazine in March 1968. His poem "Salute" was written in prison as an open and defiant reaction to increased armament around the world.

His reaction to the election and inauguration of Richard Nixon, whom he had distrusted since Nixon's days on the House on Un-American Activities Committee, was the long statement *Tyrannus Nix?* (New York: New Directions, 1968). Termed "a political-satirical tirade" by Ferlinghetti, it contains a dedication "To Pressley E. Bisland, father emeritus" who had encouraged an involved yet satiric view of politics in young Ferlinghetti. The form was a long letter to President Richard Nixon as the face of adult, television America. It is a confrontation with the lost American values and contains a wealth of allusion to political philosophers Herbert Marcuse,

R. D. Laing, Buckminster Fuller, as well as to Apollinaire, Vachel Lindsay, and Bertolt Brecht. It is perhaps most striking as a prophetic forecast of the corruption of the Watergate conspiracy, and a later appended cover for the book, "Watergate Rap, 1969–1973," brings home the irony of American political trust and mistrust. Ferlinghetti accurately refers to this work as an unheeded "populist hymn," and it echoes his earlier populist hymn of another sort—"Assassination Raga," delivered at the Incredible Poetry Reading at Nourse Auditorium with raga musical accompaniment on June 8, 1968, the burial date of Attorney General Robert Kennedy. It is a response to the "Death of TV" of both Jack and Robert Kennedy and was chanted to the raga in a synthesis of Eastern and Western requium. In a very real sense, a great many people began to look to Ferlinghetti as a populist spokesman with a large and long perspective on political and social affairs and with a bold ability to express their common conscience.

City Lights published the third issue of *The Journal for the Protection of All Beings*, the "Green Flag" issue concerned specifically with the People's Park protests at Berkeley. It rounded out the 1960s with three more books in the Pocket Poets series: Ginsberg's *Planet News*, number 23, Charles Upton's *Panic Grass*, number 24, and Paul Blackburn's translations of Pablo Picasso's *Hunk of Skin*, number 25. It was a decade in which Ferlinghetti had gained national then international attention and influence, one of prolific output and direct activist involvement. In many ways Ferlinghetti had found his public and private self in his role as poet-at-large, yet his relentless desire for growth and renewal, his existential motive, would take him into new and deeper realms in the decade to come.

LIVING BEYOND THE MYTHS

As we have seen repeatedly, Ferlinghetti combines a journalistic and mythic view of his life. It is not surprising then to have him provide the profound metaphor for his life in the 1970s. In "Adieu à Charlot: Second Populist

Manifesto" he confronts himself and his audience with the necessity for facing their lives squarely by stripping away the remnants of myths each has created as a survival tactic. He lists for himself and for those who have listened to his writing: the bohemian myth, the myth of Whitman, Hemingway, Henry Miller, Gaugin, D. H. Lawrence, Malcolm Lowry, Bob Dylan, Kerouac and Cassady, Joan Baez, Allen Ginsberg, Ken Kesey, and others, as ultimate blocks toward the final authentic coming home to himself. He sees others living these myths in the streets daily and knows them well from his own life. Thus the 1970s, the sixth decade of his life, finds Ferlinghetti a good gray poet whose drive for the authentic has brought him pain and wisdom. No less committed to his earlier values and involvements, he is perhaps more existentially whole through the outliving of his personal myths.

The Mexican Night (New York: New Directions, 1970) contains the journal writing of a lifelong relationship with the country of Mexico and contains the following dedication to his son, Lorenzo: "Should he someday come upon himself in that labyrinth of solitude." The journeys dating back to the late 1950s are surveyed for the sense of self and Mexico which emerges through experiences as diverse as smoking marijuana on a public bus, the vision of death and evil in the corpse of a dog, and his witness to the poverty and brotherhood of the Indians. It closes with his personal and mythic image of the self which endures: "It is as if I were waiting for the sea to stop its absolute incoherence. . . . I see myself in the dark distance, a stick-figure in the world's end."[57] A second book of journeys followed in 1971. *Back Roads to Far Places* (New York: New Directions) is a long poem dedicated to daughter Julie who is "on her way"; it embraces a more Eastern outlook and form, yet the journey toward self is clearly the controlling vision: "Ah how my life runs on / into the Real / back roads / to far places / lost in the traces." Such works reveal both his sense of family and his ongoing quest for self.

Ferlinghetti had made a publishing partnership in 1970 with Nancy Joyce Peters, who is a poet herself and the wife of poet Philip Lamantia. Though he smilingly refers to her as the "brains of the outfit," it is clear that Ferlinghetti regards her as a full partner in the publishing and the bookstore, the first coeditor of City Lights. Peters also has provided a sustaining friendship through some of the trying personal struggles of his later life. In 1971 Bruce Cook assessed the cultural contribution of City Lights Books as "one of the most important independent publishing ventures of the last twenty-five years," which he attributes in part to the bookstore which broke down the false barrier between the writer and his public, one of "the important pre-conditions if any independent literary culture is to begin to grow."[58] City Lights opened the seventies with Diane Di Prima's *Revolutionary Letters*, number 27 and Jack Kerouac's posthumous *Scattered Poems*, number 28, edited by Ann Charters. Ferlinghetti himself set about the great unfinished task of editing the writings of Neal Cassady, perhaps the most mythic beat figure. Cassady's writings were published in 1971 as *The First Third* by City Lights, followed by a volume of Timothy Leary's prison writing, *Eagle Brief*.

While this work kept Ferlinghetti's mind occupied, it did not protect him from the emotional strain of a collapsing marriage. He and Kirby had been unable to come to terms with each other's needs, so he moved into an apartment over the City Lights Books office on Grant Avenue in 1971. During this period Ferlinghetti's aunt, Mrs. Jean McGrath, provided family support in nearby Bolinas. Ferlinghetti's deep concern about the effects of divorce on his children may have been one reason that the marriage continued until the final divorce in 1976 when Ferlinghetti was given custody of the children. He then moved in with his friend and lover Paula Lellevand, a North Beach activist poet whom he had met in 1972. The divorce caused Ferlinghetti a great deal of personal pain as he witnessed the death of yet another myth concerning love, and it became the theme of several of his poems, "Lost Parents," "People Getting Divorced," "Great American Waterfront Poem," and "Director of Alienation."

A 1972 trip to Australia with his son Lorenzo and good friend Allen Ginsberg provided a chance for him to relax as well as an opportunity to read in the Adelaide Festival and at Melbourne and Sydney with another long-time friend Andrei Voznesensky. City Lights had just published Voznesensky's *Dogalypse*, number 29, and Ginsberg's *The Fall of America*, number 30 had just received the National Book Award for poetry, so in many ways it was a happy though busy trip. Ferlinghetti did develop a pattern of relaxing with his son on fishing and camping trips in Hawaii and along the Pacific Coast, during which he kept a journal of prose and poems.

In the mid-1970s he directed his energies and time to other projects and involvements. His largest book of poems, *Open Eye, Open Heart* (New York: New Directions, 1973), contained over a decade of work and required much effort and time in arrangement. The poems are representative of Ferlinghetti's varied forms and interests organized into four parts, a biographical life-reporting section, poems from his many trips, political poems, and a final section entitled "American Mantra & Songs" which revealed his interest in "developing chants with American English words." The writing is lyrical, satirical, real and surreal, filled with meditation and confrontation. J. M. Warner wrote in a review, "At 50 years of age, Ferlinghetti is still as dynamic, verbose, alarming, charming and unsettling as when he began writing poetry."[59] It is a major work by a major American writer. He also put through three volumes of poetry: Pete Winslow's American surrealism in *A Daisy in the Memory of a Shark*, number 31, Harold Norse's *Hotel Nirvana*, number 32, and Anne Waldman's *Fast Speaking Woman*, number 33, and published two volumes of bold short fiction by friend Charles Bukowski. A further life-art link is apparent in Ferlinghetti's pattern of establishing close personal relationships with those he publishes.

San Francisco furnished the setting for projects as Ferlinghetti launched the Poets' Theatre through City Lights. The theatre provided a site for mass readings, one of which was the Benefit Reading for the Greek Resistance at which Ferlinghetti read his anarchistic poem "Forty Odd Questions for the Greek Regime and One Cry for Freedom." At another more personal reading, this time a Memorial Reading for Kenneth Patchen (Feb. 3, 1972), Ferlinghetti delivered his beautiful and profound "An Elegy on the Death of Kenneth Patchen." Capturing Patchen's original form and bold involvements, the poem mixes lush and pointed lines of Patchen with Ferlinghetti's own existential awareness of the poet's life:

A poet is born
A poet dies
And all that lies between
is us
and the world.
(*Open*, 37)

The poem, which rivals "Pound at Spoleto" as a tribute, achieves through its recognition of self in the other a lyric poignancy. Acknowledging that Patchen's ashes had been cast upon the Pacific, Ferlinghetti releases a flow of images of wonder in tune with Patchen's own writing:

And he swings in the tides of the sea
And his ashes are washed
in the tides of the sea
And 'an astonished eye looks out of the air'
to see the poet singing there

And the dusk falls down a coast somewhere

where a white horse without a rider
turns its head
to the sea.
(*Open*, 39)

On his final visit with the ailing Patchen at Palo Alto, Miriam Patchen noted how deeply moved yet reticent Ferlinghetti remained. It was a silence eloquently broken with this elegy.

Ferlinghetti had also become engaged in the workings of the San Francisco Zen Center founded by Suzuki Roshi and was much impressed with the teachings of J. Krishnamurti, both of whom he found to be genuine and humble. Yet his political and social involvements remained direct and outspoken as he worked for the cause of the United Farm Workers of America and for such ecological concerns as the Greenpeace anti-whaling campaign and anti-nuclear power protests. One long-time concern, dating back to his 1968 *Tyrannus Nix?*, was the issue of encroachment upon freedom of speech in the arts through federally funded and controlled grant systems—The National Endowment for the Arts, the National Endowment for the Humanities, Coordinating Council of Little Magazines and Small Presses. Ferlinghetti waged a campaign, which may have lost him favor with some small press publishers and writers, through his widely published poem "Populist Manifesto" and the 1976 "A Political Pamphlet" put out by the Anarchist Resistance Press. In essence Ferlinghetti's stance is that, while these grants may have no outward strings attached, they do cultivate a dependency upon government money which may be withdrawn and for which the artist or press has already symbolically demonstrated a corrupting relationship. He warns, "The state, whether capitalist or Communist, has an enormous capacity to ingest its most dissident elements."[60] As he wrote to Stanley Kunitz in refusing to read at the Library of Congress, his principle is simple, "Guilt by complicity, as I learned it chez Camus, is I'm afraid still to be reckoned with."[61] Ferlinghetti also developed a populist stance by publishing his poems, particularly the Populist Manifestoes, in newspapers, often in the nonliterary sections of the *New York Times*, the *San Francisco Examiner*, and the *Los Angeles Times*. When San Francisco's Mayor George Mascone and Supervisor Harvey Milk were assassinated in November 1978, his "An Elegy to Dispell Gloom" appeared on the front page of the *San Francisco Examiner* and helped to dispel the violent reactions in the streets of San Francisco. Ever increasingly Ferlinghetti ties himself to the people.

When *City Lights Anthology* appeared in 1974, it brought to the surface another of Ferlinghetti's lifelong concerns by featuring a fifty-page self-edited section by the "Surrealist Movement of the United States." It should be pointed out that Ferlinghetti's coeditor Nancy Joyce Peters as well as friends

Philip Lamantia and Stephen Schwartz were members of the San Francisco Magnetic Fields group which had merged with this Chicago-based group headed by Franklin and Penelope Rosemont. The group is surprisingly pure in its surrealist theory and practice of subversive art and is a strong voice and direct conspirator in the International Surrealist Movement. Ferlinghetti's alliance dates back to his Paris days of the 1940s: "I considered myself a surrealist in Paris in those days, in as much as I considered myself anything . . . but I was a *Nadja* surrealist, rather than a Manifesto surrealist."[62] Ferlinghetti's relationship to surrealism will be explored later in this study, but it is important to note his clear admiration for their subversive and purist stance toward institutionalized constraints. His concern for providing a vehicle for the dissident voice is demonstrated in his plans for publishing a new magazine "Free Spirit: Surrealism, Anarchism, Socialism" in the 1980s. The *City Lights Anthology* also included works of West Coast writers, a tribute to spiritual leader Alan Watts, and a section of contemporary Greek poets. Jack Hirschman's *Lyripol*, number 34, poems of West Coast communism, also appeared in 1974.

Ferlinghetti's *Who Are We Now?* was published by New Directions in 1976, and it was followed by a reading tour of Mexico. The book's title illustrates well his universal questioning of self in light of public and private events. The opening poem "The Jack of Hearts" is a tribute to folk-rock singer Bob Dylan mixed with memory allusions to the late Jack Kerouac. It poses the essential question: "Who are we now, who are we ever / Skin books parchment bodies libraries of the living."[63] Ferlinghetti declares that individually—like Dylan, like himself, like Kerouac—and collectively we evolve through our questioning. The country had survived Vietnam without facing it, was faced with a new president, "The President Who Was Nothing" (*Political Pamphlet*), and seemed trapped in limbo until its citizens asked the essential questions which he posed. For himself, too, it was a time of probing immediately following his divorce and a separation of another kind. His bookstore partner of twenty years, Shig

Murao, was hospitalized, and when Ferlinghetti tried to ease him into part-time managing of the expanding City Lights Bookstore, Shig flatly quit, thus ending another myth of friendship and creating a gap in Ferlinghetti's already torn life. His life with Paula Lellevand and their combined families, and in particular their times of retreat and solidarity at Bixby Canyon, became all the more important to him.

Ferlinghetti has continued his relentless productivity and confrontation of social and personal issues through the seventies and into the eighties. The City Lights Pocket Poets Series has been expanded by Allen Ginsberg's *Mind Breaths*, number 35, Stefan Brecht's *Poems*, number 36, and Peter Orlovsky's *Clean Asshole Poems & Smiling Vegetable Songs*, number 37. City Lights is also publishing retrospective work by Samuel Greenberg, Edgar Allen Poe, Blaise Cendrars, John Reed, and Karl Marx. Ferlinghetti's own perspective on the whole San Francisco literary revolution has been provided in his photo history, *Literary San Francisco: A Pictorial History* (City Lights and Harper and Row, 1980) which he has coauthored with Nancy Joyce Peters. In 1976 he helped to found and sponsor (through City Lights) the San Francisco International Poetry Festival and was honored by a San Francisco Civic Art Festival Day devoted to his work and contribution. His record of his travels to Paris and Rome, where he participated in the First International Festival of Poetry, has been published by New Directions as *A Trip to Italy and France*. Recent activities have included participation in a Conference on Urban Literature at Rutgers University, reading at Paris's "Polyphonix 2" which honored City Lights Books' twenty-fifth year, and support of the San Francisco's Writers' collective, "Group 80." *City Lights Journal* number 4 (1978) contains a truly international collection of innovative poetry and prose.

Ferlinghetti's own writings have appeared in the *Northwest Ecolog* (City Lights, 1978), poetry and prose journal writings of his camping trips with his son along the West Coast. They, like his more recent poetry collection *Landscapes of Living and Dying* (New York: New Directions, 1979) reflect his continued concerns for man's coming to humanitarian and ecological terms with his living. There is a warm, mellow tone throughout each book reflecting a growing acceptance Ferlinghetti has found with his life. Whether it is his personal identification with the aging ancestors of "The Old Italians Dying," his overflowing compassion in "The Love Nut," or his celebration of the Chaplinesque, "the collective subjective / the Little Man in each of us," Ferlinghetti has achieved a rare animal oneness with nature and man. Though these works reflect a wiser and fuller "coming home" of the author to his long-sought self, we can be sure that their resolutions are not resignations and that his authentic and engaged quest is renewed each day.

In the recently published *Endless Life: Selected Poems* (New Directions, 1981) Ferlinghetti offers us his own perspective on his life and art. The resultant personality of form which emerges through his ongoing, open-form autobiography of consciousness provides each poem with its resonating core and the extended work with its organic unity and authority. In this ripened area of the author's conscious life-art interrelationship, in this total complex of consciousness, Ferlinghetti stands as subject and object, as author-narrator-hero combined. Mutlu Blasing in *The Art of Life* defines this role of personal yet public poet as a point of synthesis in which the subjective "I" becomes collective and mythic, aware of time and its timelessness, "not only past but present, both the observed and the observer, history and historian, hero and poet, form and life."[64] By understanding this biographical basis of Ferlinghetti's work and its resultant record of consciousness, from birth through growth to death, we grasp his comprehensive personality of form and understand his integrated life-art identity as our chief contemporary poet-at-large.

2

A Stance Toward Life and Art

> Poetics are the politics of poetry
> sticking feet to flypaper
> making everything and everyone
> hang together
> but I like live models
> like all those free feet at dog level
>
> ("Berlin")

WORKING out the dynamics of Lawrence Ferlinghetti's poetics is essential to developing an appreciation of his achievement as a writer. The task is somewhat complicated by the fact that Ferlinghetti's integral theory of art and life follows European lines, rather than the mainstream of American literature, and by the fact that his statements of poetics are rare, though direct, occurring primarily within his poetry. The challenge then is to accurately place him within a European tradition of literature, which has, nevertheless, had major American adherents, and to formulate a working theory of poetics from his open though fragmentary declarations. It is a necessary act if we are to bridge the gap between his important work and the development of a vital contemporary criticism. We should not forget that Ferlinghetti, despite his disclaimer, did a detailed dissertation on modern poetry, worked for a time as a critic of art and writing, has issued three Populist Manifestoes on the nature and needs of contemporary writing, and is also a careful editor and publisher of contemporary writing. His influence on the contemporary practice of writing is profound, if not pervasive. As Charles Olson pointed out in his landmark essay "Projective Verse vs. The NON-Projective," what leads us into a new poetics is the contemporary poet's "stance toward reality outside a poem as well as a new stance toward the reality of a poem itself."[1] Not only do Ferlinghetti's poetics provide the true path to his methods and achievement, but they also illuminate the working poetics of much of the contemporary poetry of engagement.

Perhaps the best prose key to Ferlinghetti's own poetics is the introduction he offered to his translations of Jacques Prévert's *Paroles*. Prévert is an important figure in the early development of Ferlinghetti as an artist. The differences between Ferlinghetti and Prévert have been pointed out by critics Kenneth Rexroth and Samuel Charters[2] and are highlighted by Ferlinghetti's own assessment of Prévert's weakness for sentimentality, triteness, and surface naturalism—faults which nevertheless are linked with Ferlinghetti's own writing. It is, however, the similarities between these two bohemian artists that are most revealing. From his first discovery of Prévert, ironically on a paper tablecloth in a restaurant in St. Brieuc, Ferlinghetti sensed a radical defiance of the norms of literature and art. He suggests, "Prévert spoke particularly to the French youth immediately after the War, especially to those who grew up during the Occupation and felt totally estranged from Church and State,"[3] and he finds the perspective applicable to America: "Since then we have had our own kind of resistance movement in our writers of dissent—dissent from the official world of the upper middle-class ideal and the White Collar delusion and various other systemized tribal insanities" (*Paroles*, 3). Having embraced Prévert's poetics of dissent, Ferlinghetti adopts a necessary subversive stance toward art: "There are those who have always considered Prévert no more than a Surrealist clown . . . And he is finally put down by today's poets and critics for committing the cardinal crime of too much clarity in a world whose very Absurdity (Cf. Camus' *Myth of Sisyphus*) Absurdly cries for an expression of that Absurdity in all its arts" (*Paroles,* 5). Refusing to render Prévert historically obsolete, Ferlinghetti confirms in him the contemporary and philosophical relevance of his stance. His "Translator's Note" was written in 1964 when Ferlinghetti had thoroughly digested and enlarged his own poetics with the existential philosophy of Albert Camus and Jean-Paul Sartre. Thus grounded in this desperate yet vital view of life, the position of poet of dissent was dictated by the times, as Ferlinghetti explains, "no other life-alternative, nothing else possible, poetry the only self-solution, the last and only resort."[4] As Karl Malkoff explains, "Even in Ferlinghetti's most explicit aesthetic statements, art is not defined in terms of itself but rather is grounded in the necessities of human experience. It is because we live in 'the empty air of existence' that the poet must take his risks. And because he is aware of the enormity of human suffering and the absurdity of the human condition, the poet has a commitment to his world as well as to his art."[5] For Ferlinghetti, as for Prévert and the surrealists, Camus and the existentialists, the act of writing is directly tied to the act of living—the condition of the world and the poet's consciousness. The poet is clearly not free to construct a tower of art, but must work first to save the world by changing it.

The visionary role of poet-prophet is intricately bound to his function as actualist of the public nightmare. Ferlinghetti therefore praises Prévert: "Still there are many so-called poets around these days who have need of such a seeing-eye dog in the street. Prévert remains a great 'see-er' if not a seer. He writes as one talks while walking" (*Paroles,* 5). In "5" of the early *Pictures of the Gone World* we find Ferlinghetti's flat declaration that "A POEM IS A MIRROR WALKING DOWN A STRANGE STREET." This line was taken from a long unpublished statement of poetics, "The Street's Kiss: Aphorisms on Poetry (Ars Poetica)," from the summer of 1955. In it Ferlinghetti was working out the dynamics of his own functional and immediate aesthetics: "Poetry is a high house echoing with all the voices that ever said anything crazy or wonderful. . . .

Poetry is the pure speech of everybody's exile." In his 1958 "Note on Poetry in San Francisco" for *Chicago Review* he further defined his concept of an urgent street poetry: "It amounts to getting the poet out of the inner esthetic sanctum where he has too long been contemplating his complicated navel. It amounts to getting poetry back into the street where it once was, out of the classroom, out of the speech department, and in fact—off the printed page. The printed work has made poetry so silent."[6] Prévert's quality as outspoken consciousness reflector, echoed in Ferlinghetti's image of the "Hungry Eye" of the above poem, unites the role of the poet-of-the-street with that of the oral poet. The poet is to be out there in the world—seeing it and saying it. This called for a radical change in both the content and methods of his art.

In a poem that has become synonymous with Ferlinghetti's plebian stance toward life and art, he charts the dog's life of the poet in positive terms:

DOG
The dog trots freely in the street
and sees reality
and the things he sees
are bigger than himself
and the things he sees
are his reality

The poet catalogues in objective detail those reality images from common life:

Drunks in doorways
Moons on trees
. . . .
Fish on newsprint
Ants in holes
Chickens in Chinatown windows
their heads a block away

Yet the young dog-poet is also conscious of what he records and affected by what he sees and hears:

Although what he hears is very discouraging
very depressing
very absurd
to a sad young dog like himself
to a serious dog like himself

Like Ferlinghetti and Prévert, "He will not be muzzled" by repressive institutions such as the policeman around the corner or Congressman Doyle of the House Committee on Un-American Activities; in fact, "Congressman Doyle is just another fire hydrant / to him." Yet the real concern of this Beat, existential dog is to record and reflect reality:

touching and tasting and testing everything
investigating everything
without benefit of perjury
a real realist
. . . .
with something to say
                                        about ontology

something to say
                                about reality
                                                and how to see it
                                                                and how to hear it

Finally the dog stills himself into the symbolic stance which Ferlinghetti has adopted all along:

looking
            like a living questionmark
                                    into the
                            great gramaphone
                        of puzzling existence.
                                                (*Coney*, *67–68*)

Rarely has any poet stated so clearly and with such characteristic ease the artist's role which he has claimed. The poem has all the colloquial crispness, direct commitment, and dangerous lucidity of Prévert at his very best. Ferlinghetti has declared himself as the open and public realist daring to speak our common truths.

Besides castigating mutual targets of simple-minded nationalism, institutionalized authoritarianism, the hypocrisy of moralistic sexual attitudes, military aggression and a general and modern waste of life, Prévert and Ferlinghetti share in their development of a new language of poetry. Michael Benedikt's description of Prévert's functional diction presents a strikingly apt parallel with Ferlinghetti's own method: "The poet's own diction is an implicit rebuke to this [sterile formality]: casual, colloquial, and fluid, alive with sudden shifts of mood, it moves with ease from sentiment to irony, anger to tenderness, flatness to a kind of ecstacy of delicacy, transmitting the poet's ideal, which is that of a kind of transformed earth: perhaps an Eden."[7] Using the full range of spoken and verbal dynamics, both poets are concerned with a remaking of life through remaking art into an immediate and functional means, one which actually changes the nature of life by changing our means of perceiving and expressing it.

The parallel to Arthur Rimbaud as well as to the French Surrealist Movement is obvious in this effort to revitalize art and life. It was Rimbaud who chiefly asserted this transforming function for writing to "change life," as he worked towards a visionary poetry of action. As Paul Schmidt declares of Rimbaud's ideals, "His writings are the notes of a quest, a search for a kind of perfection only children believe in, an attempt to find an absolute freedom."[8] In the alchemy of language which Rimbaud passed on to the surrealists, he seeks a method in tune with the needs of the times. What Ferlinghetti claimed from Rimbaud, besides a visionary and yet functionally vital sense of art, was a new boldness about language and a strong sense of idealistic innocence. As Samuel Charters points out concerning Ferlinghetti's world view, "His own idealism is an oblique expression of the same innocence that has deeply influenced [Gary] Snyder and [Lew] Welch. It is not an expression of ignorance, but a refusal to accept the society's corruption."[9] Ferlinghetti, the poet who boldly declares the madness of the streets, is also the poet who awaits "perpetually and forever / a renaissance of wonder" (*Coney*, 53). His idealism remains intact because he refuses to compromise his faith in life's potential. It is the basis of his pacifist, anarchist, and ecological stand. This concept of "wonder" has a firm foundation in the French Romantic tradition of Rousseau and later Surrealism, in the British Romanticism of Wordsworth, Coleridge, and Blake, as well as in American romantics Emerson, Thoreau, and Whitman. Ferlinghetti found it echoed in Eastern philosophy and in contemporaries such as E. E. Cummings, Thomas Wolfe, William Carlos Williams, Kenneth Patchen, Robert Duncan, and Jack Kerouac. As an integral part of a world view, it embraces faith in the freedom, spontaneity, and innocent questioning of the child and a ready acceptance of the validity of the imagination. Life's unity and man's divinity are affirmed in the child's open response to the universe which he beholds, as Kenneth Patchen describes it, in his "sense of wonder, a sense of identification with everything that lived, with everything that had its being around him."[10] Ferlinghetti's faith in a transcending wonder coupled with a belief in a brotherhood of love is the basis of many of his most prophetic and positive statements. In the early "Junkman's Obbligatto" he sings and swings in breezy affirmation:

> Let us arise and go now
> to the Isle of Manisfree
> and live the true blue simple life
> of wisdom and wonderment
> where all things grow
> straight up
> aslant and singing
> in the yellow sun.
>
> (*Coney*, 59)

Such cosmic statements as "The Situation in the West, Followed by a Holy Proposal" and "Spontaneous Anarchist / Pacifist Buddhist Song" resound with the oneness of all life:

All color sound and taste and touch
all one
All form and emptiness
All living entities All sentient beings one.
(*Open*, 130)

It is a working philosophy that underlies Ferlinghetti's basic stance toward life and links him to romanticism, surrealism, transcendentalism, Buddhism, and even the beat movement. With this as a basis, even his most cutting attacks on institutions are seen in a larger frame as necessary confrontations in seeking to preserve the inherent, beatific wonder of life. It provides the basic motive for his writing, his need for dissent and his goal in expression. Karl Malkoff describes this fundamental movement in Ferlinghetti's work as "built around the tension between the poet's wish to participate in some greater unity, some wholeness that can survive the prevalent fragmentation he sees all around him, and his need to participate in deadly events of his time, his need to confront the dark heart of experience rather than turn away from it."[11] Always for Ferlinghetti one must confront the world authentically in all its terror and beauty. The dual vision of daily madness and potential wonder gives birth to the creative tension which generates the artist's immediate and mythic expression of life.

Ferlinghetti's relationship to the French surrealist movement demands some clarification here. Though he declares, "The surrealist poets were some of my earliest sources,"[12] and though he often opened his verse to surrealistic images and has written a kind of native American surrealism in his novel *Her*, Ferlinghetti is certainly not a pure surrealist and is correct in calling himself a "semi-surrealist." What he writes is always dominated by the conscious mind, not the automatism of subconscious expression, so that he produces a type of surrealism with the eyes open. Ferlinghetti explains it this way:

> What's "automatic"? I mean everything is automatic from that point of view. You sit at the typewriter and you write on the typewriter what comes to your head . . . . The old sense that

> they used "automatic" came from the trances of mediums, . . . dictation from some psychic source. Dictation direct from the psychic-spiritual force somewhere into the pen of the poet writing it on the page blind but just letting his hand go. . . . I didn't write anything from a trance state; *Her* wasn't written in a trance state; that's the only pure "automatic" writing when a person who's writing doesn't even know what he's writing; he's just an instrument being dictated to by someone or something else. If I were being dictated to by some being or force, I would *change* the dictation; it wouldn't come out the way he told me to write it. I don't like dictators, even poetic ones![13]

This alliance with surrealism will be examined later in a consideration of the works, but it should be obvious that Ferlinghetti adapts surrealism, like everything else, to his own functional dynamics. What is important to recognize here is Ferlinghetti's true sympathy with the goals, if not the methods, of surrealism. Basically, he shares the subversive motivation of overthrowing the restraints of a too-rationally controlled society. In affirming a world beyond reason he too shares André Breton's declaration that "The mere word 'freedom' is the only one that still excites me. . . . Imagination alone offers me some intimation of what *can be*."[14] In his vision of the sacredness of this life Ferlinghetti affirms an existence that goes beyond man's use and abuse of reason. He is closely aligned with contemporary philosopher Herbert Marcuse, a favorite of contemporary surrealists, in a Blakean defiance of the institutionalized "reality principle" in favor of the sustaining "pleasure principle."[15] The poet must create works that resist the overcontrol of insane rationality (absurdity) and, in fact, throw that rationality back in the face of the institutions that perpetuate it. "Poet is the anarchy of the senses making sense," declares Ferlinghetti in "The Street's Kiss." It is a frequent position of a Ferlinghetti poem, as in "23" of *Pictures of the Gone World*, in which Ferlinghetti pays his tribute to the pre-surrealist motive of the Dada Movement:

Dada would have liked a day like this
with its various very realistic
unrealities

each about to become
too real for its locality
which is never quite remote enough
to be Bohemia
Dada would have loved a day like this
with its light-bulb sun

The happy happenstance of its form and its positivistic tone give the poem a validity in intuitive pleasure. A series of reality images dance before us in accepted juxtaposition:

a dishpan hand
waving at a window
or a phone about to ring
or a mouth about to give up
smoking

Ferlinghetti concludes in a conscious recognition of the basic intuitive and analogous methods of dada and surrealism:

and its passing priest
about to pray
Dada
and offer his so transcendental
apologies
Yes Dada would have loved a day like this
with its not so accidental
analogies

It is not a surrealist or even a dadaist poem in its method, yet this street meditation like the more recent "Enigma of Ho Chi Minh's Funeral" is in perfect tune with the principal motives of both movements. Ferlinghetti's alliance with surrealism is a long one, but one that is revealed more clearly through an understanding of his close relationship with the pre-surrealist Guillaume Apollinaire.

As Ferlinghetti openly declares, his poetic vision is grounded in these bold Frenchmen, "Especially poets like Apollinaire, who was not really a surrealist. He was more or less the con man of the movement, but I think I learned more from him than others."[16] Their lives are remarkably similar in that neither knew his father, both had a Catholic upbringing, and each sought a bohemian life in the long self-quest of their lives. Roger Shattuck's insight on Apollinaire's disposition is also revealing of Ferlinghetti: "Apollinaire, in his verse and in his life, was successively a clown, a scholar, a drunkard, a gourmet, a lover, a criminal, a devout Catholic, a wandering Jew, a soldier, a good husband. These are partial revelations he made of himself. They resolve into two distinct themes: a huge gaiety and vitality which carried him through life with apparent assurance, and an equally strong but slightly muted note of tragedy and despair which was the reverse side of the same life."[17] Not only are the roles of these two men similar, but the psychological disposition is strikingly similar. It was Apollinaire who presented the strongest image of what a poet's life should be, to Ferlinghetti as well as to the surrealists. Shattuck describes Apollinaire alternately as a "poet of danger" and "hero poet": "Apollinaire, I am ready to say, exceeded even the resources of this literary device. He came close to attaining what could be called the 'automatic life.' He lived and acted out of recesses deeper in himself than most people ever become conscious of, and his heroism consisted in sustaining this way of life."[18] The analogy is certainly not forced in finding these same qualities motivating the art and life of Lawrence Ferlinghetti, a man who still loves to don the derby of Apollinaire and Chaplin. Neeli Cherkovski, Ferlinghetti's biographer, sees the same activist and "automatic life" in both Ferlinghetti and Ginsberg: "In addition Ferlinghetti and Ginsberg helped to stimulate the creativity of their contemporaries. This made them public figures. Their role was to be out in the arena, involved in the life around them, and as time would show, that is how both functioned—as poets in the world."[19]

It was chiefly then as a figure of the poet in the world that Apollinaire influenced Ferlinghetti, yet they also discover similar methods in making their engaging art. Each works with the sensuous elements of the shape and sound of the poem as a way of bringing increased attention; each seeks to broaden the language of poetry by including common language and by combining language elements to create a new yet deliberate simplicity. It is not surprising then to find two meditations on Apollinaire in the recent Ferlinghetti book *Northwest Ecolog,* which casts a long eye back on his own life as a poet. "Reading Apollinaire by the Rogue River" contains the essential identification between Apollinaire and himself as each has written poems of "the river that runs through the city / taking time & life & lovers with it."[20] Yet his fullest tribute and most profound identification is in the quiet "The Fate of the Poet." Here Apollinaire is "The Poet," a hauntingly true reminder of Ferlinghetti himself as he envisions Apollinaire yet thinks of his own life:

> His eyes are
> black bees
>
> His scraggy black moustache
> covers the crack of his mouth
> like a nest of black ants
> in the white sand of his face
>
> He
> will never
> speak again.
>
> (*Northwest,* 26)

It is a beautifully simple statement that draws from the photograph of Apollinaire's face those characteristic images so refreshingly literal and clear yet surrealistically charged that they mirror our deepest selves. Having assimilated his methods and vision, Ferlinghetti accepts Apollinaire's face and fate as his own.

As has been pointed out in the biographical section, Ferlinghetti's commitment to making a new vital art evolved as his consciousness did. By the late 1950s, the heyday of the beat movement, Ferlinghetti's art had turned to an even broader engagement with life. Partly in reaction to the prevalent "coolness" of beat hipsterism, partly in justification of his increased socio-political involvement, and partly as a natural reaction to his increased awareness of the writing and thinking of men like Albert Camus and Jean-Paul Sartre, he had come to feel it was necessary to publicly declare his stance. He makes it clear that the "wiggy nihilism of the Beat hipster, if carried to its natural conclusion, actually means the death of the creative artist himself," and that engagement was essential, "because Jean-Paul Sartre cares and has always hollered that the writer especially should be committed. *Engagement* is one of his favorite dirty words. . . . Only the dead are disengaged."[21] This deliberate commitment which broadened the socio-political sphere of the poet, came after his long political tirade "Tentative Description of a Dinner to Promote the Impeachment of President Eisenhower" for which American poetry audiences, even around San Francisco, rebuked him for taking poetry into an unseemly area. Sartre had received similar aesthetic chastisement for his engaged stance, which he sought to express on both a philosophical and aesthetic basis. Besides the existential imperatives of living authentically in the world and accepting the responsibilities of freedom, Sartre found an aesthetic ground for this engaged writing. Declaring that "there is no art except for and by others," Sartre clarifies that the act of reading is always a "synthesis of perception and creation" and that "since the artist must entrust to another the job of carrying out what he has begun, since it is only through the consciousness of the reader that he can regard himself essential to his work, all literary work is an appeal. To write is to make an appeal to the reader that he lead into objective existence the revelation which I have undertaken by means of language."[22] Aesthetically for Sartre, as for Ferlinghetti who felt less the need to justify, the artist's engagement is made valid because all art is a plea for the reader to freely join in the conscious act of creation. All art is thus an imperative, and as Sartre concludes, "The work of art is a value because it is an appeal."[23]

Ferlinghetti dramatically asserted the rights of engagement in the publication of Allen Ginsberg's *Howl* and in its subsequent defense, "considering the barren, polished poetry and well-mannered verse which had dominated many of the major poetry publications during the past decade or so, not to mention some of the 'fashionable incoherence' which has passed for poetry in many of the smaller, avant-garde magazines and little presses. *Howl* commits many poetic sins: but it was time."[24] The functional immediacy of life supplants the value of art for art's sake as the primary standard of art. Ferlinghetti's engaged stance as a poet and publisher embraces such new standards as the work's vivid directness, its topical yet universal application to life, and its affective value to stir consciousness and bring about change. Or, as he stated in 1958, "Finally, in some larger sense, it all adds up to the beginnings of a very inevitable thing—the *resocialization* of poetry."[25]

Ferlinghetti's debt to Sartre and Camus for the philosophical basis of his aesthetics of engagement he has readily declared, but he was equally affected by his American alliance with his immediate elder of the avant-garde, Kenneth Patchen. His tribute to Patchen as "a loud conscientious objector to / the deaths we daily give each other" (*Open*, 37), suggests his long and deep admiration for Patchen as the voice of an unrelenting public conscience. Beginning in the Greenwich Village days of the 1940s, Ferlinghetti had found in Patchen as well as E. E. Cummings and Henry Miller artists who remained fiercely independent of schools and political ties and who offered an American counterpart to the European artist of engagement. "I am the world-crier, and this is my dangerous career. . . . I am the one to call your bluff, and this is my climate,"[26] declares Patchen in his poem "EARLY IN THE MORNING." Patchen's own theory of engagement is based on an essential commitment to life through love (including the sexual), brotherhood, and a faith in the unity of life whereby the poet brings about "the ascendency of person out of chaos and non-being through feeling, through love."[27] Ferlinghetti follows Patchen's example and that of earlier American populist poets Vachel Lindsay, Edgar Lee Masters, and Carl Sandburg, in holding no institution as sacred above life. He makes his own pointed and eloquent blasts at social and political systems which devalue life. Like Patchen, Ferlinghetti is not naive, for both record vividly the vision of evil which they witness in the world. Following the contemporary tradition of Patchen, Kenneth Rexroth, and later Allen Ginsberg, Ferlinghetti is that outspoken conscience who confronts us with prophetic visions of potential beauty amidst the daily wreckage of our lives, and who, as Edward Lucie-Smith exclaims, "has the courage to get up and say aloud the thoughts which all are thinking."[28]

The tenets of Ferlinghetti's socio-political stand are made clear in the numerous direct and transparent statements of his writings, including the recent "Populist Manifesto" poems. Moreover, in an interview with poet David Meltzer, he offers an explanation of his perspective. Shunning the political illiteracy of most poets, he clarifies his own belief that "capitalism is an outrageously *extravagant* form of existence which is leading to an enormous ecological debacle unless it is completely changed. . . . The world ecologically cannot afford capitalism anymore. It's absurd. . . . The resources won't stand it."[29] Like Thoreau, Ferlinghetti favors the concept of a pacifist anarchy that is ecologically sound, and as a necessary step in that direction he embraces "a form of humanitarian socialism: not authoritarian, but a nontotalitarian socialism. I'd like to think it could be a kind of Buddhist socialism."[30] Socialism is sought as a means of restoring equality and freedom to the masses, his populist concern. Capitalism is condemned as well for the alienation it has fostered through consumerism. In the early "Autobiography" poem he warned of "the close identification / of the United States and the Promised Land / where every coin is marked / In God We Trust / but the dollar bills do not have it / being gods unto themselves" (*Coney*, 63). This vaudevillian though pointed criticism is given a deeper thrust in the recent "Director of Alienation" in which he presents a compelling image of American society as a sea of outsiders bent on consuming their way into an identity; "You wanna belong / You gotta have it" is the formula he reads. In this materialistic quest each person descends into Macy's department store basement where he or she begins the cannibalistic ritual to "Consume your way up / until you're consumed by it / at the very top" at which point they leap off the roof "waving plastic jewels and genitals" (*Who,* 9). Ferlinghetti's method is to attack the obvious by driving it into our consciousness through a vivid telling image. His audience in this and many other broadside poems is not the critic in the classroom but the man and woman in the streets. Through graphic directness and imaginative projection he engages them.

In his long poem "The Situation in the West / Followed by a Holy Proposal" he turns his vision of universal love and anti-nationalism into the direct invective:

> And blessed be the fruit of transcopulation
> and blessed be the fruit of transpopulation
> and blessed be the fucking world with no more nations!
> . . . .
> we'll all still have the sun
> in which to recognize ourselves at last across the world
> over the obscene boundaries!
>
> (*Starting,* 65)

Both symbolic image and direct denunciation are used in "Dissidents, Big Sur" where the images of nature—of hummingbird and sky—are swallowed up in the aftereffects of the polluting "metal monster," the American automobile. And the dissenting crows, symbolic of resistance, all too soon "wing away on wind / and are sucked up / and disappear / into the omniversous universe. / Even as any civilization / ingests its own most dissident elements" (*Who,* 41). Added to the images of ecological and economic waste is the warning of this final image, the political control of free speech through ingestion. This concern becomes a focal point of the populist manifestoes of the 1970s and serves to highlight the dynamics of Ferlinghetti's open poetics of engagement.

The first "Populist Manifesto," which was issued in April 1975 and appeared in countless publications and was broadcast on radio, fundamentally takes to task the poetry of all schools which has not been dealing practically and immediately with the issues of contemporary life. His cry for poets to "come out of your closets, / Open your windows, open your doors" is necessitated by a world view in which Rome, San Francisco, and Moscow are symbolically burning. Pressed on by the immediacy of the times, he declares that it is:

> No time now for the artist to hide
> above, beyond, behind the scenes,
> indifferent, paring his fingernails,
> refining himself out of existence.

He finds that too many poets are playing literary or esoteric games when direct action is necessitated by the temper of the times:

> We have seen the best minds of our generation
> destroyed by boredom at poetry readings.
>
> Poetry isn't a secret society,
> It isn't a temple either.
> Secret words & chants won't do any longer
> . . . .
> Time now to open your mouths
> with a new open speech,
> time now to communicate with all sentient beings.
>
> (*Who*, 61, 62)

Demanding that the poetry be of the streets, engaged, and outspoken in its commitment, he calls for a new visionary writing that echoes Whitman's "sense of sweetness and sublimity." His stance and directive are clear as he defines that new writing:

> a new wide-open poetry,
> with a new commonsensual 'public surface'
> with other subjective levels
> or other subversive levels.
>
> (*Who*, 63–64)

No institutions, not even avant-garde circles, are held sacred in his bold demands for a new engaged and engaging writing. It might reach other suggestive levels, but it must begin primarily as committed communication predicated on his definition:

> Poetry the common carrier
> for the transportation of the public
> to higher places
> than other wheels can carry it.
>
> (*Who*, 64)

It is certainly a functional and populist aesthetics which not all would accept but which each must answer, and it is the one which Ferlinghetti's writing should be evaluated upon. Paralleling Ferlinghetti's engaged art with the social satire of French writers Raymond Queneau and Jacques Prévert, Kenneth Rexroth defines the work in its broader social and aesthetic contexts: "Many contemporary poets, perhaps the most significant ones, have simply left the society, deserted it as doomed, or already dead. Ferlinghetti is very much inside it. He feels its evils as directed against himself; as they say, he takes it personally. . . . He is there. He sees the napalm fall. He hears the jokes in the locker room. He is the man on the street. To many poets of the counter culture all this seems to be happening to another species as it is rushing itself to extinction, but not Ferlinghetti."[31] Ferlinghetti's work is thus viewed as necessarily involved in the struggles of life, where in fact, its value is determined. It is to be judged not on established and isolated aesthetic patterns, but on how the poet molds his art to the needs of life, on the essential truth and challenge with which he engages his readers. If Ezra Pound made poetry into a modern art, Lawrence Ferlinghetti has worked to make that modern art a vital instrument of conscience and change.

Though elsewhere he works out his own oral, mythic, satiric, and open-form poetics (as we shall see in the next chapter), in his populist declarations he is wide-open in form as long as the writing has a public surface. In his "Second Populist Manifesto," which appeared in March 1978 as "Adieu à Charlot," (*Landscapes*, 41–45) he carries through his declared mission. However, the tone is less phlegmatic as it clearly sees the direction poetry must take as inward, into "the deep sea of the subjective." And yet it is not the personally idiosyncratic which is needed or the self-gratifying confession, but "the collective subjective / the Little Man in each of us." As a means of restoring public surface to aesthetic depth, he strips away the separate myths of modern civilization and returns us to ourselves and our authentic sense of our collective life. It is Whitman again who provides the vision and example as Ferlinghetti calls these "poets of another breath" to reclaim their original high purpose, "The subjective must take back the world." This has been the direction of his own recent work, though it has existed all along in his writing—to touch the universal within oneself.

In his Third Populist Manifesto, "Modern Poetry Is Prose (But It Is Saying Plenty)," he again takes to task the lost values of the contemporary poet and reasserts the need for a poetry that sings of the soul, the spirit of humanity, "The Street's Kiss." Analyzing the damaged psyche of contemporary man in which "the boat of love breaks up / on the shores of everyday life / And the Collective Unconscious / remains uncollected," he turns to the poet's visionary need to restore spirit to life. Citing examples of Whitman, Sandburg, Lindsay, Wallace Stevens, Langston Hughes, Kerouac, and the Blakean Allen Ginsberg, he asks for a poetry that sings once more:

> And so wails today a still wild voice
> inside of us
> a still insurgent voice
> lost among machines and insane nationalisms
> still longing for the distant nightingale
> that stops and begins again
> stops
> and begins again
> stops
> and resumes again
>
> It is the bird singing that makes us happy.[32]

In his own rhythmic sound echoing (and Ferlinghetti has always been a lyric poet of the inner ear) he suggests the example that might prove the rule. Repeatedly his manifestoes are rich in allusions as he tries to shape a tradition that more closely binds the poet's art and life.

Understanding the dynamics of Ferlinghetti's revolutionary view of the poet-at-large not only provides the truest approach to his art and achievement, but it also reflects the evolution of a radically new image of the contemporary poet of involvement. Poet-critic David Meltzer, who interviewed Ferlinghetti along with William Everson, Kenneth Rexroth, Michael McClure, and Richard Brautigan in his study of *The San Francisco Poets*, is thus able to draw this revealing composite portrait of the poet of engagement:

> The poet's work is to activate the mind to its full measure of perception & receptivity. . . . That's what poets do, what we all do, who are awake & resist the dark dead thought brings. . . .
>
> The poet is a revolutionary because he is constantly subverting corrupt institutional languages with his art. He can make the life-denying rhetoric of power politics void by singing one coherent, true song. The words connect in a man so that he stops and thinks. . . .
>
> A poet comes to his tribe with song & if the song is good, if the words work & sound right together, the tribe is renewed, restored &, for a moment united and free.[33]

In this testament by a younger poet one can sense the unmeasurable impact which Lawrence Ferlinghetti has had in shaping a new poetics of action. He is the poet of engagement who integrates his life and art in the enlarged role of the hero-poet as: oral poet, poet of dissent, poet of the streets, poet-prophet, populist poet, actualist of the public nightmare, super-realist, political poet, international and visionary poet of consciousness, tribesman. As Cherkovski sums up, Ferlinghetti is the poet out "wandering through the world from a central point, making good use of an ever astonished eye and an extraordinary ear. . . . The poems he created are living artifacts of contemporary consciousness."[34] Ferlinghetti's voice is distinctly contemporary and authentic.

His engaged stance dictates his radical roles and methods, and it results in some of the most powerful and popular writing of the contemporary period. We move now to a closer consideration of those works and the methods he developed to fulfill this revolutionary vision of life and art.

3

The Poetry

> The talking poet is the singing poet; he who talks to himself cannot be heard in the streets. The only singing poet is the talking poet; the only singer is the street singer, the only poet is the street poet.
>
> ("The Street's Kiss")

RARELY has any poet's work received such wide popular acceptance and such limited critical appreciation as Lawrence Ferlinghetti's writing. While the public generally views the work as immediate, alive, and relevant, the academic and poet-critic generally attack it as being simplistic, sentimental, undisciplined, and in open violation of the conventional poetic form. Some critics, caught in the quandary of how to respond to the radically new values of this engaged poetry, have sought to detract from the writing by naïvely branding the poet as "one of those spiritual panhandlers" or "an egoistic trifler."[1] Others such as Crale D. Hopkins and Vincent McHugh, who are more in tune with Ferlinghetti's methods and intent, respectively view the writing as "striking, powerful, convincing," and Ferlinghetti as "an original and a natural. A rare conjunction and in light of his astonishing gifts, correspondingly valuable."[2] Hopkins locates the critical dilemma squarely: "It cannot be judged by conventional literary standards, however. Whether or not it is indeed poetry can only be answered when a comprehensive definition of that word is agreed upon—a situation not yet achieved."[3] Revolutionary in its form as well as its content, Ferlinghetti's writing is a deliberate and open challenge to the status quo of both art and life. As Hopkins points out, it is clearly based on a new definition of the very concept of "poetry." Apocalyptic in its conception, opposed to any traditional veneration of art, it is dedicated to no less than a radically new affirmation of the world and the word. Until we accept the genuine challenge of this poetry and deal with it earnestly and fully, we perpetuate the gap between experimental art and its critical appreciation. We labor in the dark. The existing art forms must bear the attack of experimentation if they are to remain vital. For Ferlinghetti they are clearly humanities which have failed to humanize us, and they are crying for reform. His art is most truly defined then by the protean forms which he has created to fulfill his revolutionary vision.

As we have seen in considering Ferlinghetti's life-art stance, his work is generated from the tension between things as they are and as they might become, the basic existential and romantic thrust of the work. He is both the realist and the idealist seeking to engage and regenerate life in his audience. Just as surrealist, expressionist, and naturalist painters have chosen to sacrifice certain "painterly" qualities for the immediacy of their art (the subject to artist to audience bond), so Ferlinghetti's engaged poetry sacrifices certain "poetic" qualities for its direct impact—its movement toward heightened consciousness that leads to action. Yet, while certain conventional poetic values are sacrificed (and we expect to hear the wounded cries of unsympathetic critics), not all are abandoned. Rather, they are *recast* with a more essential and deliberate molding of form to meet the goals of his vision. In fact, what emerges in Ferlinghetti's poetry is a more immediate rhetoric of form and function based on both its transparent values of essential action and its inner logic of emotion and thought. He thus develops methods to fulfill his integrated and tripartite vision of an art which is characterized as: 1) *authentic*—existentially true to the artist's candid sense of life; 2) *engaged*—grounded in broad and common human experience yet directed towards active transformation; 3) *visionary* in its pursuit of wonder—the positive potential of human existence. Characteristically in this practical and rhetorical poetics, "the poet like an acrobat" risks everything, including absurdity, in his relentless pursuit of "taut truth" (*Coney*, 30). More than any other contemporary poet, Lawrence Ferlinghetti writes truly memorable poetry, poems that lodge themselves in the consciousness of the reader and generate awareness and change. And his writing sings, with the sad and comic music of the streets. To appreciate his work we must recognize and examine his methods, his practical poetics of engagement.

Oral Messages

Three of the chief characteristics of Ferlinghetti's poetry—its oral basis, its satiric intent, its development of the authentic voice—are integrally bound. "The breath, response, the personal rhythm of Ferlinghetti's line—the immediacy, the directness of his style as he turns to tell you something. I don't think anyone else has the tone of Ferlinghetti—the flat, dry, laconic and compelling tone-sound of his voice."[4] Samuel Charters locates here the distinctive feature and the united effect of a Ferlinghetti poem in its personal, immediate, and expressive voice. Ferlinghetti creates a contemporary basis for the tradition of the Homeric, Celtic, and Druid minstrels. He becomes the contemporary man of the streets speaking out the truths of common experience, often to the reflective beat of the jazz musician. As much as any poet today he has sought to make poetry an engaging oral art, releasing recordings and organizing and performing at public readings. Poet Alan Dugan comments, "Oral poetry has to fit the speaker's voice. At its best it can be true of the poet, his audience, and their common situation. . . . Mr. Ferlinghetti's verse is perfectly suited to his style of delivery, and his style is effective and engaging."[5] More than an entertaining or bombastic claim on the audience's attention, oral poetry, as Ferlinghetti practices it, must bring together the poet, his vision, and his audience in a shared experience through the poet's authentic voice. The oral message is to exist in both spoken and written form.

From the outset Ferlinghetti makes it clear that one direction his writing will take will be the oral: "The printed word has made poetry so silent. But the poetry I am talking about here is spoken poetry, poetry conceived as oral messages. It 'makes it' aloud."[6] Reacting against the atrophy and in-group nature of much contemporary poetry, Ferlinghetti conceived of an oral poetry to fulfill his goals of engagement, vision, and the authentic while it also revitalized the poetic word.

More immediate precedents for an oral poetry may be found in the colloquial bluntness of Prévert and Rimbaud, in the "intimate yell" of Russian poet Vladimir Mayakovsky (whom Ferlinghetti had studied in researching his dissertation), in the personalism of Whitman, the populist denunciations of Carl Sandburg, Vachel Lindsay, and Kenneth Patchen, in the drive for a poetry of American speech of William Carlos Williams and Kenneth Rexroth, and in the spontaneous and spoken style of fellow Beat writers. It was a form which each poet revitalized with his own personality and vision. Yet with Ferlinghetti, as with E. E. Cummings, it became a conscious and direct development of a form. It brought the poet off the page and into the life of the reader, giving the work a spoken directness through its immediate sense of audience and sound. Like the pied poet of old, Ferlinghetti uses and develops the oral form to reach and affect the widest possible audience.

One of the ways in which the oral form is developed is as a viable vehicle for satire. Like the jazz musician who uses exaggerated musical devices and counterpointed underscoring in the satiric comment of a piece, Ferlinghetti uses mocking alliteration, internal and multiple rhyme, puns, incongruent diction levels, and comic allusions to present ironic insight and to highlight the absurdities of the life he mirrors. He often creates the persona of the wizened comedian who, as Alan Dugan points out," makes jokes and chants seriously with equal gusto and surreal inventiveness, using spoken American in a romantic, flamboyant manner."[7] As Dugan observes, a comfortable position for Ferlinghetti is achieved in the stance of being "half a committed outsider and half an innocent Fool."[8] Using this simple, vaudevillian persona, he is able to effectively question conventions without threatening his audience. Like a Beat Huck Finn, he questions institutions while he "asserts the primacy of the anarchic individual as exemplified by himself as speaker,"[9] thus creating a voice that is a responsive instrument for social criticism while also turning the elements of conventional poetic form on itself for satiric effect and ironic comment. Rexroth accents this position analogous to the jazzman's satiric stance as cultural outsider when he declares of Ferlinghetti, "At its best his poetry, more than anybody else's, captures the rhythms of modern jazz, perhaps because he shares so many of the deeper life attitudes of the best jazz musicians."[10] Using spoken rhythms and deliberate satiric devices he creates a convincing and appealing voice that adds color and dimension to the poetry of social criticism. As we shall see, Ferlinghetti like the jazzman, creates an oral form that is equally open to humor, searing invective, and beautiful lyric suggestion.

The prime examples of this oral and satiric style are the "Oral Messages" of *A Coney Island of the Mind*, works which were conceived and developed "specifically for jazz accompaniment and as such should be considered as spontaneously spoken 'oral messages' rather than as poems for the printed page" (*Coney*, 48). However, the position of comic commentator is one that Ferlinghetti repeatedly comes back to throughout his writing, most often in the broadside poems treating the issues of the times. Repeatedly we find ourselves in the easy oral confidence of the poet "outside

Mike's place" looking out at the comic-sad world and puzzling over the absurdities of our day. He begins "I Am Waiting" from the "Oral Messages" section of *Coney* with:

> I am waiting for my case to come up
> and I am waiting
> for a rebirth of wonder
> and I am waiting for someone
> to really discover America
> and wail.
>
> (*Coney*, 49)

The short phrasings are based on speech, rather than on the open-form expressionism of much of his other verse. Close repetition focuses the attention on the verbal phrasing and its variations, drawing out of the prose an American spoken poetry. Not only is the phrase "I am waiting" repeated three times in four lines, but there is an abundance of close vowel echoing and alliterative *c*, *w*, and *r* sounds. We have a characteristic hip street talk lingo in the "really" intensifier and, of course, the anticipated "wail" of discovery. The mixed diction of the flat "waiting for my case to come up" and the abstract "rebirth of wonder" accents the cultural absurdity by ironic juxtaposition. The poem is rich with slang expressions given a poetic and satiric accent by their positioning:

> and I am waiting
> for the American Eagle
> to really spread its wings
> and straighten up and fly right.
>
> (*Coney*, 49)

American culture as it is reflected in common speech is both a subject and a method in his oral messages. When he tells us he awaits "the living end," it is a phrase that underscores the absurdity of the times through repeated allusions to war, bombs, religion, and death, much in the same way that Eliot projects world destruction "not with a bang but a whimper" in "The Hollow Men." Similarly, the Second Coming becomes an expression of open idealism tainted by societal movement toward self-destruction. The rich texture of the poem is thereby developed through broad and satiric allusions to this "Age of Anxiety" evidenced in projected reversals: "for Billy Graham and Elvis Presley / to exchange roles seriously," "for the Last Supper to be served again / with a strange new appetizer." Political forecasts look "for the Salvation Army to take over" and in ironic staccato, "for Ike to act." America is established as the context for absurdity through geographic and historical reference to the gaping Great Divide and the mechanized "reconstructed Mayflower," "with its picture story and tv rights / sold in advance to the natives." Particularly effective in this 1958 poem is the reference to the South, where he is waiting "for Ole Man River / to just stop rolling along," "for the deepest South / to just stop Reconstructing itself / in its own image" and "for a sweet desegregated chariot / to swing low / and carry me back to Ole Virginie." Here Ferlinghetti incorporates the music and language of the culture and turns it around on itself. It should be immediately apparent that Ferlinghetti's use of cultural allusions varies sharply from the obscure intellectualism of T. S. Eliot's *The Waste Land*. Ferlinghetti's allusions are common and deliberately transparent to help mirror the society he portrays and to add coherence to his perceptions. They are as often from baseball, rock music, and films as they are from literature, politics, and art. A. Poulin observes that Ferlinghetti's use of allusions as literary and cultural cliches has much in common with the formula used in ancient oral poetry.[11] It is a reflecting device which enriches and authenticates the reality of the poem. Ferlinghetti's celebrated swinging line keeps drawing the reader out, then brings him up on himself and his accepted ignorance. Following the pun of an awaited Aphrodite who will "grow live arms / at a final disarmament conference," he brings the poem around to its final arresting vision:

> and I am waiting
> for the last long careless rapture
> and I am perpetually waiting

for the fleeing lovers on the Grecian Urn
to catch each other up at last
and embrace
and I am waiting
perpetually and forever
a renaissance of wonder

(*Coney*, 53)

In a poem about anticipation and perception—"about reality / and how to see it" as he declares in "Dog"—when the reader has also learned to expect the ironic climax, Ferlinghetti makes the grand ironic leap and closes instead with an image of the lyrical beauty that is ever present. The reader rides in the consciousness of the oral spokesman who convinces with his verbal acrobatics as well as with his cutting truth.

In an accompanying piece, "Junkman's Obbligato," much like his "Autobiography," Ferlinghetti's clownish guise is accented with a near-vaudevillian word play. In the "Hurry up, it's time" atmosphere of Eliot's *The Waste Land* he urges us all out into the street reality where "Your missus will not miss us," where we meet the "flowery bowery" with refrains of "My country tears of thee." Such obvious multiple rhyme and punning punctuates the irony effectively, yet it is not a detached vision which he projects, for he also exposes the reality of those who

Stagger befuddled into East River sunsets
Sleep in phone booths
Puke in pawnshops
wailing for a winter overcoat.

(*Coney*, 55)

Thus his alliterative devices are also capable of blues singing, as Ferlinghetti's oral spokesman seeks to capture it all in "our tincan cries and garbage voices." His junkman assures us that:

Another flood is coming
though not the kind you think.

There is still time to sink
and think.

The rich allusive parody of Eliot's vision is updated with references to the cultural clatter of *The New York Times Book Review, Life* magazine, "Good Will Industries," and the spokesman bids symbolic adieu:

So long Emily Post.
So long
Lowell Thomas.
Goodbye Broadway
Goodbye Herald Square.
Turn it off.
Confound the system.
Cancel all our leases.

(*Coney*, 58)

The whole gamut of American culture echoes itself through the junkman. Yet he too is capable of turning from the oral satiric tone to a lyric singing as he closes with a regenerative vision:

Let us arise and go now
to the Isle of Manisfree
and live the true blue simple life
of wisdom and wonderment
where all things grow
straight up
aslant and singing
in the yellow sun.

(*Coney*, 59)

All the echoing devices of alliteration, internal rhyme, punning, allusion, juxtaposed dictions and oral phrasing are leading the voice to accentuate and authenticate an act of transformation. As Ihab Hassan comments of Ferlinghetti's oral style, "Putting aside the clownish guise, he can burst into sudden anger at sham or injustice, burst with the authentic power of poetry. Like E. E. Cummings or Kenneth

Patchen before him, he can convert extravagant wit or protest into some human perception of wonder and generosity."[12] The comparison to Cummings and Patchen is extremely appropriate, for all three are verbal acrobats capable of a rousing and cutting satire as well as deeply human gestures in their writing. Each wins his audience with outspoken directness clothed in wit.

While Ferlinghetti's oral style is most often used for satiric effect, it is also effectively employed to create an authentic voice capable of direct invective and a kind of mind-talk, an oral stream-of-consciousness. He locates the work for the reader in the solid sense of a spoken voice. Repeatedly we are brought to the realization of J. M. Warner, "Ferlinghetti is still as dynamic, verbose, alarming, charming, and unsettling as when he began writing poetry. His rhythms are rough, colloquial to the point that reading his poetry aloud is absolutely essential to get at the source of his meaning and the sense of his metamorphic content. . . . Ferlinghetti shouts it, chants it, rails it, and either wins you over or revolts you. All with common language that in his context becomes often surreal and unerringly hits your eye and heart."[13] One of the poems which Warner responds to is the long and direct political statement of "A World Awash / With Fascism and Fear." The poem is an excellent example of the use of direct invective in an authentic oral voice. It is a cry for freedom against the deliberate or ignorant agents of fascism and oppression which he vehemently lists:

> And the Basques cry for freedom
> And the Jews cry for freedom
> Husbands cry for freedom
>   And women cry for freedom
>   And illuminated Heads cry for freedom
>   And faggots burn for freedom
>   And men are everywhere shut up
> And the world rolls on lousy with fascism
>   The jails groan with it
>   and governments groan with it

And wherever there's a flag with red in it
the people holding it up
                groan with it.

(*Open*, 88)

The poem blisters with insistent directness and echoes with verbal repetition (assonance, alliteration, parallelism)—essentials of memorable political statements. He is also able to turn a phrase through punning, as in "where even unions are rank with the file of force." The phrasing is so tight and direct that the reader must surely flinch with the searing exposure of repressed truths:

not to mention the unsilent undergrounds
    of speed & smack & cocaine
and Charles Manson & Hell's Angels into junk
            ripping off the world
And there are no ends but means.

(*Open*, 89)

Ferlinghetti is Ferlinghetti here, the public poet-spokesman declaring his views and truths with all the authority his directness of perception and expression can earn. In poems like this, the populist manifestoes, and the numerous socio-political broadside poems, Ferlinghetti refuses to pull his punches with a comic persona. Instead, he is the engaged and authentic spokesman molding an invective into an immediate and oral affront. His short spoken phrasing, his echoing poetic devices, his open and involved stance all compound to make the poem authentic.

In a rare account of his creating a work, "Genesis of *After the Cries of the Birds*," Ferlinghetti tells how crucial it is for him to find the voice for a poem. He is at Bixby Canyon on New Year's Eve searching for the beginning of the poem:

Pen poised over Nothingness. Nothing to say and not enough to say it with. Voice not as full as I had wanted it, . . . yet no other self-voice to turn on through, to sound through, over & over, my own perceptions, world-view, trauma & charisma, evidence of eye, heart (the heart some days a bird turning about, about to

> fly, turning & turning upon itself, other days a stone imbedded in flesh, sinking, weighted), nothing to say which has been said before, since nothing at all has yet been said, all still to be perceived, all still to be articulated, all still darkness & ignorance even here on the West Coast of time . . . Nevertheless! . . . Poem begun then in alienation by the Man Outside, as all tough poems must be.[14]

This remarkable documenting of his method of creating reveals just how integral are the elements of voice and heart, statement and personal stance, as Ferlinghetti finds himself in the combined act of perception and articulation, the essential act of his voice saying it. Also declared are the gaping ignorance and the blatant need for an expression of the times which defines the motive for his authentic, engaged, and visionary art.

Quite often this need for an expression of the times is met by the poem which manifests itself as an oral stream-of-consciousness, Ferlinghetti's own mind-talk. The poem "Berlin" provides a good example:

> A song a line a free phrase
> keeps recurring
> Under the Linden trees . . .
> Under the Linden trees . . .
> As if everything had begun over
> as if I had it to do
> all over
> here where I'm still walking & looking
> for the great indelible poem.
>
> (*Starting*, 53)

Struck by a phrase, the speaker repeats it while his mind works with it, recording the act of thinking out loud. Present participles ripple as "over" and "over" resound, and the whole poem moves quietly along spoken rhythms. His quest for the poem leads him to question, "Where is it gone / Is it here in Woolworth's," and in this richly allusive environment he meditates on the surface details and the deeper questions of self and sense. Woolworth's department store offers a strange analogy to the situation in Berlin where a mystery stirs:

> if only the Chinese printer
> hadn't pied our fortunes
> claiming they were Inscrutable
> and all looked alike to him
> So I'm reduced to Greater Woolworth's
> a microcosm of sweet America
> What a scene
> Fantastic display of
> soft toothbrushes
> herds of women
> Sweet valley where I sing my song
> of free enterprise.
>
> (*Starting*, 54–55)

The marvelously colloquial joke of the Chinese fortune cookie writer is made more subtle by the ongoing dazzle of objects and meanings as the poet seeks to connect and sing. We are brought into the act of creation, the struggle for significance is shared. The tone is not desperate or comic, but open and active, like the dog on the streets, tasting and smelling everything. There is a moment of reflection when the poet-voice recalls other beginnings:

> as when my mother held me
> on a lovely balcony
> and waved my hand for me
> at another grand parade
> (How wonderful to think
> God loved us
> if we prayed).
>
> (*Starting*, 56)

The thoughts gently flow without interruption following associative leaps in the emerging pattern of thought reaching expression. The poem now rises from within, "a love poem I had begun / where gone dumb poem / wrought from the dark in my mother long ago" as the poet reaches through the German refrain into his own lyric:

> God, come back, Innocence of the World
> a song a line a free phrase
> in autumn capitals
> their avenues of leaves ablaze.
>
> (*Starting*, 57)

The poet has captured the happening of the poem in all its momentary promptings and oblique manifestations. In this open mind-talk the possibilities for expression and form are as varied and vital as the experience of the poet. The tone enlarges as the poem progresses, rising to the lyric and metaphoric final images. One is forced to turn to the explicatives of Jack Kerouac in describing such bardic song, "They are CHILDREN. They are also childlike graybeard Homers in the street. They SING, they SWING."[15] In a spontaneous and open innocence the poet works his way toward a shared significance, yet, as Kerouac is quick to point out, the writing has its discipline, "typified by the haiku (Basho, Buson), that is the discipline of pointing out things directly, purely, concretely, no abstractions or explanations, wham wham the true blue song of man."[16] When it all comes together, as it does here, Ferlinghetti's oral method is inextricably bound to himself as poet talking in the world. The structure is integral with the poet's awareness and rich in the flow of words meeting perception. It is an engaged position with wide, emphatic, comic, and lyric possibilities.

Unlike most poetry where the tone and manner are locked in with the first line, Ferlinghetti's poetry is as varied as the consciousness of the perceiving poet. In a recent work from *Landscapes of Living & Dying* he renders poignantly the tragicomic significance of "The Old Italians Dying":

> For years the old Italians have been dying
> all over America
> For years the old Italians in faded felt hats
> have been sunning themselves and dying

You have seen them on the benches
in the park in Washington Square.

(*Landscapes*, 1)

Beginning with the colloquial refrain, beautiful and simple, "For years the old Italians have been dying" an irony is drawn in soft tones of "faded felt hats" as they sit "sunning themselves and dying." He draws us into this ritual as he is surely drawn into his ancestral sense of self, "You have seen them." He moves close and deep, like the haiku, in the telling concrete image:

You have seen them
the ones who feed the pigeons
                    cutting the stale bread
                      with their thumbs & penknives
the ones with old pocketwatches
the old ones with gnarled hands
                                and wild eyebrows
. . . .
the grappa drinkers with teeth like corn.

(*Landscapes*, 2–3)

Ferlinghetti's heart and voice have found each other here in this realistic tribute. The images cut as deep as the old thumbnails or the rows of corn teeth. In his renaming of the old men he creates a song out of speech for which he adapts his open-form typography to allow a reflective pacing with oral phrased qualifiers. In Norman Mailer's classic statement of the hip existential artist, "The White Negro," he provides an insightful definition of what it means to "swing" with a subject: "For to swing is to communicate, is to convey the rhythms of one's own being to a lover, a friend, or an audience, and—equally necessary—be able to feel the rhythms of their response. To swing with the rhythms of another is to enrich oneself—the conception of the learning process as dug by Hip is that one cannot really learn until one contains within oneself the implicit rhythm of the subject or the person."[17] Ferlinghetti seeks to assimilate his subject, its rhythms, its truths, by an oral process that swings through its united response. The elegiac tone is a triumph again and again in Ferlinghetti's writing, whether it is in tribute to a literary or political friend or just to these old men who echo his own humanity. And the reality and wonder of their lives is written

on the face of a church
as seen in a fisherman's face
in a black coat without sails
making his final haul.

(*Landscapes*, 4)

What Ferlinghetti has done with the oral tradition of poetry is to give it new meaning and form by adapting it to contemporary needs. In his most recent Populist Manifesto, "Modern Poetry Is Prose (But It Is Saying Plenty)" he laments the loss of song in modern poetry—"it has no *duende* / no soul of dark song / no passion musick"—which he equates with a loss of spirit. A simple examination of Ferlinghetti's poetry will immediately reveal how much it is attuned to sounds and rhythms, the sustaining oral and lyrical quality of his verse. From the comfortable and direct stance of his oral style he truly makes the spoken word sing and swing.

OPEN FORM—ABSTRACT EXPRESSIONISM

WHILE such terms as "projectivist," "field composition," and "open form" apply to Ferlinghetti's poetic process, they were theories which evolved concurrently with his early work, which is more closely allied to that of E. E. Cummings and the abstract expressionist painting movement. The broken line visual patterning of virtually all the pieces in the 1955 *Pictures of the Gone World* are predicated on another theory than his oral style. It is a recurring form which Ferlinghetti uses throughout his writing career as a type of second voice. More subtle in its visual-aural form, its achievement must be approached through an understanding of three currents—the lyrical shape and sound form of E. E. Cummings and William Carlos Williams, Ferlinghetti's assimilation and adaptation of the theories of abstract expressionist painting applied to writing, and finally, his own evolution of an intuitive open form style. The key is in an understanding of Ferlinghetti as both a writer and painter, as artist. Though he uses the typewriter as both a paint brush and a scoring instrument for his composing, his interest lies beyond pictorial effects into the realm of achieving a further and fuller life-art bond.

From the early 1940s Ferlinghetti was enthused about the writings of E. E. Cummings and William Carlos Williams which sought to achieve a new synthesis of sight and sound on the page. While Williams worked through imagism toward a capturing of the inherent poetry of American speech in the variable foot, Cummings developed a daring verbal dramatics that was nonetheless lyrical, though perhaps more colloquial in effect. Like Apollinaire, Cummings defied conventions by moving the words about the page to achieve maximum effect. While both Cummings and Williams were prime influences on Ferlinghetti's early years, and were among the first whom he sought to publish at City Lights, Cummings is the dominant force, for as Ferlinghetti states, "Cummings' American language is more colloquial than Williams' was . . . His speech was more American lingo, street talk sometimes."[18] Two of Ferlinghetti's declared theories of composition come together here, "'open-form' typography . . . to indicate the breaks and hesitancies of speech as I hear it in the poem"[19] and his belief that "style is a feeling for the weight and arrangement of words on a page."[20] He, like Cummings and Williams, was working toward a fuller synthesis of sight and sound, as in "13" of *Pictures of the Gone World* where he renders the woman he has come upon:

'We *think* differently at night'
she told me once
lying back languidly
And she would quote Cocteau
'I feel there is an angel in me' she'd say

'whom I am constantly shocking'
Then she would smile and look away
light a cigarette for me
sigh and rise
and stretch
her sweet anatomy
let fall a stocking

One feels in the space around and between lines the poet speaking these lines slowly to a friend, capturing the woman's soft phrasing and the movement of the moment. Like Cummings it is a form that blends fine lyricism with straight pictorial imagery. The expressionistic form captures the emotion of the poet in the moment as the eye, the heart, and the voice unite in the spontaneous act of perception-recognition-creation.

In 1948 and 1949 Ferlinghetti was studying art in Paris, experimenting with nonobjective art which he later rejected, as he declares in *Her*. By 1951 he was doing reviews of the San Francisco art scene for the New York based *Art Digest* and doing his own painting of semi-abstracted nude figures in his San Francisco waterfront studio. Influenced by the work of Franz Kline's bold and simple black and white forms, he opened further to the abstract expressionist art that thrived around San Francisco. Mark Toby, Mark Rothko, and Clyfford Still were each associated for a time with the California School of Fine Arts in San Francisco. Not only did the work of the abstract expressionists affect the painting of Ferlinghetti, leading him to bold primitive yet expressionistic form in black and white, it allowed him to open his poetry to a fine assimilation of abstract expressionism and open-field composition. As Neeli Cherkovski records, "Ferlinghetti was impressed by the daring and clarity of emotion which these artists were able to express in their work."[21] In a recent interview Ferlinghetti offered some explicit clarification of his poetics: "Nonobjective painting isn't based on an object, so this is a complete misnomer when it comes to applying it to my poetry because this is very objective poetry. Some of it was social-realist poetry, some of it was lyric-realist poetry. It definitely wasn't nonobjective. But what could be called abstract expressionist was the use of space so that each poem was on the page as in a white field, and the space between words was the amount of silence between those words when the poem was spoken. . . . And also the line breaks would dictate where the phrase should be broken off."[22] Locating the practical poetics in the phrasing and sound function of space on the page, Ferlinghetti goes on to clarify his poetic tie to abstract expressionist art: "And there was a continuous line from the beginning of the poem to the end, like a thread of paint in a Jackson Pollock painting. And so you have what I call Open-Form composition, whereas Robert Duncan uses the term Open Field. . . . That's what they were doing, Open-Form painting—Franz Kline, Pollock, Clyfford Still, de Kooning, people like that. There's Open-Form painting."[23] From these painting and writing cross-influences emerged the natural development of Ferlinghetti's open-form, abstract expressionist style.

The open-form composition which Ferlinghetti had been working out from his assimilation of Cummings and Williams sought to maximize the use of space and word position on the page. Though developed prior to or concurrently with the composition by field theory of Robert Duncan and Charles Olson, they are strongly analogous. The field composition poetics developed from Ezra Pound's work with the Chinese ideogram and out of the Imagist and Objectivist focus on the direct rendering of the thing in itself. For Olson, as for Ferlinghetti, the poem is viewed as an energy field: "A poem is energy transferred from where the poet got it . . . by way of the poem itself to, all the way over to, the reader, . . . a high energy-construct and, at all points, an energy discharge."[24] The kinetics of this poetry, like the action painting of abstract expressionism, viewed the work of art as a spontaneous act of creation. Instinct and experience tells you what is right; impulse and chance are valued as means of liberating the inner necessity of the artist, much like the improvisation of the jazz musician. Kenneth Rexroth, speaking of the abstract expressionist artists of the period, defines the work as "an object in its own right which showed forth . . . the direct expression in the material of paint of the personality of the artist in action."[25] For the poet it was words and space which vitalized the surface of the poem on the page and expressed his own emotional and intuitive recognition. Olson describes the process: "ONE PERCEPTION MUST IMMEDIATELY AND DIRECTLY LEAD TO A FURTHER PERCEPTION, . . . get on with it, keep moving, keep in, speed, the nerves, their speed, the perceptions, theirs, the acts, the split second acts, the whole business, keep it moving as fast as you can, citizen."[26] Thus, while abstract expressionist artists like Kandinsky and Jackson Pollock splashed and poured and dribbled their paint on the canvas, open-form poets used the typewriter as a type of intuitive divining rod to allow the words to find their place upon the page. Kandinsky's view of the "inner necessity" as the guiding force to creation holds that the work achieves its form as a correspondence between vision and gesture, movement and color. The structure is thus determined by the spontaneous and intuitive act of recognition which the artist enacts in his work. It is, to be sure, a personalist, expressionist, neo-romanticist approach to creation and was directly influenced by the theory and practice of surrealism. The work achieves both an expressive individuality and a universality in its tapping deeper levels of consciousness. As Olson explained it for the writer, "the projective act, which is the artist's act in the larger field of objects, leads to dimensions larger than the man."[27] For Ferlinghetti it is the means of achieving that "pure subjective / the collective subjective / the Little Man in each of us" (*Landscapes*, 45).

The union of these parallel movements of abstract expressionism and field or open-form composition, which we see most apparently in the New York Poets John Ashbery, Frank O'Hara, and James Schuyler, actually underlies the eclectic and "impurist" nature of contemporary poetry. What is most striking about Ferlinghetti's practice is that it evolved independently and prior to the New York Poets. As each abstract expressionist brings his uniqueness to the work (Pollock's spontaneity, Mark Rothko's meditative reductions, etc.), so in Ferlinghetti's work we find a personality and expression uniquely his own.

In "8" of *Pictures of the Gone World* Ferlinghetti, the painter-poet, creates his own word painting spun out of his reaction to the painted women of Sarolla:

> I cannot help but think
> that their 'reality'
> was almost as real as
> my memory of today
>
> when the last sun hung on the hills
> and I heard the day falling
> like the gulls that fell
> almost to land
>
> while the last picnickers lay
> and loved in the blowing yellow broom
> resisted and resisting
> tearing themselves apart
> again
> again

The poem, which begins with a central focus on "Sarrola's women in their picture hats / stretched upon his canvas beaches," brings the meditative poet to a new sense of personal reality. In this tone of reflecting consciousness the poem moves toward a quiet epiphany in content and form. The line becomes the pattern of thought finding itself in the strong central block of reality impressions which focus in form, then enlarge once more as the poet's emotion dictates expression. The sense of the lovers "in the blowing yellow broom" is timed to reinforce the extension of time just as the still motion of their "tearing themselves apart / again / again" dramatizes the moment of poignant recognition for poet and reader. There is a slow cinematic sense to this rendering of a day's significance captured in objective terms yet through the artist's emotional thought—in memory. It is both lyrical and concrete as the phrasing meets the mood, meaning, and movement of the awareness. The poet and his form do not obtrude; rather, they meet in the shared recognition and expression of the poem's content. Through spacing, phrasing, line positioning, as well as an Imagist sense of detail, the poem becomes a moment of shared clarity.

Ferlinghetti's response to a Morris Graves painting provides another occasion for expression in "11" of *A Coney Island of the Mind*:

It is a wild white nest
in the true mad north
of introspection

where 'falcons of the inner eye'
dive and die
glimpsing in their dying fall
all life's memory
of existence

and with grave chalk wing
draw upon the leaded sky
a thousand threaded images
of flight.
(*Coney*, 25)

Ferlinghetti's bold mixture of abstract and concrete serves to blend thought and sensory content in an emotive and intuitive form. There is the characteristic sense of the line in contact and motion as the spontaneous expression emerges, as he "swings" with it. Yet here in particular is a fine sense of sound embracing content as the *i* and *a* vowels dominate and create an airy tone. Color is strong also, as Ferlinghetti finds his own equivalent for Graves's expressionistic works. One feels the light and whiteness all through this piece, especially in the "chalk wing" image of the birds, which is reinforced by "bled white wings" and "whitebone drone / mating in air." The abstract expressionist work characteristically hits the viewer with a dominance of impression, and Ferlinghetti has captured Graves's mode here as he exclaims the artist's "imagination / turning upon itself / with white electric vision." Repeatedly in these picture poems Ferlinghetti finds a written form to capture and release intense vision and shared recognition.

Used little in *Starting from San Francisco,* predominantly oral messages, the open-form, abstract expressionist method becomes the dominant approach of *The Secret Meaning of Things*. In "Through the Looking Glass" Ferlinghetti uses this expressive form to capture a further level of consciousness, the drug experience. This three-part poem explores three stages of the LSD drug experience: "I. Imagining LSD," "II. LSD, Big Sur," and "III. After-dream." The poet's semi-clinical approach suggests the investigative nature of this 1967 experiment with the "mind expanding" hallucinogenic. In part I, the poet records his imaginings while flying above Chicago. The factual, conscious reality dominates, though the lines express the rush of thought:

And Sunday Chicago appears
                                        at end of Autumn carpet
              stuck to great flat blue cloud
                                           of Lake Michigan
                                               stretched out
   Rich resorts & Lakeshore fronts
              beaches lapped forever
                        pavilions asleep in time.

(*Secret*, 25)

In part II, image impressions of the true LSD experience at Big Sur come in a more pronounced form expressed by one and two word lines with broad spacing:

Intolerable arabesques
                                   coming & coming & coming
                                             on & on
                                                        toward me
                                              onto me
                                                   over me.

(*Secret*, 29)

The consciousness is only able to emit exclamatory words in isolation as the language appears to fail the vision:

Relentless
  Ineffable!
        Coming down now
            re-echoing
        gliding down
            those landscapes
      & arabesques of earth
    seas reglitterized
  seen thru a silkscreen overlay
      sun stricken!

(*Secret*, 29)

There is a great deal of sound repetition, and one senses a motion to the flow of consciousness, a sort of doubling back on itself, out and in, within an onward flow. The subconscious is where the experience is truly flying, and we are left with only a few gestures at expression, as Ferlinghetti regrettably admits it is "some dharma / whose name I could / conceivably sing / yet cannot yet decipher" (*Secret*, 30). The final "After-dream" is a short still poem in traditional form, yet deeply mythic in content. Ferlinghetti puts his form to use here in what proves to be one further exploration of *The Secret Meaning of Things*.

A finer poem from that collection is "Moscow in the Wilderness, Segovia in the Snow." It is a poem that makes clear how deeply Ferlinghetti's content as well as form are influenced by the abstract expressionist vision. This long and beautiful poem captures the sense of modern Russia's reality and myth through the poet's deep and mixed consciousness of it. Using his favorite position of the poet out walking (or riding or flying) in the world, Ferlinghetti takes this night journey into the heart of Russia where images freely associate within the experiencing poetic consciousness, all while the strains of Andre Segovia's classical guitar resound with the strange, beautiful, and mad music of the place. Linked together in the poet's consciousness are the realities of Russia (then and now), Segovia (the musician artist and his music), and the poet himself sitting aboard the "black bus" touring "Midnight Moscow." More than a surrealistic juxtaposition, the realities are connected in the poet and manifested in the form the poem takes. Immediately the reality of the bus inflates within the poet:

> Segovia comes on
> like the pulse of life itself
> Segovia comes on thru the snowdrifts
> and plains of La Mancha
> fields & fields & fields
> of frozen music
> melted on bus radios
> Segovia the instrument
> driving thru the night land.
>
> (*Secret*, 41)

The images are a deep weaving of conscious and subconscious, physical Russia and expressionistic music. In such images of "fields / of frozen music / melted on bus radios" all three reality levels merge. The smooth, even sense of "fields & fields & fields" depicts the poet's sense of the flattened landscape.

> Segovia warms his hands
> and melts Moscow
> moves his hand
> with a circular motion
> over an ivory bridge
> to gutted Stalingrads.
>
> (*Secret*, 41)

The worlds freely float within each other, in fact, are bound to each other by the poet's full awareness and by the rightness of the form on the page. The reader surrenders to the masterful control of the poet in the authentic act, just as the poet surrenders to his deepened perception. We cross the bridge of the guitar into Stalingrad as Segovia—indicated by a strong left margin—takes over the primary role of the poet, and notes:

Stone Mayakovsky stares
thru a blizzard of white notes
in Russian winter light
Segovia hears his stoned cry
and he hears the pulse in the blood
as he listens to life as he plays

(*Secret*, 42–43)

Ferlinghetti convinces us with this intuitive imagery and form so evenly modulated along the flow of the music and the journey of inner necessity. Increasingly the subjective view of the artist, Segovia, is trusted as the truest interpretation of the distant Russia, yet it is the poet's view of Segovia that we also trust:

His music has a longing sound
He yearns & yet does not yearn
He exists & is tranquil
in spite of all
He has no message
He is his own message
his own ideal sound.

(*Secret*, 44)

"He is his own message" explains the poet, and it is true of guitarist, poet, and Russia. As we flow along the expressive surface of the poem, as in music, we surrender to the mood and meaning of the artist. Ferlinghetti interprets Segovia interpreting Russia:

He is saying
There's a huge emptiness here
that stares from all the faces
All that is lost must be
looked for once more.

(*Secret*, 45)

And Ferlinghetti delicately turns the key which releases the terrible irony of the mystery of Russia and of Segovia and his music:

On the steps of a jail
            that looks like a church
                  he finds a white bird
What is important in life? says the bird
Segovia says Nada but keeps on playing
            his Answer.

(*Secret*, 46)

It is all an inexplicable mystery which Ferlinghetti has been able to render and yet not penetrate, for to penetrate would be to violate the subjective truth. Like the early picture poems, this large painting of Moscow and Segovia is accurate to the reality of emotional thought, sensory intuition, and to the personal mythology of the artist. It is a landscape of consciousness. Partaking of the mystery of life, it presents that mystery openly for our subjective recognition. Like all great art, it reaches beneath the surface of life to the inexpressible. It is a major poem and a fine example of the unobtrusive art that underlies Ferlinghetti's best work.

As he seeks to transmit the spontaneous sense of life and art, Ferlinghetti's use of the open-form, abstract expressionistic mode undergoes repeated application and metamorphosis in form. In *Open Eye, Open Heart* there is an entire section of mantra and songs which achieve a subtle oral and visual form. In the delicate "Nine Shaman Songs Resung" a mystical and meditative mood is engendered, as in the melodious chant of the "She-shaman princess":

Swinging her mesmere lamp
            her incense burner
                  on a gold chain
   She drops her thumb-ring in the Sea
And turning
      and turning
            stretches her body burning
                        toward me.

(*Open*, 134)

The lyric echoing rings within the poet's perception as he sings of the sensory and emotive rise of desire. In *Who Are*

We Now? Ferlinghetti turns his responsive form to the paintings of Gustav Klimt. "Short Story on a Painting of Gustav Klimt" presents the poet carried into a poetic tale of romantic tone and delicate and subtle gesture like Klimt's lush works. The painted details are not merely spoken, they are enlivened by the deepened consciousness of the poet:

And the woman the woman
turns her tangerine lips from his
one hand like the head of a dead swan
draped down over
his heavy neck
the fingers
strangely crimped
tightly together
her other arm doubled up
against her tight breast
her hand a languid claw
clutching his hand
which would turn her mouth
to his.
(*Who*, 15)

Ferlinghetti has found a diction suited to the haunting beauty of the subject, and his form provides the ideal medium for rendering the suggestive story behind this expressive art. The line seems to break with the fine sensitivity of a heart beat—a mental, sensory, and dramatic recognition. This form is duplicated in "The 'Moving Waters' of Gustav Klimt" which follows it. Repeatedly his form captures and releases the beauty of another artist in that integrated moment of perception and apperception.

In *Northwest Ecolog* Ferlinghetti takes his method another step, this time outdoors to render the meditative response of man and nature. Like the artist with brush and canvas, Ferlinghetti paints the word pictures of his awareness landscape. In "Wild Life Cameo, Early Morn" he brings us into the place:

By the great river Deschutes
on the meadowbank greensward
sun just hitting
the high bluffs
stone cliffs sculpted
high away
across the river.

(*Northwest*, 9)

A clarity and stillness is engendered in the subtle markings of the poet's awareness. Using a type of mental phrasing, approximate to Williams's variable foot, each line drops into its complement and balances itself. The flow is toward a focus as the poet notes:

six white-tail deer
four young bucks with branched antlers
and two small does
mute in eternity
drinking the river

then in real time raising heads
and climbing up and up
a steep faint switchback
into full sun.

(*Northwest*, 9)

The pacing and bare detail are deliberate and clear. There is a "switchback" to "real time" and a central awareness in "full sun," as the poet notes through binoculars, "as in a round cameo,"

There is a hollow bole in a tree
one looks into
One by one they
drink silence
(the two does last)
one by one
climb up so calm
over the rim of the canyon

and without looking back
disappear forever
Like certain people
in my life.
(*Northwest*, 9–10)

Drawn back in the poet's brief awareness at the close, we sense the expression of personal recognition which the form of the nature meditation has provided. The analogy to the Japanese verse of the haiku and tanka is apparent, yet Ferlinghetti has integrated the Western form and Eastern approach in this finely tuned poem. Like the hand-scrawled haiku journal writing of the earlier *Back Roads to Far Places* (1971), Ferlinghetti's application of open-form composition to nature subjects is a triumph in *Northwest Ecolog*, which includes his own bold and expressive sumi drawings from nature. The forms are integrated in the man who creates them.

In "A Sweet Flying Dream" from *Landscapes* Ferlinghetti further adapts his form to the sense of vision and flight contained in the dream. The lines are intuitively placed to release the energy of the poem experience and to confirm the reality and motion of dream. The flight is of two lovers "in an archetypal dream / of flying":

We
drifted
wafted easily
We
flew wingless

Full of air
our hair
buoyed us

We
trailed our slim legs
in streams of silver air.
(*Landscapes*, 24)

The reader is caught in word flight, participating in both the liquid sense of the experience and the act of recreating it through the poem. The rhythms and sound echoes are close yet light, a gentle singing in cerebral phrases. The life and art unite in the shared act of recognition and recording. In his open-form abstract expressionism Ferlinghetti has vitalized the visual surface of the poem and maximized phrasing effects so as to render the experience of consciousness whole. In painting his perceptions he has created a form which engages the reader in an authentic search for awareness and expression.

The Surrealism

From the start, Ferlinghetti's vision of art has been directly influenced by the work of the French surrealist movement, especially the work of Rimbaud, Apollinaire, Prévert, Cendrars, and Eluard. As he admits in an interview with David Meltzer, he has also been affected by a "native American Surrealism"[28] practiced by such writers as Henry Miller, Djuna Barnes, and Kenneth Patchen. As we have seen, the basic surrealist stance of engaged subversion directed against societal restraint and toward a vision of wonder and transforming love is at one with his own. Yet he is careful to call himself a "semi-surrealist poet,"[29] meaning that his vision of art includes and yet goes beyond the principles and bounds of surrealist theory as set down by the movement's leading spokesman, Andre Breton. As he has declared, Breton's chief influence on him was through the model of the semi-autobiographical *Nadja* and not through his manifestoes. Indeed, most of the influences above existed, by precedent or ultimate theatrical transgression, outside the bounds of official surrealism as Breton defined it. However, what we discover on closer examination is that Ferlinghetti not only embraces basic principles of the surrealist vision of art, but he also incorporates surrealist methods of creation into his anti-novel *Her* and into his poetry. Based on the surrealist theory of the *inner model*, parallel to the abstract expressionist concept of "inner necessity," he frequently engages in spontaneous or automatic writing to release subconscious sources, creating, through irrational analogy and intuitive juxtaposition, the powerful surrealist image.

In addition to publishing the writings of the surrealist movement in the United States, as well as the work of American surrealist Philip Lamantia, Ferlinghetti has published the surrealistic work of Americans Pete Winslow, Bob Kaufman, and the semi-surrealistic experiments of Allen Ginsberg, William S. Burroughs, Jack Kerouac, Frank O'Hara, and Gregory Corso. His long friendship with Philip Lamantia and Nancy Joyce Peters (Lamantia's wife and City Lights coeditor) has brought increased interest in the possibilities of surrealism as a means of mass transformation in the 1970s and 1980s. Ferlinghetti suggests, "The whole thing comes together after all these years. We talk and think about some word better than surrealism. At a time when daily reality far exceeds 'literary' surrealism, there really isn't any better term. I mean, maybe there is, but no one has thought of it yet. Superrealism? Hyperrealism? Unrealism?"[30] Certainly a primary problem facing contemporary criticism is the need to come to terms with the surrealism that pervades so much of contemporary writing. We can, nevertheless, discover the place of surrealist theory and methods in the work of Lawrence Ferlinghetti, the surrealism that does exist in his verse.

Chief among the surrealist methods of creation and of evaluation of a work is the artist's use of automatism. In the 1924 "Manifesto of Surrealism" Breton boldly defined: "SURREALISM, n. Psychic automatism in its pure state, by which one proposes to express—verbally, by means of the written work, or in any other manner—the actual functioning of thought. Dictated by thought, in the absence of any control exercised by reason, exempt from any aesthetic or moral concern."[31] Though the definition of surrealism expanded from this early formulation, it never varied from its faith in the automatic method of creation. Believing in a personal and yet universal mythology that existed in the subconscious, the surrealists found this unfettered release of thought a true source of the "inner model." What is not generally understood is that the various surrealists have each developed a personal approach to the use of automatism. While Benjamin Peret is judged as the most automatic in his pure, almost trancelike, devotion to spontaneous expression, and Robert Desnos practiced automatic speech, as fine a poet as Paul Eluard used automatism as an initial exploration point from which he recorded images that were later consciously woven into surrealist poems. Ferlinghetti, who was chiefly influenced by Apollinaire, Prévert, and Cendrar, poets who allowed much more conscious direction to their writing, follows Eluard's example of using automatism as a source, yet consciously working the poem later as a blend of conscious and subconscious thought. Speaking of Lamantia's reaction to his surrealistic writing, Ferlinghetti flatly admits, "I had the feeling he thought I was doctoring up my spontaneous visions and putting 'thought' in it—making it no longer a pure surrealistic product. In fact, I *was* doctoring them up."[32] Thus Ferlinghetti produces a combination of subconscious-conscious thought with the emphasis on the conscious, a surrealism with the lights on, if you will, as he demonstrates in "4" of *A Coney Island of the Mind*:

In a surrealist year
                    of sandwichmen and sunbathers
                         dead sunflowers and live telephones
     house-broken politicos with party whips
     performing as usual
     in the rings of their sawdust circuses
     where tumblers and human cannonballs
                              filled the air like cries
                    when some cool clown
                              pressed an inedible mushroom button
and an inaudible Sunday bomb
                              fell down
catching the president at his prayers
                                   on the 19th green.

(*Coney*, 14)

Such an opening declaration, "In a surrealist year," makes it clear that the poet is conscious of the nature of his perception, and, as the poem proceeds from juxtapositions of "sandwich-men and sunbathers / dead sunflowers and live telephones," it clearly becomes a conscious and symbolic thought. Thus we follow from the surrealistic image of a circus of "tumblers and human cannonballs" to the contemporary allusion of "an inedible mushroom button" and a president who prays on the golf course at the "19th green." Ferlinghetti is using imagery tapped from the subconscious to make a calculated and powerful statement, as in: "while out of every imitation cloud / dropped myriad wingless crowds / of nutless naga-saki survivors" (*Coney*, 14). The approach is much like Jacques Prévert's *Paroles* in which he combines a journalistic eye for external social detail and cultural event with an internal eye and ear for imaginative confirmation and release. Thus in Ferlinghetti's translation of Prévert's "Picasso's Magic Lantern" we find lines that capture "The mad terror of the trap in the eye of a bird / . . . A window on the ocean opened like a oyster / . . . A railroad ticket with all its baggage / . . . The caressing squirrel of a nude girl" combined with direct allusions to "The face of Andre Breton the face of Paul Eluard" and such conscious thematic reflection as "Of a world dead on its feet / Of a world condemned / And already forgotten / . . . Of a world without knowledge of how to live but full of the joy of living" (*Paroles*, 65–77). Like Prévert, Ferlinghetti personifies the poetic awareness which reflects the surface as well as the deeper realities of the integrated consciousness. His source is the outer and inner worlds. Automatism liberates the latter.

While Ferlinghetti's use of spontaneous writing can be traced throughout his works as a frequent source of imagery and an intuitive parallel to his open-form, abstract expressionist method, it is most pronounced in two books, *A Coney Island of the Mind* and *Open Eye, Open Heart*, where it appears in varying degrees. In the "A Coney Island" section of the former work Ferlinghetti borrows his title from Henry Miller's *Into the Night Life* and advises the reader that the works reflect "a kind of Coney Island of the mind, a kind of circus of the soul" (*Coney*, 8). Much like a surrealist work which he admired, *The Poet in New York* by Federico Garcia Lorca, this work charts the "surrealist landscape" of America. He records in "3" the "mindless prairies / supermarket suburbs / steam-heated cemeteries / cinerama holy days / and protesting cathedrals / a kissproof world of plastic toiletseats tampax and taxis" (*Coney*, 13). Clearly Ferlinghetti is consciously allowing the images to jar the reader by prompting their surrealistic charge, yet they are mirror images of a popular culture and not deep images of the subconscious. Yet by poem "24" he has given over to automatism more fully as he elicits images of:

> We squat upon the beach of love
>   among the beached mermaids
>   with their bawling babies and bald husbands
>   and homemade wooden animals
>   with icecream spoons for feet
>   which cannot walk or love
>   except to eat.
>
> (*Coney*, 39)

The images are more irrational, more self-generating, less interpretive or consciously reflective, and they therefore draw a deeper reaction from the reader's subconscious recognition. Yet here is revealed one of the major problems with Ferlinghetti's surrealism, that it often violates the surrealist approach to symbolism. For the surrealist the image simply means what it is, its symbolism is only connected in an inexplicable subconscious recognition, the sparks or magnetic waves which surrealists espouse. Too often Ferlinghetti seems to be working his own surrealist image source in a conscious attempt to interpret while he writes. This is against the grain of surrealist automatism which seeks to short-circuit the conscious rational mind in favor of the marvelous and the beauty of the subconscious. The poem reflects Ferlinghetti's ability on occasion to tap this truer source of the surreal and to trust its irrational image impact and flow.

In *Open Eye, Open Heart*, a book that reflects the gamut of Ferlinghetti's poetic abilities, his trust in the surrealism of experience is even more apparent. "An Imaginary Happening, London" is full of the subconscious power of automatism in such images as:

> The moon makes hairless nudes
>
> An alabaster girl upon her back
> becomes a body made of soap
> beneath a wet gypsy
>
> Suddenly we rush
> thru a bent gate
> into the hot grass.
>
> (*Open*, 45)

The poem follows a dream flow of inexplicable images and events that lead inward. Irrationality is given its reign as compulsion and transformation project the surrealist thrust of the pure automatism. The poem is unfathomable and clear. Yet the most dramatic, and most purely automatic work in the book occurs a few pages later in a three-part, trilingual celebration, "TROIS POÈMES SPONTANÉS SUR LA FORCE DE FRAPPE DE L'AMOUR A SIX HEURES DU MATIN" [Three Spontaneous Poems On the Force of Love At Six in the Morning]. The work rivals the most automatic writing of the surrealists, and finds its closest analogy in the celebrated first surrealist text, *Les Champs Magnetique* by Andre Breton and Philippe Soupault. Judged on the surrealist criteria of the authenticity of the motive and on the intuitive trust in the automatic method, it is purely surreal. Part three is included here with an accompanying translation of the Spanish and French:

> III.
>
> Ceremonial de la vida cassée comme un oeuf in a black bowl the yolk-soliel se leve encore ces croque-notes casques marchent toujours in the light of it Squads Right le monde takes a turn for the worse Remember the Maine chambered nautilus couldn't turn once it started in any direction et j'suis venu de Spain cet hiver les cloches sonnent toujours et on sait pour qui mais on n'entend plus on danse toujours to dead drums au Café Tambour

Place Bastille le bald garcon batte son oeuf sur le comptoir de sa vie casse-croûte the drum-world turns apres la pluie plaque des miroirs brises où on voit rein que les pieds nus des celebrants figes en énternité figures faces fixed in the dawn stagger onward titubant strung our egg-yolk in the sky et le monde rentre dans l'obscurité du soleil jeu perdant ballon tournant au ciel disparu au-dessus des toits fumes mais l'éclipse des cons va-arriver quand même.

(*Open*, 57)

[Rite of life night broken like an egg in a black bowl the sun-yolk rises again those cracked-noted casques marching forever in the light of it Squads Right the world takes a turn for the worse Remember the Maine chambered nautilus couldn't turn once it started in any direction and I have come from Spain this winter the bells toll forever and they know from whom yet they no longer understand they dance forever to dead drums at the Cafe Tambour Place Bastille the bald waiter beats his egg on the counter of his snack life the drum-world turns after the rainy plate of broken mirrors where one sees only the naked feet of celebrants congealed in eternity figures faces fixed in the dawn stagger onward weaving strung out egg-yolk in the sky and the world reenters the obscurity of the sun losing game balloon turning in the sky vanishing above the smoking roofs but the eclipse of idiots is about to arrive just the same.]

Particularly striking here is the juxtaposition of three languages within the flow of dream consciousness. Images, expressions, events, even commands spew out of the poet's subconscious, often echoing each other, as in the egg, sun, baldness, and the sense of impending (morning) awareness that pervades the moment. The absence of punctuation and the multi-lingual presentation attest to the poet's authentic trust in subconscious communication which exists outside a conscious concern for audience communication. The poet's faith in chance revelation outweighs his need or concern for explication, and yet the work projects powerful images confirming inner desire and wonder. There is the true "go with it" feel of surrealist creation ushered in by the sense of imminent delivery and arrival. The irrationality of the language is an affront to a rationally reduced reality. The surrealist poem is the surrealist act, and this poem is pure surrealism.

Having verified Ferlinghetti's reliance on the spontaneous creation of automatism, we can examine the characteristic surrealism that results in the surrealist image—a triumph of juxtaposition, analogy, and word alchemy. Ferlinghetti has always had and used the ability to transform reality through the irrationally true image. In "11" of *A Coney Island of the Mind*, for example, he presents shocking images of the "spirit birds": "these droves of plover / bearded eagles / blind birds singing / in glass fields / . . . And a masked bird fishing / in a golden stream / . . . And then those blown mute birds / bearing fish and paper messages" (*Coney*, 25–26). In seeking to capture the world of painter Morris Graves in analogous word images, Ferlinghetti follows the subconscious impulse into the "glass fields" of the surrealist image. The effect is powerful, not because it is irrational, but because it is intuitively right; it shocks us into a subconscious recognition. The images are freely associated in the subconscious, "fields" and "glass" for example, yet pulled forth together in a compelling analogy. The surrealist concept of juxtaposition of distant realities in the image, Lautreamont's celebrated "chance encounter of an umbrella and a sewing machine on a dissecting table," involves more than irrationality. According to Reverdy, "The more the relationship between the two juxtaposed realities is both distant and true, the stronger the image will be—the greater its emotional power and poetic reality."[33] The instinctive truth of the automatic method where the realities are associated and linked in the subconscious provides what Andre Breton called the essential spark or "light of the image."[34] The power of the image is thus weighed in its ability to produce and confirm the marvelous. The surrealist image is thus a surrealist act, a witness and talisman to the surreality of experience. It is part of the word alchemy of Rimbaud in which the surrealists not only recreate language but use that language as a tool to recreate the world. When Ferlinghetti tells us in "Euphoria" that "I see my roll-up tongue upon a string / and see my face upon the stick of it / as on a pendulum about to swing / a playing-card image with bound feet" (*Starting*, 11–12), he is tapping subconscious energy in an image-making gesture where reality is confirmed from within, and from the reader's shared sense of that recognition.

As suggested earlier, Ferlinghetti often "uses" the surrealist image in an otherwise straight piece of writing to accent incongruence or confirm wonder, and he often violates surrealist practice and theory by using or mixing the image with conscious symbolism, for he is the eclectic and "impurist" poet who takes and gives influences from a truly international perspective. Nevertheless, he is, as we have seen in the case of automatism and the surrealist image, capable of creating the pure surrealist poem as well as developing new forms of surrealist expression.

Another aspect of the surrealist use of language is the use of analogy. It is integral with the surrealist vision and practice; as Paul Eluard explains it concisely in "Donner à voir," "Everything is comparable to everything else. . . . Everything finds its echo, its reason, its resemblance, its opposition, its development everywhere. And that development is infinite."[35] More than an extension of metaphor in which one thing is consciously perceived in terms of another, for the surrealist the analogous view sees the one thing contained in the other. It is the unifying principle of their world view in which all things interconnect. Rationality for the surrealist has imposed a non-real barrier between all things, in particular between the objective and the subjective realities, between physical reality and the dream. In our imaginatively free subconscious all things connect, as they do in dreams. Much of surrealist art is thus directed toward manifesting this irrationally interconnected world, just as Ferlinghetti does in his surrealistic anti-novel *Her*. In fact, the surrealists developed a game of perceiving "the one in the other" as a type of training, rite, and celebration of the analogical method. The player would be required to describe an object (privately derived) in terms of another (which the group had decided upon). Thus surrealist artist Toyen would be required to spontaneously stretch her vision by describing an ice skate—in terms of a comb: "I am a toothless COMB used with the feet to part level and very tough hair."[36] Following this analogical vision and use of language, in which "like" is seen as a verb of action, the surrealists produce the characteristic telescopic images in which concrete and abstract, external and internal, things actual and imagined, are linked: "Windmills of mirrors and of eyes / Islands of breasts furrows of words / Caressing snow of strength / Faded ponds of fatigue."[37] Having established this basic method and motive of surrealism we can examine how Ferlinghetti used and developed it in his own most surrealistic writing.

The analogical image is common in Ferlinghetti. In "25" of *A Coney Island of the Mind* we confront the "flesh of air" and a world characterized as "a blather of asphalt and delay." In "Underwear" we recognize "poetry still the underwear of the soul," and in "Berlin" the poet tells us that walking through Woolworth's department store is "like dying / inside an amoeba." In the more recent "Several Surrealist Litanies" we confront the "glove compartments of the moon" and a "bread-breasted woman" as the "trees turned to ashfoot bodies" and "leaves turn to toast." It is an imaginative extension based on the surreality of experience and charged with humor and wonder.

More broadly, the analogical view of experience is integral with Ferlinghetti's vision of life and art, and it is deeply imbedded in his stance and method. We see it in such major poems as "Berlin" where the situation in Berlin and in Woolworth's department store are strangely linked, in the combined world of "Moscow in the Wilderness, Segovia in the Snow," in "Where Is Vietnam?" in which American diplomacy and aggression are described in terms of Lyndon Johnson's ranching practices, in "Baseball Canto" where American aggression against its minorities becomes linked and revealed through a San Francisco Giants baseball game and Ezra Pound's *Cantos*. In "One Thousand Fearful Words for Fidel Castro" the Cuban revolution and San Francisco street life stand mutually revealed, and "Las Vegas Tilt" exposes the American soul in combined images of Las Vegas gaming and the earth's quaking. The list is long and true, and, though he often engages in what might be termed allegory or extended metaphor, most often it is an analogical vision that precipitates the revelation of the poem, as in the classic "Enigma of Ho Chi Minh's Funeral."

In "Enigma of Ho Chi Minh's Funeral" the poet begins in the realm of his local street reality: "I am walking down the middle / of Telegraph Avenue Berkeley," but we are also in the abstract reality "in the middle of the surrealist enigma / which is Ho Chi Minh's funeral." Ferlinghetti rather self-consciously tips his hand in the reference to a "surrealist enigma," but he moves from there into a description of two realities in terms of each other as literal Berkeley blends with the revolutionary thoughts of Ho Chi Minh and North Vietnam. The analogy brings the subconcious emotional thought of the poet into his conscious awareness. He hears revolution screaming a third-story window record player and notes "When the mode of the music changes / someone throws bathwater out / with a burning baby in it." The realities of the Vietnam War in this 1969 poem are made super-real to our consciousness and conscience by the release of images of repressed horror. The juxtaposed realities are further linked when "An old friend I never knew very well / comes up & kisses me / waving her new Black baby / A black tank trundles by / waving its red light / and whining electronically / Back in Genoa Street." There is a leap from this image of terror brought home to Andre Breton's *Nadja*, "Nadja opens the door of her womb / to a great poet / It is illuminated by a very small light bulb / neither black nor red." In his taped reading of this poem surrealist poet Philip Lamantia is mentioned as the "great poet," the revolutionary, surrealist, Berkeley poet as an appropriate analogy in himself. The poet in the poem then thinks of Yevteshenko's warning on the tyranny of Revolution when "another Nadja named Nataska Nevsky / comes to bid me a red-eyed goodbye / on her way to a bed / in the home town of Dostoevsky." The literal and imagined become webbed in the fabric of consciousness, and the poem ends in perhaps the most powerful and personally authentic image of the integrated realities. Joining the parade "in my red Volkswagon teepee" he notes "The photo of Ho seems to be saying ho-ho / hollowly," and as he finds himself "Waving a small black flag / which turns red subsequently / I run over my family / accidentally." The immediate echo of this shockingly matter-of-fact though nonetheless tragic ending is to that of Yevtushenko's earlier warning that "truth is no longer truth / when the Revolution incidentally / sets fire to a loved one's roof" (*Open*, 83–84). Ferlinghetti has used the methods of juxtaposition and analogy to expose a broader reality and a deeper truth. He has captured both the "unreal" atmosphere of our times and the "super-real" subjective truth where the subconscious manifests itself. It is a method developed by Ferlinghetti and given definitive expression in this poem which extends the vision of surrealism through Ferlinghetti's dedication to authentic wholeness. While it is not pure surrealism, it is pure Ferlinghetti.

Sueño Real

1.

In the eternal dream-time
                    a fish dreamt ocean
                        a bird sky
And I stand on the beach in the land
        where all is still frontier
And hold an aluminum bird in my hand
And don't dream sand
                running through my head
                        as through an hourglass.
(*Open*, 16)

Ferlinghetti thus opens his ten-part visionary poem in the surrealist atmosphere of dream reality where life elements interconnect without question. The lyric flow of image to image, accented by the rhythmic line flow, connotes an air of acceptance—the familiar self-confirmation of the marvelous.

Each segment of the poem interweaves a fabric of irrational association led on by the inner voice:

6.

Loony surrealist dream
    of a lead soldier in a
        tin cowboy hat
    riding over
        the burnt horizon
        backwards on his horse
In his hand he holds
        a small white horse
        bearing a small white cowboy
            between its teeth
And this cowboy is singing
            'Life is a real dream.'

(*Open*, 18)

The poem progresses along the lines of inner need as matter and movement inseparably follow the thread of recognition. The open-form composition brings its own intuitive rightness to the inner vision. The refrain line, "Life is a real dream," does not obtrude, but seems unquestionably true in the pervading stream of subconscious. It leads to an expansion of meaning:

9.

I know that I don't dream
  'Life
    dreams me'
It is life
    that dreams around me
The leaves breathe
        the hills breathe
There is a willow aflame
            with sun
There are a series
        of waterproof mouths

And my words are
myself. . . .
(*Open*, 19)

Like the whole surrealist process, trust is prerequisite here, which Ferlinghetti confirms in his solipsistic concession that "Life / dreams me." In the poem's doubling, its fusion and extension, its transparency and balance, it demonstrates that this faith leads somewhere, that one need only follow as Ferlinghetti does to the inner self where "my words are / myself." The physical world of leaves, hills, willow are all quietly transformed from within by the surrealist vision of the marvelous where desire and wonder connect and vibrate. The final segment of the poem attests to the process as a "Transliteration of inanimate objects / into real beings . . . / by a stream impossible / to decipher." We have in this fine poem Ferlinghetti's fullest resolution of the surrealist methods and vision with his own as explication and application give way to revelation. Automatism, surrealist image, analogical experience, and surreal vision all come together in this new synthesis, the poem as action. It is Ferlinghetti's own long quest which results in his integration of surrealist methods to achieve both a subjective and subversive form to both reveal and transform reality.

FILMIC SCENES

FERLINGHETTI'S filmic scenes, his cinematic renderings of life overheard and reflected upon, represent a synthesis of his orientation and training as journalist and poet. Much like James Joyce's "epiphany" and "epicletti" scenes which capture life's character and significance through naturalistic detail, Ferlinghetti's filmic scenes reveal him as a master of locating and rendering unobtrusively life's revealing moments. They provide yet another voice and form for his verse, one that is more attuned to his populist concerns. Quite often these scenes, with their visual excitement, function as cultural mirrors containing and reflecting the sense of the times. His own fascination with filmic reality in *Her* and in his filmmaking experience with the 1960 *Have You Sold Your Dozen Roses?* are exhibited in these filmic scenes which adapt the techniques of cinema—cuts, detailing shots, sight and sound correlation, pans, sequencing, focusing—to the reflective form of poetry. He creates a form which, like film, excels in both documenting and commenting on reality. He is an adept poet-journalist with a cinematic sense of life.

In both *Pictures of the Gone World* and *A Coney Island of the Mind* Ferlinghetti is wrestling with the essential question of the relationship of life and art. Both works contain a liberal mix of naturalistic detail and artistic sensibility. It is not surprising then to find here the first use of the filmic scene. In "6" and "8" of *A Coney Island* we find Ferlinghetti's masterful delivery of two San Francisco street scenes. "6" locates us "in front of the church / of Saint Francis" in time to witness the men "putting up the statue / of Saint Francis." Reading like a scenario, the poem projects the scene:

in a little side street
just off the Avenue
where no birds sang
and the sun was coming up on time
in its usual fashion
and just beginning to shine
on the statue of Saint Francis
where no birds sang
And a lot of old Italians
were standing all around
in the little side street
just off the Avenue
watching the wily workers
who were hoisting up the statue
with a chain and crane
and other implements
And a lot of young reporters
in button-down clothes

were taking down the words
of one young priest
who was propping up the statue
with all his arguments.
(*Coney*, 17)

This carefully modulated montage of detail shots is heightened by the use of open-form composition where everything emerges in some unspoken relationship to each other through the poet's consciousness. There is a cast of extras in the old Italians and button-down reporters; there is a sight-to-sound correlation between the striking silence ("and no birds sang") and the priest's arguments. Though there is no dialogue, a primary feature of later examples of filmic scenes, there is the correlation of activity which is deliberately brought into focus and blended with the other detail shots. The tone is expertly controlled by the time lavished on isolated shots (through the open-form abstract expressionist phrasing), and one is made quietly aware of the moment's significance when unobtrusively the camera strays to what everyone is ignoring, the young woman, "a very tall and very purely naked / young virgin / with very long and very straight / straw hair / and wearing only a very small / bird's nest . . . passing thru the crowd / . . . her eyes downcast all the while / and singing to herself" (*Coney*, 18). Whether symbolic or surreal, the scene has been given a visionary thrust through the juxtaposition of characters. Ferlinghetti, with a fine sense of timing and image, uses filmic devices to both document reality and to extend it through the controlled and multiple focus.

In "8" the scene is Golden Gate Park, and the reader is brought into the filmic focus of a meadow, "which is the meadow of the world" where a man and a woman enter for a picnic of grapes and oranges. One begins to see the scene mythically when we are brought back into the documentary tone of the detail shots. It is reported, yet a significance seems to be just eluding us:

And then
he took his shirt and undershirt off

but kept his hat on
sideways
and without saying anything
fell asleep under it
And his wife just sat there looking
at the birds which flew about
calling to each other
in the stilly air
as if they were questioning existence
or trying to recall something forgotten.
(*Coney*, 20–21)

The poet-filmmaker controls our attention and mood as we follow the camera's eye to the final revealing detail shot of the wife:

and finally looking over
at him
without any particular expression
except a certain awful look
of terrible depression.
(*Coney*, 21)

Tone and mood are made one as we close-up on her forlorn face, the reality behind the detail and action. This use of character in almost a mime fashion is a primary feature of Ferlinghetti's experimental drama. Like the Chaplinesque silent film portraits of emotion and attitude through gesture, these characters and this scene pulls at us for unknown reasons. Ferlinghetti has poised, with a director's or editor's sense of associative control, a strange and telling scene. This same sense of cinematic transcription is evident in many of the other early works such as "20," "The pennycandystore beyond the El" and "Dog," the latter filmed as part of the National Educational Television "U.S.A. Poets: Ginsberg and Ferlinghetti" on the streets of San Francisco with Ferlinghetti and his dog Homer. "The Old Italians Dying," which is a sort of update on the "6" poem of *Coney*, has also been made into a film featuring the San Francisco scene and the poet reading by Herman Barlandt.

In the long poem "Bickford's Buddha" from *The Secret Meaning of Things* Ferlinghetti gives the filmic scene a deeper dimension of personal reflection. The poem, which was "Writ on the back of a map of Harvard College," as Ferlinghetti attests, is a record of his day at Harvard before a Boston reading. The camera moves much quicker here, flashcutting as he moves about Bickford's Harvard Square from the Harvard Co-op down the street, where he records: "And a threeyear-oldgirl on a sidewalk / licking the chocolate spreckles off / a gooey ice-cream cone / peering through the open back-door / of a drycleaningshop / where some sort of big belted wheel / was going round fast," down Plympton Street into the Grolier Bookshop, past the front of Bickford's Cafeteria, past classrooms, past the statue of John Harvard to the Fogg Museum to the Kirkland House, then off to his Boston reading as "The sun slips down" (*Secret*, 11–19). Sights and sounds are picked up in his "Observation Fever / omniverous perception of phenomenon / not just visual." We hear people talking, view the posters of poets, observe the students working at study and revolution, confront a guard who throws Ferlinghetti out of the Lamont Poetry Room for not owning a student card, watch as the many characters, including "A bearded student buddha / in blue-jeans beads & sneakers," tread by. And yet this cinematic panorama in motion is not simply documentary; it is centrally located in Ferlinghetti's consciousness which is simultaneously wrestling with "the secret meaning of this day," with thoughts of buddha and poetry "in the Dublin of America." It is a stirring poem of fun and observation as the poet-journalist is out walking and filming. His technique runs parallel to Jack Kerouac's "sketching" technique of picking up all the spontaneous images and impressions of an experience.

In *Open Eye, Open Heart* Ferlinghetti takes his poetic camera and sound system into the heart of America for two restaurant scenes in the poems "In a Time of Revolution for Instance" and "The Astonished Heart." He has chosen an ideal spot to watch and overhear America, a Ramada Inn in Lawrence, Kansas. The poet-observer is there as first-person recorder for both poems. In the former he has "just ordered a fishplate at the counter when / three very beautiful / fucked-up people entered" (*Open*, 10). He picks up their subtle gestures with a subjective camera that records the hair styles, dress, postures, and the woman's gentle smile and lips that move in mime from the back of the restaurant. However, using a final objective camera eye, the poem just steps back from these "beautiful people" in a restaurant full of "little people" who are "quietly eating their quite ordinary / lunches" (*Open*, 12), and wraps it off. The poet's final sexual fantasy is as unreal as the whole scene, and all of it is rendered in a final montage of observations.

In "The Astonished Heart" Ferlinghetti provides a parallel piece about a couple "in the next booth" undergoing their own private tragedy and joy. Close-ups of the man and woman project into flashcuts of scenes of desire, "with her long look / out a window / through the Stanford Station's neons toward the plains / where somewhere soon / they will lie together hot / under the sun at noon." Ferlinghetti even sets up the dissolve shot here in a filmic fade "into the astonished heart / of America" (*Open*, 15).

Another cafe film-poem takes place in the ten-part "Overheard Conversations," where the scene is documented as "In the U.S. Restaurant & Café Sport, San Francisco, Listening to Barlow Farrar, Tony Dingman & Others." The literary chatter is recorded accurately amidst the common interchange of an American restaurant:

Knock at your own risk
        and duck if you're in the way
  That's
            my philosophy
                                she tittered
              as two too cool young guys
                                                saunter in
                  and sit down at the next table
                        smoking Luckies and looking around
                                                        without expression.
                                                                (*Who*, 25–26)

The whole poem is a sensory mixture of sights, sounds, even

smells of the food. The objective tape recorder is left running as each segment begins with a speaker other than the poet-narrator. It picks up talk of Mao, movies, Mexico, tennis shoes, and poetry workshop talk. In this "random colloquial clapping / by one hand" Ferlinghetti captures the culture in a filmic mirror that has all the verbal dynamics of a Robert Altman film with eight microphones open at once. The reality of it washes over us.

In his most recent collection, *Landscapes of Living and Dying*, the poet records four cinematic portraits: "The Old Italians Dying," "Holiday Inn Blues," "Cloning at the 'Hawk & Dove'" and "Two Scavengers in a Truck, Two Beautiful People in a Mercedes." This increased use of filmic scenes testifies to his populist goal of attaining a poetry of "new commonsensual 'public surfaces'." The poet must be out there, at-large, in the streets recording life. In these particular pieces he spans the realities of San Francisco's Washington Square, a South Carolina Holiday Inn, a Washington D.C. bar, and finally the traffic of San Francisco's streets.

In "Two Scavengers" Ferlinghetti renders a still-life study filmically, an animated photograph of garbagemen and socialites at a stoplight at "Nine A.M. downtown San Francisco." They are captured at the moment of looking at each other, the consciousness of self and other, and finally of the "great gulf" between the lives of Americans. This is all told wordlessly but in detail shots montaged to a peak of recognition. We see "two garbagemen in red plastic blazers," the couple "the man / in a hip three-piece linen suit / with shoulder-length hair & sunglasses / The young blond woman so casually coifed / with a short skirt and colored stockings." We shift back to the physical details of the scavengers, then the "cool couple," and finally "for an instant / holding all four close together" (*Landscapes*, 26–27). That's it, Americana reál.

In perhaps his most developed filmic scene, "Holiday Inn Blues," Ferlinghetti combines all his cinematic techniques in a poem that captures the heart of America in its pervasive loneliness. The film-poem opens on the "weird ritual" practiced nightly in any Holiday Inn, America. The popular culture references are strong. Beyond the invitation to "Come

Dance the Fuzz Off Your Peaches!" in the cave-like lounge, lies the reality of:

a country-rock group working out
an Elvis Presley singer
bellows at four dim couples dancing
two of them doing rock-style
not touching
or looking
at each other
as they thrash about
as if each were trying
to keep his or her balance
on some erratic highspeed treadmill
The other two couples
wrapped around each other
in the local bear-hug style.

(*Landscapes*, 18)

Again the description is close to scenario or filmscript directions, capturing in the open-form timing and phrasing the emptiness of the camera's gesture and motion. This is a dance devoid of expression. As the two "middle-age ladies" are escorted back then shovelled into their seats by the men in lumberjack shirts, the poet-filmmaker follows the women into a flashback of their lives. One has a fat husband and three grown children and "a lady barber from Asheville / who specializes in blue hair and blue gossip," the other is a too willing receptionist to an old dentist. Back on the dance floor, the ladies are being sought after once more by another pair of manly suitors:

the men hanging onto them
as if they were
absolutely starved for affection
on a life-raft somewhere
clinging to them like life itself
or their mothers
yet they are absolute strangers.

(*Landscapes*, 19–20)

The ultimate inexpressible loneliness of American life haunts those lines, all told explicitly in the empty gestures of their ritual. Ferlinghetti knows that all he need do is show it. His receptive consciousness records the significance of the common. As the band leader banters and the singer starts his Buddy Holly numbers, Ferlinghetti lets the whole scene writhe in the hollowness of their quiet desperation. Amidst the electronic antics of the rock band he projects the couples into desperate embrace, "lips clinging to each other / like suction cups." Though there is no beauty here nor any authentic emotion, it is for love that the poem cries out:

> We've fallen into
>   Dante's Inferno
>   burning for love
> We're trapped inside
>   Bosch's Garden of Delights
>   groaning with love
> We're lost
>   in Burrough's loveless Soft Machine
>   with tongues alack
>   for love.
>   (*Landscapes*, 20)

In this filmic epiphany which elicits the poet's response we are made to face the charade of love; we see and hear the acts of alienation in a cinematic mirror. A slice of American life is expertly documented and revealed. In these filmic scenes captured by the poet-journalist we come not only to see and hear life, but to know it.

THE PROSE POEM

FERLINGHETTI is certainly not one to respect any artificial genre distinctions. One finds a liberal mixture of prose and poetry, for example, in *Mexican Night* and *Northwest Ecolog*, as well as a blending of forms in the haiku journal form of *Back Roads to Far Places* and the poetic prose passages of his anti-novel *Her*. Lawrence Ferlinghetti has also become one of America's leading practitioners of the international form, the prose poem. In fact, an examination of Ferlinghetti's diverse innovations with the prose poem form provides an excellent introduction to the possibilities of this anti-formalist writing as well as a further revelation of Ferlinghetti's broad achievement.

In Michael Benedikt's "Introduction" to *The Prose Poem: An International Anthology* he suggests the impossibility of defining the form other than by its chief features. Charm, intensity, humor, everyday speech and associative leaps mark the prose poem which carries a visionary thrust in its attempt to record the fluctuating motions of the conscious and subconscious mind.[38] Situated in the writer's inner voice, the prose poem is an extremely open, organic and original form. It has gained a wide popularity among contemporary American audiences and writers, as seen in the work of W. S. Merwin, Russell Edson, Michael Benedikt, Robert Bly, James Tate, and others. In Ferlinghetti's hands it becomes a subtle, versatile, and powerful form. Tracing its evolution is a revealing task.

In "29" of *A Coney Island of the Mind* Ferlinghetti presents his first prose poem, a spiralling verbal flow that focuses on the love quest in a society characterized by quick-paced emptiness. The prose poem is remarkably like the most poetic prose of his anti-novel *Her* and contains the same basic themes and forces. There is no punctuation and the lines run together in a rhythmic stream of consciousness filled with strong currents of cultural and social allusions and illusions:

> but they go right on trying to get it all the time like in Shakespeare or The Waste Land or Proust remembering his Things Past or wherever And there they all are struggling toward each other or after each other like those marble maidens on the Grecian Urn or on any market street or merrygoround around and around they go all hunting love and half the hungry time not even knowing just what is really eating them like Robin walking in her Nightwood streets.
> (*Coney*, 44–45)

The final allusion in this merrygoround of loss is to Djuna Barnes's novel *Nightwood* which Ferlinghetti has suggested had a profound influence on the form of *Her*. Particularly, in the character of Dr. Matthew O'Connor, whose consciousness stream borders on the surrealistic, we have a prototype for Ferlinghetti's experimentation. And yet Ferlinghetti provides his own characteristic flare for the rich suggestiveness of allusions and the impact of spoken language. The prose poem closes with the associative images and symbols released from the subconscious:

> and then comes tumbling down the sound of axes in the wood and the trees falling and down it goes the sweet cock's sword so wilting in the fair flesh fields away alone at last and loved and lost and found upon a riverbank along a riverrun right where it all began and begins again. (*Coney*, 45–46)

Captured here is the cyclic motion of longing and loss in a form which echoes its theme of loneliness. It is a form that he will develop fully in *Her*.

In *Starting from San Francisco* Ferlinghetti is working the prose poem to other ends. He has developed what might be termed the Whitman (later Ginsberg) refrain, the long-lined breath units comparable to paragraphs of thought. He uses this most pronouncedly in "Tentative Description of a Dinner to Promote the Impeachment of President Eisenhower" where the invective is given momentum by the cyclic repetition of his charges against the Eisenhower administration. Poetic devices of repetition (consonance and assonance), puns, and word echoes are used to dramatize the absurdity and to heighten a public sense of irritation:

> And after it became obvious that the President nevertheless still carried no matter where he went in the strange rain the little telegraph key which like a can opener could be used instantly to open but not to close the hot box of final war if not to waylay any stray asinine action by any stray asinine second lieutenant pressing any strange button anywhere far away over an arctic ocean thus illuminating the world once and for all. (*Starting*, 42–43)

The "And . . ." clauses compound themselves into a climactic case for the fast-speaking poet of rebellion. The other prose poem of this volume is the narrative "The Great Chinese Dragon" in which Ferlinghetti uses the Chinese dragon of San Francisco Chinatown parades in a parable of Chinese-American culture. It too makes use of the Whitman refrain and the "And . . ." clauses as it narrates in prosey form the mythic event and interpretation of a minority race in America. The dragon is given a philosophic, political, even phallic interpretation as it exhibits each year a richly imagistic and non-American vision:

> And he is a monster with the head of a dog and the body of a serpent risen yearly out of the sea to devour a virgin . . . and he is the great earthworm of lucky life filled with flowing Chinese semen and he considers his own and our existence in its most profound sense as he comes and he has no Christian answer to the existential question even as he sees the spiritual everywhere translucent in the material world and . . . (*Starting*, 39)

Ferlinghetti finds in the prose poem a loose form for spoken narration yet a form which can readily be given poetic charge through rhythmic devices and word play, street songs that contain the directness of prose yet the intensity of poetry. Both works are visionary yet ordinary, generating a creative tension for the reader as the poet's consciousness seeks and finds a voice to express the reality about him.

Open Eye, Open Heart, with eight prose poems, demonstrates the further explorations the poet makes with the possibilities of the form. Besides the multilingual "Trois Poèmes Spontanés" which achieves a visionary intensity through the flow of automatism, there is the lyrical and poignant tribute of "Pound at Spoleto," a prose poem that organically blooms into a climactic poem. Within the same "Poems in Transit" section, Ferlinghetti also includes a new prose poem development—the four-part "Poems from 'Russian Winter Journal'." The mixture of poems (2 and 4) with prose poems (1 and 3) is reminiscent of *The Mexican Night* journal writing in which the poet seeks to render the various realities of locale and thought in matching forms. Like the filmic scenes of a roving consciousness, here Ferlinghetti has eye and heart open to the rich suggestive depths of a winter Russia. One can also sense the poet with his tiny journal notebooks scribbling in near finished form the poems and prose of his observations. He is caught up in the double life of Russia's surface and the interior realities as his own mixed consciousness delivers the form.

He begins the "Poems from 'Russian Winter Journal'" with a simple listing of images surrounding the abandoned amusement park "In Khabarovsk above the Amur River":

> a great deserted merrygoround park with empty Ferris wheels, airplaneride whirligigs with little planes with empty cockpits on ends of long booms attached to a central turntable (empty planes stalled high in air), abandoned pavilions & summer esplanades high over the beach and frozen estuary waters, the beach covered with snow, heroic statue of some hero in a greatcoat & boots striding forward with a great hound wolfdog leading him but all fenced in a little snow-covered plot among winter trees full of stiff brown leaves frozen. (*Open*, 62)

And yet, even in this running catalogue of details including the very specific "100-foot-long six-foot-high white canvas banner in Russian proclaiming 50TH ANNIVERSARY OF THE GREAT OCTOBER REVOLUTION!" (*Open*, 63), we are aware that a reality deeper than the factual is invading the poet-journalist's report. In the vivid colors and somber tones of "stiff brown leaves . . . bright blue winter sky . . . Red horse missing . . . black boats deserted . . . small black & white mongrel dog" we too are swept into an impressionistic mood of time and place. It is a long (400 words) sentence of perception etched upon the poet's ripened awareness. The prose poem form lends itself to the informality of observation yet the underlying tension of awakened sensibility. We are in motion yet stilled by the lower depths of this panorama. All of this is given a final ironic cap in the solitary and absurd image: "And uptown in front of a big cafe, one young father in grey lamb wool shako & fur-collared coat hurrying along the wide boulevard sidewalk under the municipal trees, carrying one wooden merrygoround horse under his arm upsidedown" (*Open*, 63). The prose poem form reflects the perceptual growth as the journalist is quieted by the poetry that emerges. The piece is full of the humor, charm, and poetic intensity of this organic form.

There follows "2," a sharp impressionistic poem, a "Recipe for Happiness" amidst the sunny Russian cafe life "with strong black coffee in very small cups." It is a brief imagistic and tonal piece which flows into the more political consciousness of prose poem "3." This work begins with the imagist recording of Siberian wilderness as "huge frozen white butterflies—*schmetterlings* wing-to-wing over the plains & tundra, piled up like snowdrifts in the mountains, fluttered under the birches of eternal *taiga*, falling through high passes, these frozen white butterflies like the Great White Night itself" (*Open*, 65). And yet these lush images meet with the emerging political awareness at the border of Mongolia and China: "In this White Night Country the wood houses may someday be turned over by enormous Birds, as beasts sigh, rutting, and a Red winter sun pours blood out of Manchuria" (*Open*, 65). Again the poet's heightened sensibility is rendered with the reflexive ease yet intensity of the prose poem as the associative leaps draw the mind back upon itself.

Part 4 is given the title "The Old Revolution" and is a poem which squarely places the poet in the unspoken reality of Russian revolution. Ferlinghetti projects himself as a seaman on the Battleship Potemkin which is now held motionless in the midst of Siberian snowfields where "Nothing moves / And yet it won't sink!" (*Open*, 66). Time and place are rendered fluid in the poet's consciousness stream. Ferlinghetti offers in this four-part sequence from his "Russian Winter Journal" a convincing demonstration of the powerful mixture of poetry and prose, where what is important is not the premeditated polish applied to the writing, but its open release of a reflective and intuitive truth. It is a form that captures the act of poetry. The distinctions between prose and poetry are not only artificial but a block to expression.

In the "Public & Political Poems" section of *Open Eye, Open Heart* Ferlinghetti's application of the methods of the prose poem is more rhetorically direct. All are examples of what may be termed the "rolling narrative" form in which a speaker delivers, often in one long compounded sentence, an account of a circumstance or event. Much like Kerouac's "sketching" technique of spontaneous prose, Ferlinghetti's form is both loose and direct, like jazz improvisation, spun out of the poet's own authentic confrontation with street reality. It manifests itself in a flow of common speech as the public poet addresses and exposes the pretenses of the day. In "A Parade Tirade" dated 1962, the poet strings together, minus punctuation, a flow of adieu's to the signs of American hypocrisy in the passing parade. Besides the militant "america of the american legion" and the "mute poet & professors who only stand and wait," there is a farewell to the corrupted visions of Hemingway, Pound, and Eliot. Then the poem turns to salutations of "good day" to the visions of Dylan (Thomas and Bob Dylan), Pablo Neruda, Allen Ginsberg, Fidel Castro, climaxing in a morning greeting to a vision of nature and love. The prose poem form maximizes the effects of cataloging and an oral delivery. "Telegram from Spain" (24 Marzo 65) uses the telegram form to convey a message of criminal complicity in the reign of Spain's General Franco. Ferlinghetti confronts the contemporary complacency with the immediacy of italics and hard images of violation: "POLITICAL VEGETARIANS FORCED AT LAST TO FEED ON THE GREAT PORKER HIMSELF & SO THEMSELVES DEVOURED AT LAST BY CENTURY PLANTS OF THEIR OWN SOWING" (*Open*, 76). The rhetorical application of devices is strong in these functional pieces of political engagement.

"Where Is Vietnam?" and "Alaska Pipe Dream" make a stronger use of the spiralling invective of the rolling narrative form. Like his "Tentative Description of a Dinner" prose poem, the poet projects his sense of moral violation into the public consciousness through an imaginative dramatization. Caricature is a prime device as political figures perpetuate, through ignorance or corruption, their acts of transgression. Bits of dialogue are worked into the flow, as are verbal puns and surrealistic images of violence. Lyndon Johnson, for example, as Colonel Cornpone in "Where Is Vietnam?" makes the verbal slip of referring to it as "Vietmind" and "Vietmine" as his fingers touch the globe and "the surface of this world had suddenly become very very slippery with a strange kind of red liquid that ran on it across all the obscene boundaries" (*Open*, 78). The nightmare reality is too true to deny. In the 1973 "Alaska Pipe Dream" Ferlinghetti mixes oil and blood and human body waste in his cry against the governmental (Canada and the United States) greed for oil. In both prose poems his form is very prosey, yet open to poetic gestures as the overall fast-speaking flow metaphorically captures the sense of the times: "and this world went on spinning faster and faster in the same so predestined direction and kept on spinning and spinning and spinning and spinning!" (*Open*, 78). The running narrative with its protean form capable of cutting directness or undeniable imagery proves an effective rhetorical device, one he will use again and again as in the long *Tyrannus Nix?* political-satirical tirade of 1969.

In *Who Are We Now?* Ferlinghetti adapts the rolling narrative form to new content. "The Heavy" is a seemingly autobiographical piece of reporting during an afternoon in the tiny Trieste Cafe of San Francisco. There is the oral ease of detail collecting yet the compounded intensity of the emerging moment of realization. In this filmic scene a heavy Italian "Mafia godfather" garners the attention of the curious poet who projects the heavy's entire life from his face until the associations begin to reel out from the poet's own life: "he was James Joyce's Artist . . . he was Proust's solitary diner, and he was Dr. Matthew O'Connor in drag in Djuna Barnes' *Nightwood* asking 'Watchman, what of the Night?'" (*Who*, 33). It is Joycean epicleti as a prose poem sketch in which Ferlinghetti engenders sympathy by his own identification with the life of the streets. In "Highway Patrol," however, the poet takes on the character of a rambling California cowboy who unreels his proud and boisterous tale of bigotry and violence in the Sacramento Coffee Shoppe. This unusual use of a persona narrator is nevertheless effective and appropriately disturbing as the hell-bent cowboy destroys the place while boasting, "and the goddam roof catches fire and everybody in sight freaks out and runs off down the road and over the hill outa sight Man we sure as hell lit that joint up if you know what I mean All good clean fun and we died laughin' Just like in the movies" (*Who*, 38). Ferlinghetti has thus adapted the rolling narrative of the prose poem to his oral delivery and to his filmic scenes form.

In "Great American Waterfront Poem," a long and powerful work, he develops a type of prose litany for his life. In his oblique confessional portrait of his divorce, he begins with a series of thought fragments, subjects in search of predicates, as his life is waiting to end so that it can begin:

> San Francisco land's end and ocean's beginning The land the sea's edge also The river within us the sea about us The place where the story ended the place where the story began The first frontier the last frontier Beginning of end and end of beginning End of land and land of beginning Embarcadero Freeway to nowhere . . . What is the water saying to the sea on San Francisco waterfront where I spent most of my divorce from civilization in and out of waterfront hangouts. (*Who*, 34)

As Ferlinghetti turns to the concrete reality of time and place, the literal as well as the mythic, we are aware that it is the comprehensive consciousness that he is transcribing. It is a moment at which all things become symbolic, even the place names of various familiar waterfront hangouts which he chants: "China Basin Mission Rock Resort Public Fishing Pier Harbor Lunch Tony's Bayview Red's Java House Shanty Gallery Bottom-of-the-Mark Eagle Cafe Longshoreman's Hall the Waterfront dead No Work No Pay Golden Gate Pilot Boat" (*Who*, 34). As his mind unreels the language of locale, he begins to catalog physical details which unobtrusively prompt memories into his own deep quest to locate himself:

> The phone booth where I telephoned It's All Over Count Me Out The fog lifting the sun the sun burning through The bright steamers standing out in the end of the first poem I ever wrote

> in San Francisco twenty years ago just married on a rooftop in North Beach overlooking this place I've come to in this life this waterfront of existence A great view and here comes more life. (*Who*, 34–35)

It is again Ferlinghetti's perspective and voice as poet-journalist that allows him to unite realism and revelation in his work. The prose poem form proves extremely adaptable in his hands to a comprehensive sense of life. As he moves into the Eagle Cafe awaiting the telephone call announcing the finality of his divorce the poem focuses yet sways with the tension of his mood which so perfectly finds its form in the prose string of realizations that unwind: "And who's this weirdo who is myself and where does he think he's going to sail away to when there isn't any longer any Away," he asks himself while gazing into the glass of the phone booth, his "mirror of the world" (*Who*, 36). All the movements of his life peak in the ocean of his affairs as his ship beckons: "The Balcutha's whistle blows The tide is at the ebb The phone rings" (*Who*, 36). In one of his longest and most complex prose poems Ferlinghetti captures all the currents of consciousness rising from within and without to a moment of stillness. The prose poem is ideally suited to the loose and flowing form of Ferlinghetti's life.

One other feature of Ferlinghetti's development of the prose poem form deserves attention—his creation of the "prose/"form in *Northwest Ecolog*. Here the poet deliberately releases the poetry from the prose journal entries by providing a mental phrasing through the use of the slash. In "13 August 77, Siskiyou National Forest," for example, Ferlinghetti and his son Lorenzo stand in a stream watching the speckled trout, "in the shrinking hole / now no more than eight feet deep / where they lay motionless / waiting / trapped / their world shrinking / and shrinking" (*Northwest*, 29). There is no line break in printed form, only the delicate sense of phrasing which the slash accents. The poet senses the cosmic passage of time hurried on by man's ecological bungling, and with light brush strokes releases the quiet beauty of this rhythmic moment in time:

> Yet seeing now the beauty of those fish / down there below the surface / so still and lovely / in their deep dream / dappled in their last deep pool / We fish no longer / turn / and go on / into the deeper pools / of our own lives. (*Northwest*, 30)

In the measured weight of the slashed phrasings Ferlinghetti listens within and guides our attention and sense of significance. Each phrase is measured against the next in a slowing / stilling effect that draws out the poetry of language and experience. Synthesis and integration are the motives, as time after time Ferlinghetti creates a form to release wonder and beauty. As he himself exclaims, he respects no "invisible boundaries," and his many developments of the prose poem —oral, impressionistic, persona, political-satirical, rolling narrative, prose/—testify to his art and wisdom.

Overview of the Poetry

SURVEYING the gamut of Ferlinghetti's poetry convinces one of his visionary and engaged quest for the authentic. He is the public and personal poet of American consciousness whose work knows no boundaries of nationality or genre. His influences are internationally varied, yet they are directed through his personal dedication toward a common and vital art. Whether he is creating an event out of a public reading in his characteristic flat and laconic voice, blending poetry and jazz, or boldly sharing the private yet universal segment of his life, he is out there making poetry a spontaneous and communal matter. Whether it is in oral, satirical, open, abstract expressionist, surrealistic, filmic, or prose poem form, it is an authentic evolution of life and art reaching into each other. The development of his poetry through his various books and recordings thus provides a revealing summary of his poetic achievement.

Pictures of the Gone World (1955), both derivative and experimental, breaks new ground for what poetry could be while it also begins to build a Ferlinghetti style. Its self-declarative theme and form lay out the groundwork for Ferlinghetti as a writer. The "gone world" theme, a jazzman's analogy to Camus's "Absurd," lies before him, and he is in it and with it. It is reflected in his cultural mirrors, enlarged by his ready allusions, and sharply focused in the poem "26" declaration where he decidedly turns from thoughts of Yeats's Arcady to "all the gone faces/ getting off at midtown places." His is to be an art deliberately engaged in life. For precedents in theme and form he has Americans E. E. Cummings and Kenneth Patchen, but more pronounced is the influence of Frenchmen Jacques Prévert, Guillaume Apollinaire, and Blaise Cendrars. He develops his own open-form, abstract expressionist mode while also reaching into speech forms for diction and style. Though some poems go flat from a too prosey form (either from ineptness, experimentation, or engaged stance), the work is an original and solid foundation for his later developments.

His translations of *Paroles* (1958), which he had been working on for some time, show Ferlinghetti as the perfect translator of Jacques Prévert. His coming to himself as poet, through Prévert, is revealed in their shared themes and forms (street and oral, slangy and surreal, with tones of the murder as well as the joy of life); the work is full of wit and love and caring. The bird images of "Birds, At Random" and the streetwise and surreal mind-talk of "Rue De Seine" become permanent features of Ferlinghetti's work.

When selections from *Pictures of the Gone World* were combined with the poetry-and-jazz experiments "Oral Messages" and the original poems of *A Coney Island of the Mind* (1958), Ferlinghetti had enlarged his stance and developed major themes of anarchy, mass corruption, engagement, and a belief in the surreality and the wonder of life. It was a revolutionary art of dissent and contemporary application which jointly drew a lyric poetry into new realms of social- and self-expression. It sparkles, sings, goes flat, and generates anger or love out of that flatness as it follows a basic motive of getting down to reality and making of it what we can. The book is a consolidation of themes and methods which brings together the surrealist images of the "Coney Island" poems, the abstract expressionism of the painting analogies (rendered in human effects), the oral style and cultural mirrors of the "Oral Messages," the American sense of Imagism with a Joycean symbolism of subject and form. Loosely, the book forms a type of "Portrait of the Artist as a Young Poet of Dissent." There are some classic contemporary statements in this Ferlinghetti's—and possibly America's—most popular book of modern poetry. The work is remarkable for its skill, depth, and daring.

Two recordings were released in 1959: the *Poetry Reading in "The Cellar"*, which combined Rexroth and Ferlinghetti's poetry-and-jazz experiments done with The Cellar Jazz Quintet, and *Tentative Description of a Dinner to Promote the Impeachment of President Eisenhower and Other Poems*, which featured selected early works. Both came at the peak of the San Francisco Renaissance and the Beat Movement and were released by Fantasy Records of Berkeley, California. Both recordings sought to fulfill the declared goals of gaining a larger audience for poetry, and, though Ferlinghetti has lately disclaimed some of his poetry-and-jazz work as a failed experiment, there is an unmatched vitality and toughness to the fugue-like "Autobiography" in which jazzmen and poet trade statements in an ongoing flow of experience and reflection. His "Saint Francis" poem is also justly enhanced by the lyrical jazz accompaniment. More than an evolution of a new form, the experiments with poetry-and-jazz opened Ferlinghetti's work to a stronger oral form with infinite possibilities for the voice; the jazz helped to release his poetry. In *Tentative Description and Other Poems* the voice is often laconic yet engaged and full of witty turns and allusions, as the street poet speaks out. He declares in the cover notes, "All the poems on this record are, in one way or another, protest poems, written to be heard. Oral messages. And without jazz. . . . Let the poet carry it, if he can." With the exception of the long political tirade "Tentative Description" which uses a background of slowly mounting kennel drums, all the others stand on the bareness of his dry and cutting voice. Outstanding examples that reflect the range of his verbal protest are the lyrical "Pennycandystore," the existential "Dog," the Beat "Crucifixion," and the engaged declaration of "The Poet As An Acrobat." It is an historic document of the poet-performer whose voice resonates sensitivity, concern, and humor—a diction and delivery of calculated understatement—making him one of the most popular and vital poet-readers of our time.

Ferlinghetti's 1961 *Starting from San Francisco* followed Walt Whitman's lead in journeying outward as a means of expanding yet solidifying a stance. The personal and social involvements are broadened in these bold and bare poems directed toward a new engaged art for a new world. "These poems represent to me a kind of halfway house in the ascent of a mountain I hardly knew existed until I stopped and looked back at the flatlands below. Like a Zen fool lost in the woods who laughs and lies face down on the earth to find his way" (*Starting*, cover notes). Ferlinghetti thus connects his physical travels with his personal pathway to consciousness, and in the chronicle of places and dates his deepened social and political involvements are revealed. The poems are direct in their content and in their violation of conventional form. An oral style predominates, often manifested in the deeply ironic voice and in his own heartfelt mixture of radicalism and innocence. The book was first issued with a recording of the poet reading key poems, and the book does contain some important statement poems (many issued originally as broadsides) and some developments of the analogical method and the prose poem applied to engaged poetics. "Berlin" and "Situation in the West" were added later, rounding the collection to sixteen long poem confrontations which compose themselves in Ferlinghetti's evolving recognition of the evil and death in life.

The Secret Meaning of Things (1968) followed Ferlinghetti's period of experimental drama in the mid-sixties and reflects his stronger attention to irrational and intuitive analogy as a means of suggesting the "secret meaning" behind life's surface. Though the works are provocative, public, and oral, they are also more cosmic in reference, revealing a stronger influence from Buddhist philosophy. Despite the fact that the book appeared during the height of the Vietnam War, the writing is more in touch with life forces, mellowed by his attempt to be at one with his various feelings and places. The vision is both dark and hopeful in such apocalyptic statements as "Assassination Raga," "After the Cries of the Birds," "Moscow in the Wilderness, Segovia in the Snow." These six long poems continue the journey of *Starting from San Francisco* toward a deeper and clearer understanding in which the poet sees and records "All Too Clearly" the slow eternal progress of civilization.

Open Eye, Open Heart (1973) is Ferlinghetti's largest and most complete collection with material ranging from 1961 to 1973 included under four broad headings: "Open Eye, Open Heart" poems of self and tributes to Patchen, Lawrence, Whitman; "Poems in Transit," journey observations from around the world, including the impressionistic rendering of "Russian Winter Journal" and the surrealistic "Trois Poèmes Spontanés,"; "Public & Political Poems," various dated affirmations and tirades of his basic humanitarian socialist stance applied to new situations—Vietnam, Greece, Spain, and the poor; "American Mantra & Song," American English chants of extreme open statement and lyric form. It is a big book with memorable poems reminiscent of *A Coney Island of the Mind*, but with a richer feeling and form and a finer, more matured voice. Like his cosmic journey toward understanding, this work contains diversity yet wholeness, held together by a composite of approaches and forms, attitudes and visions—the tried character of his life and its oneness with his art.

Ferlinghetti delineates the territory of his last three books of poetry in his open praise of the conscious and subconscious mind as "Maxims and legends of total reality, echoing and re-echoing there, . . . Visual beatitudes, landscapes of living and dying flashed upon the dark screen" (*Who*, cover notes). *Who Are We Now?* (1976) is a vision of the times translated into image-idea in a mythic earth-self quest. Though the collection is a little uneven, it contains the characteristic mixture of prose poems, tributes, filmic scenes, general views of life, art, politics, and society, and a return to three painting-poems for Gustav Klimt and Monet. It is, however, dominated by the momentous "Populist Manifesto," which contains all the best of Ferlinghetti—his particular angle of vision amidst a stark and dark reality, and all the care and calculation of his oral and rhetorical style. The poem is an explicit and artful delineation of the new essential poetry, a statement and demonstration of his engaged and authentic art.

Northwest Ecolog (1978) takes this urban poet into the wilderness where he is equally at home with earth-life concerns and able to meditate on life and age. It is a fine, mellow book full of quiet beauty and concern using imagist and open-form composition. Nature and consciousness come together in an epiphanous stillness in which the acts of perception and apperception unite. The journal prose and the original sumi drawings reinforce the transparent yet profound approach rendering the book as pure as a stream amidst the ecological destruction of encroaching civilization. The book has a rare wholeness of effect as autobiographical detail achieves universality through the meditative form brought on by a comprehensive consciousness of the ultimate limits of earth and life.

Following his populist directive, Ferlinghetti has published many of the poems in *Landscapes of Living and Dying* (1979) in newspapers. It too is a more mellowed, aged book, yet alive in its awareness of the times. The mythic reality of life is captured in various forms—the oral street observations of "The Old Italians Dying," the satiric tirade of "Home Home Home," the prose poem tributes of "Look Homeward, Jack," the deep synthesis of political awareness and surrealist image in "White on White," and the many mass culture filmic scenes. Possibly the strongest poem in terms of statement and form is his second populist manifesto, "Adieu A Charlot." Here Ferlinghetti strips away life's false myths (social and artistic) to arrive at the personal and universal myths that have been earned through the authentic. His characteristic engaged voice is heard loud and clear above the din of contemporary poetry and poetics. Through his vision, his ever-widening involvements, and his authentic search, he finds the essential stance and thus molds the creative forms to make him America's most public and personal poet. All of this is borne out in his recent journal poems published as *A Trip to Italy and France* (1980) and by his self-selected *Endless Life: Selected Poems* (1981), which is expanded by a third populist manifesto, "Modern Poetry Is Prose (But It Is Saying Plenty)" and by inclusion of a segment from his long work-in-progress, "Endless Life." Ferlinghetti is still very much at large, with us and of us, as he tells us in "Endless Life," "For there is no end to the hopeful choices / still to be chosen . . . And there is no end / to the doors of perception still to be opened."[39] He is still engaged in writing that "endless poem dictated / by the uncollected voice / of the collective unconscious / blear upon the tracks of time!" (*Endless*, 215).

Lawrence Ferlinghetti as the smiling owner of City Lights Bookstore, San Francisco, mid-1950s.
Photograph by Harry Redl

Theatre critic and friend Kenneth Tynan with Ferlinghetti at City Lights Bookstore, 1959.
Photograph by Harry Redl
Courtesy of the Ferlinghetti Collection

A poet of many hats, Ferlinghetti at City Lights Bookstore after a four-month stay in Spain and Italy, 1965.
Photograph by Larry Keenan, Jr.
Courtesy of the Ferlinghetti Collection

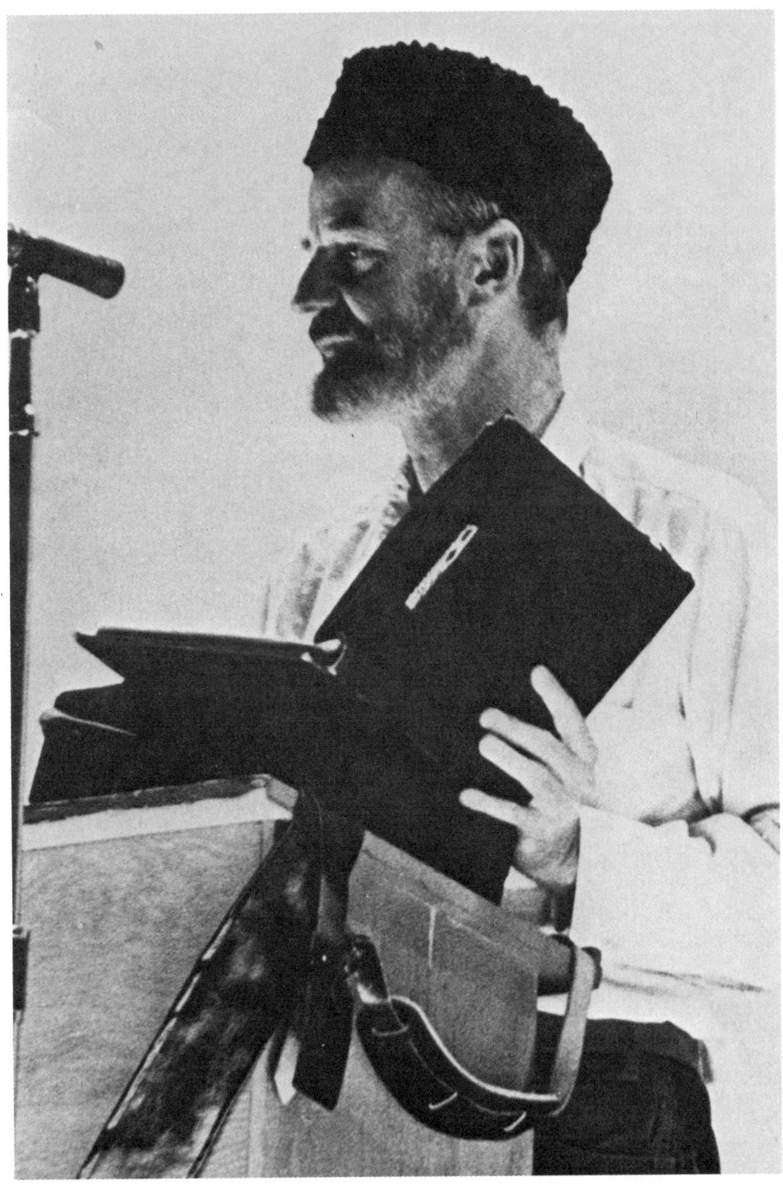

Ferlinghetti at "The Incredible Poetry Reading," Nourse Auditorium, San Francisco, June 1968. He is reading "Assassination Raga" for the first time, one month after the assassination of Attorney General Robert Kennedy.

Photograph by Beth Bagby
Courtesy of the Ferlinghetti Collection

Staff outside City Lights Books, 261 Columbus Avenue, San Francisco, 1975. *Standing*, Pamela Mosher, Mindy Bagdon, Shigeyoshi Murao, Lawrence Ferlinghetti, Bob Levy, Richard Berman. *Sitting*, Craig Broadley, Nancy Joyce Peters, Paul Yamasahi, Vermilion Sands, and Vale Hamanaka.

Courtesy of the Ferlinghetti Collection

Ferlinghetti in a photograph later used for a poster at his reading at Lone Mountain College on behalf of the United Farm Workers, early 1970s.

Photograph by Georges Hoffman
Courtesy of New Directions Publishing Corp.

Ferlinghetti at the Walker Evans Show, Museum of Fine Arts, Boston, October 1971.
Photograph by Elsa Dorfman
Courtesy of The Witkin Gallery, Inc.

Coeditor Nancy Joyce Peters and Ferlinghetti outside City Lights Books, 1978.

Photograph by Merideth Grierson
Courtesy of City Lights Books

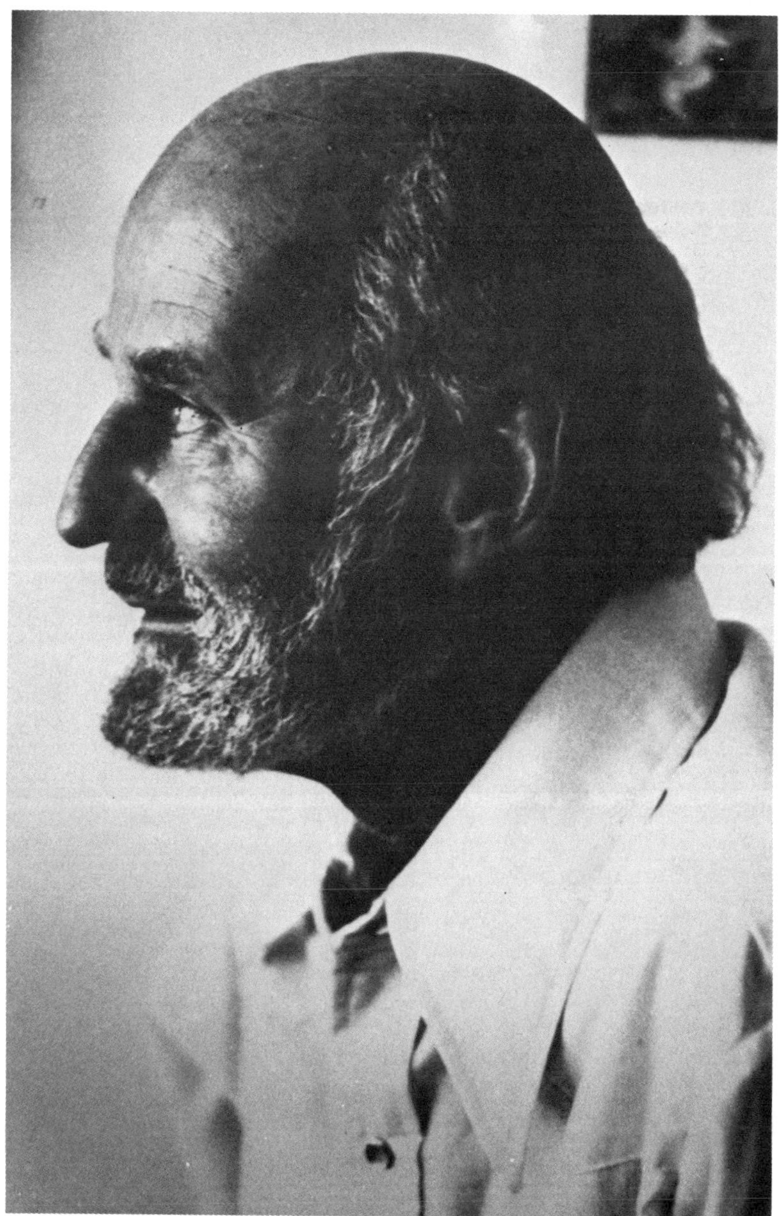

Ferlinghetti in 1980.
Photograph by Pamela Mosher
Courtesy of New Directions Publishing Corp.

4

The Theatre

This is the part of the world
where nothing's doing
where no one's doing
anything
where nobody's anywhere
nobody nowhere
except yourself
not even a mirror
to make you two
not a soul
except your own

("The Long Street")

and I have read somewhere
the Meaning of Existence
yet have forgotten
just exactly where.
But I am the man
And I'll be there.
And I may cause the lips
of those who are asleep
to speak.

("Autobiography")

Introduction

In 1962 Lawrence Ferlinghetti began a series of experiments, "plays for a new theatre,"[1] which culminated in two collections: *Unfair Arguments with Existence* (New Directions, 1963) and *Routines* (New Directions, 1964). There are nineteen brief pieces of new theatre, most of them written at a back table of the Caffè Trieste near his San Francisco City Lights Bookstore. A full-length socio-political play "Uncle Ahab," written during the late 1960s, exists only in various manuscript drafts, judged by the writer to be politically dated before it could appear. Several of the published plays have been performed sporadically around the country from San

Francisco, to Houston, to New York, and in England, Canada, and Australia,[2] yet most of them exist primarily as avant-garde literature. They are extremely international in character, openly taking their influence from Bertolt Brecht, Samuel Beckett, Jean Genet, Antonin Artaud, Eugene Ionesco, Europe's Living Theatre Company, and the film work of Chaplin. They are therefore highly eclectic in form, so that one is forced into a review of modern artistic movements in order to begin to describe them. What Ferlinghetti calls "Third Stream Theatre" is a coming together of expressionism, absurdism, surrealism, and abstractism. It approximates Revolutionary Theatre and Happenings in its use of improvisation, mime, and filmic-symbolic event. Ferlinghetti states clearly his goal: "And all to make you 'think of life.' Not a theatre of pseudo-events (which daily newspapers already are) and not a 'theatre for madmen only' yet a visionary theatre, theatre as genesis of creation, working (or playing) toward revolutionary solutions, or evolutionary solutions, acting out aspirations to some ideal existence. And not always with words, speech itself a paraphrase of thought, and even in pure miming an 'inner speech' to be heard."[3] Clearly Ferlinghetti's experimental theatre is consistent with his engaged and authentic stance as he seeks a vision to record and transform life.

Without a doubt Ferlinghetti provides the best introduction to his theatre in his explicit prefatory notes which act as manifestoes for each volume. Unfortunately the works have received poor productions and consequently very little critical attention. Richard Duerden, in reviewing the books, recognized the works as "a way of writing plays that wants to get behind established drama, to re-see the beginning, radically, as form," and praised Ferlinghetti as "clearly a good playwright. The form is proper to him."[4] Yet when the 1970 production of "Three by Ferlinghetti" was reviewed by established New York critics, Clive Barnes praised his themes as "vast and gusty, and they talk . . . about the decay and dissolution of our civilization," yet derided their form: "They are windy allegories set on some far horizon of poetic sensibility."[5] John Simon, the bulwark of American theatrical criticism, recognized "a mildly poetic, markedly absurdist, satirical but arcane atmosphere in all of them," yet found them "diffuse" despite their brevity.[6] Simon's own difficulty in coming to terms with the theatre—he finds them alternately "fairly obvious," "flirting with opacity," and "smilingly impenetrable"—indicates the general stasis of contemporary American theatre and criticism. As Ferlinghetti himself exclaims, "We have to go to Europe for the Living Theatre."[7] Ferlinghetti's continued support of a new theatre is demonstrated in his publication of work by Julien Beck and the European Living Theatre Company, the theoretical and theatrical writing of Alexander Jodorowsky, the plays of West Coast playwrights Bob Burleson, Barbara Garson, and Kaye McDonough in *City Lights Journal*, no. 3 and no. 4, as well as the City Lights collection of Artaud's *Anthology*. Lacking a critical tradition for such a new theatre in America, we must turn to the works themselves, to their international roots, and to the declarations of their author.

It is Ferlinghetti's own desire to create a critical atmosphere for new theatre which has lead him to so openly declare his influences and goals. It was Antonin Artaud who, despite his madness, was most influential as a theoretical base, principally in his *The Theatre and Its Double* and his "Theatre of Cruelty": "Everything that acts is a cruelty. It is upon this idea of extreme action, pushed beyond all limits, that theatre must be rebuilt."[8] Ferlinghetti thus locates his works in extremes, seeking thereby to arouse his audience to consciousness through a presentation of intense psycho-emotional states—eroticism, anger, terror, love. Like Artaud, he works toward release and liberation, but first through a shocking engagement. All his plays agree with Susan Sontag's declaration that, "Real art has the capacity to make us nervous."[9] Artaud explains the engaged stance and dynamics of his new theatre: "The theatre restores to us all our dormant conflicts and all their powers, and gives these powers names we hail as symbols—and behold! Before our eyes is fought a battle of symbols . . . for there can be theatre only from the moment when the impossible really begins and when the poetry that occurs on the stage sustains and superheats the realized symbols."[10] In Artaud we have the emerging currents of this Third Stream Theatre, for he, more than any other, broke down the abstract barrier between art and life in the modern quest for the authentic response. His theatre of event brought together the Surrealist goal of affronting the audience with a direct, spontaneous, and joint creation. Like the early Brechtian theatre of German expressionism and the absurdist theatre of Beckett and Genet, he sought to project inner realities and to objectify feelings and thought. His personal and universal probing of man's existential anguish has fostered what Lionel Abel has termed the "metaplays" of the absurdists. In making the stage an arena Artaud released theatre from its conventions and its overvaluing of language, and so employs the whole gamut of pure theatrical devices—clowning, filmic gestures, mime, verbal nonsense, black comedy, dream and fantasy scenes—all in a spectacle and assault on the audience. This is precisely the theatre that Ferlinghetti is working in. This new theatre is one which, as Martin Esslin suggests in *The Theatre of the Absurd*, combines comic theatre with sombre and violent content to strip the viewer of illusion and to confront him with questions rather than solutions. As Esslin states, "The relevant question here is not so much what is going to happen next but what is happening?"[11] It is a theatre of immediate presence which locates the audience squarely on the existential path through confrontation. Into this arena walks Ferlinghetti with his poetic, satiric, and existential sensibility and unleashes a renewed theatre of event.

Ferlinghetti's own declarations provide some insight to his diverse approaches. Though he reveals that his plays were written "nowhere near a stage," he affirms that they are meant to be performed, "very theatrical, in the best & worst sense" and suggests that their form and effect, either through reading or performance achieves an added significance through "curious juxtapositions of symbols & imagery" (*Unfair*, vii). He notes the progression of *Unfair Arguments with Existence* "from the representational toward a purely nonobjective theatre" (*Unfair*, viii), and ascribes to the whole work the authentic motive and direction: "Thus, feeling around on the frontiers of theatre, we may yet possibly discover some 'seeking action' in life itself" (*Unfair*, ix). Ferlinghetti attributes a general influence to the fantastic drawings of Heinrich Kley, the *manifestes du theatre* of Antonin Artaud, and the critical insights of Kenneth Tynan. The interlinking premise of the first book is the "Arguments" with existence —bold and symbolic confrontations with life enacted on the stage of the theatre or the mind.

"Notes on *Routines*" is even more explicit in its description of motive and method, and it forms a general manifesto of his new theatre. His definition of "routine" begins lightly, "a song & dance, a little rout, a routing-out, a run-around, a 'round of business or amusement,'" and symbolically deepens, "life itself a blackout routine, an experimental madness somewhere between dotage and megalomania, lost in the vibration of wreckage" (*Routines*, 1). Burlesque methods and philosophical content are thus linked for us. He continues with a metaphysical description of their form, "Routine happenings turned into dramatic action adding up to Something. . . . Routine happenstances that *turn out to be* crises, catharses, epiphanies, confrontations, manifestations, moments of truth, fatal instants . . . true realities & true nightmares, panic gods & panic clowns, destructions & disruptions, . . . liberating catastrophes, cut-ups or existence, black masses & blackouts, flips, orgasms, erections & resurrections, pot dreams & visions . . . nexuses of ordinary dramatics, nubs of plays, 'obligatory scenes' complete in themselves, demonstrations and discoveries" (*Routines*, 1–2). As Ferlinghetti warms his prose into poetry here, one senses the qualities of meditation and spontaneity that combine in these works. They are meant to be acts of life, a modern hall of mirrors in which the author and his audience find themselves. Clearly they are "metaplays" in which the form is integral with the message. Ferlinghetti links them with the free-form Happenings and the "theatre of latent barbarism" of Artaud, but qualifies them as seeking "transition from all this so-necessary dramatic anarchism to pure Poetic Action not necessarily logical or rational but with, at best, that kind of inexpressible inchoate meaning that springs from wild surmises of the imagination" (*Routines*, 2). This provision serves to expand the work in content and form as Ferlinghetti brings his poetic intuition into play more fully in this collection, instilling events and movements with a magic of gesture and image implication. His footnotes attribute influence to the drawings of Polish-French artist Roland Topor (included in the text), to the drawings of Kley once more, and to such diverse figures as R. Buckminster Fuller, Henri Rosseau, and Robert Scheer, who provided material and inspiration for the plays. The form and subjects are diverse, but the motive is clear—to make us think and feel life.

Susan Sontag's description of "metaplays" is revealing in this context, for it suggests the wide range such works include: "That life is a dream, all the metaplays presuppose. But there are restful dreams, troubled dreams, and nightmares. The modern dream—which the modern metaplays project—is a nightmare, a nightmare of repetition, stalled action, exhausted feeling."[12] Ferlinghetti's plays are equally diverse yet philosophically pointed in their symbolic enactment of conscious existence. Existential in their outlook, the plays nevertheless present a wide and original range of visions and insights into that existence. As Martin Esslin catalogs in *The Theatre of the Absurd*, the visions of man presented in Absurdist drama are integral yet diverse: "man faced with time and therefore waiting . . . man running away from death . . . man rebelling against death confronting and accepting it . . . man inextricably entangled in a mirage of illusions . . . man trying to establish his position, or to break out into freedom . . . man trying to stake out a modest place for himself in the cold and darkness that envelops him . . . man vainly striving to grasp the moral law forever beyond his comprehension . . . man caught in the inescapable dilemma . . . man forever lonely, immured in the prison of his subjectivity, unable to reach his fellowman."[13] Though Esslin is cataloging the whole range of Absurdist drama here, this is *exactly* the gamut of Ferlinghetti's own existential vision depicted in the nineteen plays which we shall now examine.

The Plays

"The Soldiers of No Country," which opens *Unfair Arguments with Existence*, is a one-act play with four scenes, and though Ferlinghetti calls it "an exercise in conventional realism," it is much closer to a Brechtian expressionist mode in its radical audience confrontation and its expression of life's inner, psychological truth. Its treatment of character, situation, and theme is close to that of British absurdist playwrights Harold Pinter and Arnold Wesker. Set in the elemental Brechtian outskirts of civilization, "A large womb-like cave somewhere," a series of obvious symbols are juxtaposed: a statue of the Virgin in a U-Haul trailer, a wall of kerosene lamps, a portable tape recorder, torn flags and car seats littered about the stage. Four displaced persons emerge—Erma in torn Red Cross dress, Toledano in priest frock, Payroll wrapped in white bandages, joined on the ledge by Denny, a war-torn paratrooper. There is an expressionist use of sounds as psychological atmosphere—bells ringing, doors knocking, insane laughing—as all the characters fail to relate to each other. This absurdist theme of communication failure and alienation is most prominent in Denny's stuttered speech:

> And everything we s-say here we s-say only to ourselves, as in a vacuum—a great vacuum, our inner vacuum, a vacuum inside ourselves, as in this cave, a vacuum inside us, a vacuum we're in, talking to ourselves! No one's listening, but we have to keep t-t-talking. . . . It's l-like we're all on a train going s-s-s-somewhere, only we don't know where, and the train's going faster and faster, and we're sealed in-in-inside. (*Unfair*, 9).

In fact, only the audience grasps the bits of significance that come from each outrageous character. Because all the characters are modern anti-heroes, the audience is left to wrestle with the ambiguity of experience and to compose the emerging significance as a societal view; we view the labyrinth from outside.

Juxtaposition is a main motif as we witness the priest's irreverent call for God to join them, "You still up there on that hot-seat, Father? Better hurry on down and get in this here cave with us!" followed by his reading from the personal and classified sections of the newspaper of love, suicide, and false teeth cement—life's daily incongruents. Awakening on the edge of the precipice becomes a basic motif as each character seeks a metaphysical arousal from this nightmare to a better dream of life. Erma states:

> And in the dream we return to where there are no nationalities—yes—as in the womb again, for in the womb we are in no country, we are the soldiers of no country, the great unborn of no country, and lead a blind life of our own, a blind life that knows no evil or hate, knows only a blind urge to love, to be born and to love and to love and give birth again. (*Unfair*, 19)

To temper the obvious and insistent theme, there is the ambiguous morass of inaction and a confusion of motives. Toledano seduces Erma on the cot right after the above speech while Payroll lies on his back singing, "Oh, there'll be tenting tonight on ye olde camp ground" (*Unfair*, 22). Toledano belches out the title's brotherhood theme, "'Oh, we are the soldiers of no countree'—blah, blah, blah—" in a drunken ramble. Characters transform themselves—Toledano strips his priest's vestment to reveal a pin-striped suit while Denny strips off his soldier's uniform, asserts his status as a military defector, and taunts Toledano for his nationalistic love of power and glory; Erma moves through sexual naivete to angry liberation. The play rises to a crescendo of burlesque activity—kicking, goosing, quacking, singing—until Erma finally bursts through the iron door followed by Denny into blinding yellow light. In the cave remain Toledano and Payroll who make absurd gestures while the cry of a baby mounts, "like the cry of a strange bird." The argument thus posed by the play is one of "the same eternal situation"

(*Unfair*, vii) in which the realities are shown and known yet perpetually ignored in favor of the shadow of illusion. The theatre experience is designed to be confrontive yet cathartic, metaphoric yet direct, with the poetic cry of hope still possible. The stage has been set.

"Three Thousand Red Ants" launches into a more abstract setting and tone—"A great big bed almost anyplace by the sea. Fat and Moth in it" (*Unfair*, 31). Much lighter in tone, though equally symbolic of man and woman's fate in an empty universe, the play pits two lovers on a bare stage with only bed, books, window, door, and binoculars. From this essentially abstract setting we sense the inevitable aloneness of existence through a succession of visions and derisions. Fat follows the message of an ant across the page, from "Man means—" to his final trailing down the gutter of the page and off the book into the abyss. This poetic sense of image and language is a salient characteristic of Ferlinghetti's theatre. There is light banter between Fat and Moth who share each other's love but not each other's vision. As Fat searches his books for one on "Improvisational Philosophy," Moth begs for attention. Symbols of red ants, Red Chinese, cracked eggs, doorways, windows, shipwrecks, and retold dreams all have the viewer playing with meaning, and yet there is a pervasive emptiness of impotence and neglect that leaves the couple forever split—like the red ants and the black—between Fat's binoculared vision of the crack in God's eye and Moth's rebuff that the "little crack" is his own. Like a dream, the symbolic fragments of the play exist in a larger metaphoric feeling about life. It is intellectually playful while more deeply it rises like the bell at the close—in alarm. It is Ferlinghetti's ontological "parable of the crack in everybody's egg or universe" (*Unfair*, viii) and his most often produced play.

Perhaps the next most theatrical and most often produced of his plays, "The Alligation" is a bit of existential absurdity and symbolic American parody focusing on three characters—Ladybird, Shooky (an aging alligator-man), and Blind Indian. The action takes place in Ladybird's symbolically set house complete with harp, television, American flag, and an active telephone connection to the outside world. There is a great deal of theatrical business with characters coming and going, windows being broken, doors flung open, characters stroking each other and rolling about the stage. Subject and theme are initially linked in the definition of "Alligation" provided by the author: "any connexion, situation, relationship, obsession, habit or other hang-up which is almost impossible to break." (*Unfair*, 48). Though the play includes multiple levels of interpretation depending on the identity of Shooky who "may also be 'represented' as a Man in a Union Suit; his skin may change color; his suit may be striped" (*Unfair*, viii), it is essentially a study of the paralysis of dependency where one is kept from the rights of his or her identity by a cultivated inauthenticity. Ferlinghetti instructs directors simply to "follow their Sisyphitic Noses" (*Unfair*, viii). Though the play depicts a final reversal (Shooky mounts Ladybird who has been smother-loving him), it is essentially a cry for help and understanding in the darkness as Blind Indian "like a bad memory" entreats us in the dim television light of America. While the play is a bit overworked for theme, it has an engaging energy of action and thought.

"Victims of Amnesia" presents a surrealistic battle between the systematic rationality of a hotel desk clerk and the vital irrational force embodied in an amorphous young woman. Outer society is symbolically portrayed in the quickened pace of feet passing the basement window and in the clerk's frequent universal projections of "Everybody . . ." and "Nobody . . ." in this hotel for "Transcients," the victims of amnesia. A tone of loneliness and longing pervades the play, as in the philosophic interaction:

> Clerk: I know someone who wants a room when I see one, and you, my dear lady, have that look.
>
> Marie: My dear man, but everybody has that look—(*Unfair*, 68)

Ferlinghetti notes his indebtedness to Andre Breton's surrealist novel *Nadja*, both for the subconscious sense of symbol (light-bulb-birth-snake) and event (the recurring amnesiac roomer), but *Nadja* acts only as a suggestive prompting for Ferlinghetti's own subconscious projections. He brings about his own intuitive juxtapositions. There is also an obvious reference to the Dada movement and the irrational pleasure principle in the baby's reply to the night clerk's questioning of her origins—"Da-da-Da-da—" (*Unfair,* 80). This is also inherent in the play's basic overthrow of rationality—repeated actions, absence of cause and effect, an absurd display of rationality (the night clerk's insane military drilling and his degenerating sense of systematic control over experience). In this absurdist dada-land there is the regenerating motive of the young mystical woman who follows Breton's pattern of re-entering the hotel, calling out her name, and having the clerk remind her of her room number. To this Ferlinghetti adds the irrational dimension of having the woman physically regress each time to a younger period of her life—all the way to infanthood. However, what is most moving is the play's surrealistic sense of inexplicable image and event which Marie achieves in scene two. Ferlinghetti instructs that the scene "must be played with intensity. . . . Every attempt must be made to convince the spectators of the literal reality of what is happening, since it does happen & is real" (*Unfair,* 73). It is this surreality of experience which must be maintained in the repeated acts of labor and birth of the successively smaller light bulbs. There is the train whistle, Marie's juxtaposed humming, groaning, singing, and her shockingly matter-of-fact dropping of each bulb from the hotel window. It is a thoroughly inexplicable act most reminiscent of the surrealist segments of Luis Buñuel and Salvador Dali's 1928 film *Un Chien Andalou.* In dreamlike repetition the large and medium bulbs crash onto the quickly darkening stage at the play's close, leaving the audience transfixed in the final surreal image: "Clock tolls endlessly in the darkness. Train whistles far off. In the darkness a very small light bulb is lowered very slowly and hesitantly down the stairwell. It grows brighter and brighter as the houselights come up" (*Unfair,* 83). The play is a surrealist text in its basic affront of rationality and in its ability to move and transform the audience through the subconscious sparks of recognition which it elicits. It confronts rational limitations and extends reality in an irrational arc of energy. Like the surrealist image, it seeks no authority for being other than its own imaginative projection and our subconscious confirmation.

"Motherlode" is a one-act existential parable done almost exclusively through the monologue of a Miner on a yellow desert peninsula. Several existential themes are woven here into a basically modern quest for the authentic life. The Miner, who ages before us, is actually a pre-conscious Sisyphus figure lacking direction and haunted by visions on this last frontier. Borrowing an epigram from Philip Lamantia, Ferlinghetti asserts the basic metaphoric pattern of waste and disillusion—"that crotch was once a vision of love." Struggling with failing sight and hearing, the Miner reaches toward the authentic, confiding, "Seems like I never git down deep enough, exactly—really underground, . . . Seems like I'm climbing all the time, somehow, instead of getting deeper and deeper" (*Unfair*, 93). The work literally echoes with metaphors, analogies, and puns on several thematic levels: following the veins of this leg-like peninsula, the Miner later lectures the Photographer on the legs of his nearly nude model; life is "like being stuck on flypaper—long, long brown, sticky road and all that"; the beatific smiler is seated upon a modern portable toilet; the uncovered skull in scene two receives a host of black-humor puns, such as, "Staked out your claim way ahead of me, eh, old timer? . . . Lost your head in the bargain, eh?" (*Unfair*, 94). Two supporting characters, Schmuck and Little Schmuck, add the trappings of mass culture, a veritable collage of contemporary life: "Large wristwatch. Large college ring, right hand. Sunglasses. Cigar. Transistor radio in carrying case, turned on. Camera in carrying case slung from shoulder. Very small portable TV under arm. Financial newspaper in one coat pocket, large picture magazine rolled in one hand" (*Unfair*, 97). As Ferlinghetti suggests in the "Notes," "*Motherlode* is a curious little calamity, questioning (on the surface) an obvious premise: In order to attain what one wants in this world, in order to live the way one wants to, one must go underground; not to do so, or to be lured into the open may be fatal" (*Unfair*, ix). The play is more than this. While the Miner digs his path underground, he also prospects his illusions of sexuality and love with the cardboard and later live model. Scene three brings about the dawning of consciousness as the Miner states his existential uncertainty: "Is we or ain't we? Is it or ain't it all a—big old dream? Big old hairy-ass dream and illusion!" (*Unfair*, 101). Using the recurring symbol of the birds to guide the audience, Ferlinghetti has them echo the essential answer of "live, live," and, despite the Miner's absurd murder by Little Schmuck, the birds appropriately "nested now in crotch of wood, lisp, 'Love, love!' very distantly, like an echo of themselves" (*Unfair*, 104). Ferlinghetti thus blends existential theme and symbolic mode in this Beckett-like portrayal of man in his ambiguous, ambivalent, yet essential struggle for the authentic.

The final two works in *Unfair Arguments with Existence* are brief scenarios much closer in form to the "routines" of his second collection. These short impurist works complete a cycle by further blending a kind of absurd-symbo-surrealism and thereby producing some powerful, though often inexplicable, images of an existential encounter. "The Customs Collector in Baggy Pants" presents a sustained phallic joke in a seven-page soliloquy by the Customs Collector, who has entered the women's room in search of his lost instrument. In this clownish, vaudevillian situation the Customs Collector mixes seduction and anguish in his cry for a phallus which is alternately referred to as: "this strange and wonderful diamond of hope," "a fine old home-wrecker of the greatest sensitivity," a "fine upstanding diamond-head needle and divining rod," and more philosophically as "this here Ghost of Love, this very totem-pole of love always rises," but also as a gun, a snake, a mobile, a codpiece, a hardened criminal, a warhead, a ship's head, "my death's head," even a Christ-like spirit arisen. What saves the piece from being sheer ribaldry are the deliberate allusions to the situation as "this lifeboat full of flush-toilets which we call civilization," "this fit of existence called life" (*Unfair*, 107, 109). In fact, the play is a general archetypal echo of the sexual-existential-identity relationship so boldly developed in his anti-novel *Her*. The tragicomic tone, with the screams amidst the flushing, creates a tension as the ridiculous swells into symbolic significance.

"The Nose of Sisyphus" is an even tighter scenario consisting of two pages of mime instructions. It is a fascinating but obscure work, surreal yet symbolic, as a large-nosed Sisyphus "in sweatshirt, track pants & gym shoes" attempts to push a globe of the earth up a children's sliding board. To his side is an equally puzzling group of surreal characters attempting to climb a children's jungle gym in a strong wind. We have fashionable ladies, gypsy fortune tellers, striptease artists, Indians, subway riders, railroad switchmen, and ski champions, all in full regalia. At one point Sisyphus shouts these absurd-surreal instructions: "Nailed Foot! Broken Hoboken! Gringo Hat Check! Bent Banana! Blue Baboon! . . . Brainpan Plumbing! Dream Crapper!" (*Unfair*, 118), which the gang of citizens chant back at him while straining in the wind. This event, reminiscent of the Happenings of the 1960s, is all brought to a climax when *Big Baboon* appears in a baseball cap shreeking a whistle. He tears off the fake nose of Sisyphus and leaves him to run off stage calling for "Light! Light! . . . Kiss! Kiss!" Baboon then confronts the audience with a whistle and roar as he throws the nose at them. This certainly qualifies as Artaud's Theatre of Cruelty and Event for its bewildering assault on the audience's sensibilities, yet its direct allusions to Sisyphus and its use of surrealistic speech make it a puzzling, complex work. Perhaps for that reason alone it is the most original and one of the most powerful pieces in the collection. It presents dramatically an unavoidable confrontation with some of the underlying psycho-socio-philosophic problems of seeking meaning amidst the madness—the overriding theme of all the plays in Ferlinghetti's collection of *Unfair Arguments with Existence*.

"Hurry, hurry, hurry, the show's about to begin to turn into Something Else. See the Bearded Lady & your lives stretched before you." So bids the author's "Notes" to his second collection of experimental drama—*Routines* (1964). These twelve extremely short bits of theatre (most only a few pages) are eclectic in form, "between oldstyle drama and spontaneous Action or improvisation" (*Routines*, 2), using the gamut of theatric and filmic devices. Aspiring to "a visionary theatre, theatre as genesis of creation, working (or playing) toward revolutionary solutions, or evolutionary solutions, acting out aspirations to some ideal existence" (*Routines*, 2–3), the book moves through objective to non-objective, social to surreal, political to poetic, all tying the audience to its broadened view of existence. Most of the routines are moments of awareness highlighted by dramatic action and punctuated by abrupt blackout endings.

The cover drawing by Roland Topor of two men wrapped in the same extended head bandage provided the original idea for the first routine. "Our Little Trip" aspires to the state of free-form Happening and Poetic Action. The audience is given blankets and asked to lie under them as part of the extended reality of this new theatre. They stir restlessly until "two figures grunt & roll over & rise up . . . dressed in conservative suits with black ties & shoes." The two figures from the cover drawing thus speak incoherently:

> FIRST FIGURE (as if reciting): Getting and spending we lay waste our trousers, and our little trip is rounded with a slip—into eternity—
>
> SECOND FIGURE: Oh, she had the look of longing to lay her lips on me—(*Routines*, 5)

Their motion like their dialogue is a turning away, enacting the play's primary and transparent theme of man's inability to communicate. This theme is directly and repeatedly stated by the Question Man who shouts: "How did you choose your mate?" and "There's a two-to-one chance you don't know *who* your mate is!" In counterpoint to this directness is the mime of two other jointly and completely bandaged characters who manage to unwind across the stage. As a further expansion of the levels of awareness on which the play operates, a loud speaker delivers a section from R. Buckminster

Fuller's *Nine Chains of the Moon* in which man is described in the language of computer technology. The speech begins as a kind of reduction to absurdity but ends as a declaration of complex beauty—the overriding motif of the play. When the Question Man broadens his dialogue with allusions to T. S. Eliot and Samuel Beckett's own questioning of man's identity and his ability to communicate, he is met by the metaphoric chant:

> Oh we are wounded, wound, unwound!
> Oh the way we wear each other down
> Oh the way we wind each other up,
> And wound each other, wind each other down.
>
> (*Routines*, 8)

The two figures reemerge naked but for their linking head bandage as they begin winding toward each other. In the union and communion of the two the Question Man raises his voice to address the audience, "Will or will not the individual endure, the free ego, the individual identity, will it always somehow manage to reassert itself in spite of all" (*Routines*, 10–11). The play is thus a symbolic and poetic statement of hope as the couple complete their little trip, embrace, then lie together moaning lowly. Clearly Ferlinghetti is sounding the collective "Our" of his title, reflecting a basic affinity with Camus's brotherhood of rebellion in which *we exist* together.

In this initial play which forms the keystone for the rest, Ferlinghetti combines symbolism, surrealism, existentialism, absurdism, and expressionism. Asking the play's basic question "What is man?" (*Routines*, 7), he creates a theatre beyond words: "And not always with words, speech itself but a paraphrase of thought, and even in pure miming an 'inner speech' to be heard" (*Routines*, 3). His premises are clear, his methods direct, and his results as mixed as his approaches.

Seven of the remaining plays are pure mime in a variety of modes. "Swinger" presents lyric and irrational images of a nude woman dancing as a great bull fiddle pendulum swings in a slow dawning of light. As the music climaxes, she passionately embraces the bull, and the audience is left with a dreamlike image of desire. "Sleeper" begins like a Picasso painting, "A big STRING BASS painted white, lying in a deserted place. Full moon." Two lovers, one classical and one representing jazz, proceed to make love and music with the bass—Bach or Teleman and Miles Davis or Ornette Coleman. There is a resolution for lovers and music in "Gunther Schuller's Variant of John Lewis' 'Django' (or other confrontation of jazz and classical)" (*Routines*, 20), as the two lovers hold each other walking off. More than a parable of musical modes, it is a symbolic projection of the resolution of those forces which generate that music. Again the stage becomes a painting in the final image: "A lion enters, comes up close and looks down at the Sleeping Gypsy. There is an effect of moonlight, very poetic" (*Routines*, 20). "The Jig Is Up" is an expressionistic rendering of blacks bagging Southern whites in garbage trucks as one strikes up "Swing Low, Sweet Chariot" on the harmonica, and the truck drives off. Again Ferlinghetti shows little regard for the confines of staging and creates short filmic enactments of themes.

"Non-Objection" makes a play on "Non-Objective" art as First Real Painter and Second Real Painter emerge from their baby carriages equipped with hand mirrors and brushes to begin self-portraits by dipping paint from a tub full of black paint and one dead nude. The two begin to parody each other into more and more non-objective painting of large black squares. In desperation they move beyond their canvases to the entire back wall which they attack with brooms. When they collapse on stage, hooded figures emerge with coffins to trundle them off crying, "The End! The End!" Thus Ferlinghetti, the former art critic and artist who had worked his way through non-objective art, does the non-objectivists one better in a theatrical form which comes complete with an objective drawing of the play's floorplan. "Ha-Ha" begins with a "Cinematic Prologue" taken from a scenario by Elliot Paul which appeared in his *transition* magazine in 1928. The analogy to the scenarios, which were popular at this time, when surrealist film was emerging, is revealing of Ferlinghetti's own form. The play could only exist as a film, perhaps only as a scenario, yet it is very moving and magnetic as it seeks to bridge the gap which Ferlinghetti foresaw, "the strangest problem still how to get real depth of emotion into such visually exciting & seemingly superficial scenes" (*Routines*, 3). Elliot Paul's prologue has all the lyric and irrational energy of surreal actions. The scene is a frosty European city where the screen bisects nurses pushing numbered baby carriages; "as each carriage arrives in front of a rathskeller door, a large boot, attached to a leg which is partly off-screen, kicks it into the air" (*Routines*, 29). The carriages pass through clouds and land in the north Atlantic where "One by one they are run down by the camouflaged cruisers" (*Routines*, 29). The surrealism borders on symbolism, a fitting prelude to Ferlinghetti's own little scenario with a sharp pacifist theme. Like Paul, and like his peer Kenneth Patchen, Ferlinghetti would awaken his audience by a fierce and symbolic enactment of the universal waste of war. The tone is absurd yet emotionally real. A Statue of Liberty which has become a furnace for war is kept burning by the shovelling of babies onto its coals. The mothers carry their babies strapped to their bosoms or close to their uterus in transparent netting. And while boatloads arrive to feed the furnace their young amidst the martial music, a Laughing Record is heard among the explosions which grow progressively louder. It is a bit obvious (part of Ferlinghetti's point), yet it is made disturbingly real in these haunting expressionistic images, including the cool jazz version of the national anthem in the finale.

These plays were written around the time of the Cuban Crisis, and they reflect Ferlinghetti's progressively direct involvement in political issues. This is immediately apparent in three plays. "An Evening at the Carnival" is an expressionistic and hopeful vision of Fidel Castro's rise to power in Cuba. "Servants of the People," the longest play in the collection, was meant to be performed "Any place people assemble" (*Routines*, 36), and it pits the nationalistic, super-patriotic shouting against the actual speech of activist Robert Scheer at a Cuban Crisis rally in San Francisco in 1962. It is a strong piece of political theatre, historical yet universal in its application. Particularly effective is Ferlinghetti's rendering of the youthful crowd which vibrates from extremes of unconcern to fiery resistance. It exposes the excessive government control through its manipulation of the Cold War myths, and it attacks the weak-willed liberals who cannot find the truth to lead. The play could and should have been an effective film. Its depiction of a political rally and riot are revealing and symbolically true. The final political drama, though more an outright declaration of the resistance, is "BORE," standing for Brotherhood of Radical Enlightenment. It is outrightly subversive in a non-violent manner as it lists peaceful methods for the "disruption of institutionalized events," or the business as usual of the American system. Ferlinghetti takes his drama into the streets in an attempt to organize a public resistance to an oppressive capitalism. This includes an attack on those who distort peace into an institutional tool for control of the masses and an affront to the control exercised by religion and Church, which is illustrated by a final Topor drawing of a brick-like cleric. This is Ferlinghetti white-hot with the burning immediacy of the times.

One of the most effective of the remaining plays is "Bearded Lady 'Dies' / Sprouts Wings / and Flies Off / UNKNOWN PILOT STEALS SHOW." Clearly not a drama but a narrative prose poem, it is cast in the style of a journalistic report of a strange occurrence at a "fashionable downtown gallery yesterday" (*Routines*, 34), and it freely flows through irrational event and surreal image into a sustained piece of storytelling. It is lighter in tone, in fact carried by its lyric humor, much like the prose poems of Henri Michaux. There are the surrealist actions: "The lady then was placed on a seesaw, and unsuccessful attempts were made to arouse her by rocking the seesaw." Anonymous Bosch proceeds to paint her: "He painted a huge face on the lady's front side, making the breasts into eyes" (*Routines*, 34), until she resembles the circus Bearded Lady. There follows, as naturally as a dream, a pilot who inflates her and her white wings which are then placed upon the cross. Finally, in symbolic subversive stance, the narrator tells us that "the combined forces of police, FBI, and CIA" stand perplexed and amazed before the significance of this all too "strange incident." Perhaps Ferlinghetti, who was seeking a more immediate theatrical form for his imaginative visions, might have given many of them a more palpable form through the open and responsive prose poem tale.

Equally surreal is his play "His Head" based on the accompanying Topor drawing of a little girl bandying before a blindfolded gentleman a stick on which rests the head of a woman. As the man begins a romantic ramble of young love, the head is placed on a turntable where it sings to the man who seeks to kiss it. Very close to his experimental novel *Her*, the scene graphically presents the surrealist theme of vigilance of desire. This theme is picked up again in "The Center for Death," yet with more black humor and in a prose that flows into the poetic. This play combines almost all of the ingredients of Ferlinghetti's experimental drama. There is the expressionistic setting in a tropical island where billboards present existential messages, where the characters either mime symbolic gestures (a woman strips off a succession of brassieres, a man a bandage of jockstraps) or recite "in a broken kind of litany" a barrage of absurd calls ("Life! Life!" cry the man and woman; "Time! Time!" cries the Watch Salesman). The Doctor of life/death passes out pills while a Sax Player blows "a very strange and lyrical refrain" (*Routines*, 24). The whole play rises to a frenetic pace climaxing in a fountain of irrational speech:

> Watch Salesman: "Tick of consciousness! Stoned strokes—"
> Unveiled Woman: "Sweet silent thought—"
> Sax Player: "Baboon dreams! Robot perceptions!"
> Unmasked Man: "Ecstasies of absurdity—"
> Apple Seller: "Paper bones, paper flesh, someone inside—"
> Unveiled Woman: "Light in me! Clear light! Body of Radiance!"
> Unmasked Man: "Things into Emptiness—"
> Apple Seller: "Someone inside! Flame life!" (*Routines*, 25)

In this tirade of broken speech Ferlinghetti holds forth the beauty, despair, and the mystery of living. As "The sax wails in unknown ecstasy" and "A Curlew cries in the end of day. Gone into that place of enormous ignorance" (*Routines*, 25), Ferlinghetti draws together his mirror fragments of the theatre of life.

5

The Prose

> *The world comes to a stop but also lights up.* Our consciousness is the projector, the moment of attention, which focuses on successive images, and each is a truth yet there's no Truth discernible as a whole. Consciousness is merely the act of attention; it understands nothing in itself. There's *no scenario, but a successive and coherent illustration.* My projector is being hurled thru the dark.
>
> (*The Mexican Night*, 14)

THOUGH quickly classified a poet, the title is clearly generic, for Ferlinghetti has produced a surprising amount of solid prose writing. There are published and unpublished travel journals, novels, political-satirical tirades, and critical writings. These works, which often border on or include poetry, provide new and direct avenues to an understanding of Ferlinghetti and his achievement. They also demonstrate an engaged and open inventiveness in his creation of valid and immediate new art forms.

JOURNALS

DURING his student days at Chapel Hill, Ferlinghetti began keeping notebooks, and he has continued to use them as working notebooks for his writing, as travel journals mixing journalistic detail and poetic expression, and finally as dream notebooks. His office includes a huge box of these, kept on pocket spiral or fine hardcover notebooks. One begins with the lament, "You have to go to Europe to find a notebook with any soul," indicative of the importance he places on these books of self record. In many of the unpublished notebooks one finds quotes from his reading mixed with first drafts of poems, minute details of place, and self-talking reflection. The writing appears to come easily and quickly; however, in one 1972 Mexico journal he confesses, "And why do I voyage so much? . . . And write so little? The travel between the lines is enormous." A typical entry is this reflection which he writes as prose, yet marks as poetry (a device he will use later in *Northwest Ecolog*):

> Lima, Peru—Feb 1960—
> "I am young and have lost / many countries,
> I am old and may / find them again /
> in myself." (2/4/60)

The journals and notebooks are all linked by this overall self-searching, the prime motive of his writing. There is a sense in which he seeks to face life by putting it down in writing, much as the transcendentalists Emerson and Thoreau had done, only with the direct personalism of Whitman. *The Mexican Night: Travel Journal* (New Directions, 1970) and *Northwest Ecolog* (City Lights, 1979) are the two published journals, though at one time he and New Directions had projected the publication of his many travel journals under the encompassing title, "Writing Across the Landscape." His "Santa Rita Journal" from his brief prison confinement following an anti-war demonstration did appear in *Ramparts* magazine (March 1968), and is exemplary in its mix of the personal and political in a poetic sensibility. Among the unpublished notebooks are: the extensive "Russian Winter Journal" which includes, among other items, the poetic "Trans-Siberian Nights" and the three prose poems which appeared in *Open Eye, Open Heart*; several scanty dream notebooks entitled "Papa Dreambook," most aborted after a few pages; a "Big Sur Notebook" from 1962–63; "The Night Writing" and several journals from his trips to Mexico, France, Italy, Spain, and Hawaii. Even his Navy logbooks have been saved, perhaps an influence on his record keeping. Ferlinghetti makes good use of these notebooks, often returning for fragments to generate or to be included in later work, such as his work-in-progress "Her Too." *A Trip to Italy and France*, a long sequence of forty poems, has appeared recently from New Directions. His prose journal writing can be revealed through an examination of *The Mexican Night* and *Northwest Ecolog*.

The Mexican Night is actually a compilation of many short trips to Mexico beginning in the late 1950s and ranging throughout the 1960s. Yet, much like Jack Kerouac's *On the Road*, it becomes essentially one sustained self-journey, one continuing symbolic confrontation with a land which echoes the writer's own deepest identity. The book bears the dedication to son Lorenzo, "should he someday come upon himself in that labyrinth of solitude," and the labyrinthine allusion is well suited for this book. The book is metaphorically deepened by the poet's sensitivity to his own personal symbolism. With allusions to Malcolm Lowry's *Under the Volcano*, Albert Camus's *Myth of Sisyphus*, and to mythic beat figure Neal Cassady, Ferlinghetti plunges into a country of fragments and extremes: "My soul in various pieces and I attempting to reassemble it, mistaking bird cries for ecstatic song when they are really cries of despair. And poetry a precession of waterbirds in flight mixed with motor accidents, o drunk flute o golden mouth, flower in the bunghole, kiss kiss in stone boudoirs. Voice lost & dreaming, door floated over the horizon. Where am I?" (*Night*, 1). Enlarging yet complicating his vision is the use of marijuana and peyote, and the result is an apocalyptic mixture of hard sensual detail and mythic significance.

The concrete reality is captured whole, as in this Plaza scene at San Miguel (8 March 1969):

> The policeman's traffic whistle in the dusk in the Plaza of San Miguel de Allende, sounding like hollow bird cries, the trees of

> the Jardin full of boat-tailed grackles, beautiful blackbirds crying out all at once in the last of the sunset, flocks of them swooping down upon the Jardin . . . The cooing of turtle-doves under the eaves . . . The grackles in the Indian laurel and jacaranda trees, and the sound of armadillo guitars . . . The Conchero dancers in the dusk under the jacarandas . . . A tall young Indian prince, very bronze and very beautiful, with long bronze legs, dancing with an Indian maid in feathered headband, her eyes bloodshot . . . The faint rattle and whir of their ankle bells, echoing hollowly, fills the sweet air. (*Night*, 45)

In this epiphany of color and sounds amidst the subtle gesturing of the dancers Ferlinghetti presents one of his many levels of style, the concrete lyrical. As persuasive as this style is, it is but one tract in the montage of consciousness whose levels include: political, mythic, peyote, concrete-historical-objective. Each level seems to add a piece of the truth yet never the whole. The poet sees and describes this process just as he is bound by it. Our consciousness is described as an act of attention to a succession of separate images; it is analogous to "one of those cyclops searchlights mounted on flatcars, piercing the sky yet reaching only so far and no farther, no matter how powerful" (*Night*, 14). Awareness is a process in which "we continuously improvise our existence, make up our lives as we go" (*Night*, 14–15); it is reality as revelation with the poet-journalist recording the flow. We are in a mythic and coeval perspective which releases visions without being confined by them as definitions. Of these visions, a few reach an archetypal awareness. Perhaps most pronounced is the phoenix cycle of death and rebirth which each successive journey to Mexico brings and toward which the entire book projects. For example, the October 24, 1961 entry begins with a sense of arrival and awakening and closes with this image: "A dead dog lay on its side by the entrance, flies in his eyes, up his nose—the Lion that didn't make it" (*Night*, 4). While the poet is moved to revulsion at the atmosphere of despair, ("Dirt streets of shitcity! It's like dying") he is also aware that "the people here smile at each other . . . as if they still had some great slur of hope somewhere" (*Night*, 6).

A second archetypal awareness of place and self is the poet's recognition of the elemental forces at work. He watches the people of the streets move about their lives rubbing against his own and concludes: "It is *innocence*, it is their seeming *innocence* which presents itself incessantly. . . . All sit there still groping into the falling dusk. Innocence persists, insanely intarissable, in spite of all. The road does not end. It is as if the radio were not playing at all. There is a stillness in the air, in the light of the dusk, in the eyes fixed forward, in the still end of life, an intolerable sweetness" (*Night*, 18–19). Like a Zen koan, life presents itself in all its irrational matter-of-factness with its persistent melodies of light and dark, innocence and evil, which the poet recognizes and releases. Basic patterns within this larger life cycle are the necessary turning away and the repeated arrival, which reach a climax in the poet's yelling to the sea in "Baja Revisited." Here he meets the harsh image of "a huge seagull with wings outflung and bent back as if still hurtling down through air . . . emblematic, plumed serpent phoenix, life . . in the ocean's long withdrawing Om. . . ." (*Night*, 54–55). If not a resolution, the poet-journalist has at last reached an acceptance of land and life, and he returns regenerated: "He who travels on peninsulas must expect someday to turn back. It is as if I were waiting for the sea to stop its absolute incoherence. . . . I see myself in the dark distance, a stick-figure in the world's end. . . ." (*Night*, 57).

The Mexican Night is a remarkable book even without the stunning and stark life drawings which the author provides. It combines aspects of the novel, poetry, and poetic prose, frank political statements on the injustices and suppression of the student revolution during the Mexican Olympic Games, and a salute and elegy to rebel leader Ché Guevara; all this encompassed within the mythic yet personal journal of the self in a land enveloped in the night's darkness yet bathed in the sun's reality. Ferlinghetti has created a most pliant form to give expression to his profoundly entangled consciousness.

Northwest Ecolog (1978) chronicles a different time and consciousness—the life-earth awareness of trips up the Pacific Coast in the late 1970s with his son Lorenzo. In sharp contrast, it is mellowed and clear, gelling as the poet's own awareness and acceptance of life had come together. Twelve poems, five journal entries, and seven drawings from nature comprise this extremely tight book. Using the "prose/" method for heightening the poetry in the prose and for rendering his sketches and reports in subtle mental phrasings, Ferlinghetti brings about an emotional thought form that ties reader and writer in the momentary comprehensions of the journeying. Just as Jack Kerouac favored the dash as a replacement for conventional punctuation in capturing the flow of consciousness, so Ferlinghetti uses the slash to heighten the moment and keep the momentum fluid. In "7 August 77," for example, he captures the rhythm and imagery of a "redneck" cowboy bar where relationships float about the room in smokey vagueness:

> She laughs real loud / and everybody up and down the bar hehaws / Even the huge elk's head mounted on the wall seems to be snorting / The barlady's breasts heave up and down in the heat / her gold teeth shine and seem about to fall out on the counter as she continues roaring / The jukebox suddenly adds its voice. (*Northwest*, 12–13)

As images knock about like sounds, the moment rises as in a Joycean epicletti, and, "The barlady breathes in my ear hoarsely 'Have another beer dearie' / I do / The barlady throws her head back again / There is a far off roaring as of the sea" (*Northwest*, 13). It is another of Ferlinghetti's filmic scenes rendered whole and clear through the journalist's cultivated eye and the poet's inner ear.

Other entries include an account of recovering the clothes of a young boy who had drowned and a depiction of the feel of a raft trip:

> We shoot the first rapids in the rubber raft, get hung up between boulders in the middle of a riffle, lose an oar, get loose and recover it, go on to Galice / And on down, as on a rollercoaster, laughing & shouting, some hilarious god in charge of us. (*Northwest*, 15)

The slashes, or absence of them here, control the pace of events and perceptions, as well as rendering the underlying feel of the journey. The form becomes a reflex of the man who lives the experience, and Ferlinghetti proves the best of companions. Placed intermittently among the drawings and poems, the prose sketches provide the ongoing sense of plot. The book's effect as a whole is like that of photographic slides, or a series of motion picture shots which fade out and come up again in shining light. And controlling and holding it all is the author's meditative tone—a synthesis of Buddhist acceptance, nature and Americana detailing, literary self-reflection, and an ecological awareness and oneness. The book becomes a revealing chapter in the author's existential movement toward life's completion in death. The prose is a responsive and integral form for this expression.

Political Satire

In 1969, pressed on by a period of political deception, repression, and war, Ferlinghetti compiled another major statement, a "political-satirical tirade" similar to his "Tentative Description of a Dinner to Promote the Impeachment of President Eisenhower." Entitled *Tyrannus Nix?*, it is a long handwritten letter to then President Richard Nixon, who had since his days on the House Un-American Activities Committee been a particularly distressing enigma of political corruption for Ferlinghetti. In what predated and forecast the coming fall of the Watergate Scandal, Ferlinghetti levels a direct and satiric assault on the accepted madness which he felt had been ruling the White House and the country. His dedicating the book to his "father emeritus" Pressley E. Bisland, who was a long-time admirer of the writings of Mark Twain, suggests an apt literary parallel. Like Twain, the author wields a sword of wit against social pretense and moral decay. A closer, though ironic, analogy is suggested in Ferlinghetti's own allusion to Vachel Lindsay's long 1920 "populist hymn" (*Tyrannus*, 1) to William Jennings Bryan, the populist midwestern spokesman. Ferlinghetti quickly clarifies, "A Bryan-Nixon parallel is incidentally obnoxious" (*Tyrannus*, 75), yet the form is similar. Though Lindsay casts his work as a multisectioned poem and Ferlinghetti writes a prose letter, both address their work directly to the historical figure and indirectly to the people of the nation, and both are full of rich contemporary imagery and filled with historical allusions. The tone is opposite, as are the figures and the motivation for writing. Other declarations of the writing's form come in Ferlinghetti's reference to it as a psalm "fraught with freedom" and his confession, "I got the talking blues" (*Tyrannus*, 38, 24). The talking of the book was appropriately recorded as a video-film by National Educational Television in 1969, and it captures the conversational tone and flow of heightened talk.

The work is poetic in its movement from section to section, in its basic metaphoric-symbolic use of language, and in its extensive use of allusions (documented in the long "Notes: to allege various thefts and plunderings" (*Tyrannus*, 75). To Ferlinghetti, who never forgets a good line, the use of quotes and allusions serves to broaden the statement of the poem, just as its actual message is intended broadly as "a curse and a cry to any old President or any old general or any assassin or lover who happens to be running things" (*Tyrannus*, 72–73). Thus Ferlinghetti makes frequent allusions to a wide range of commentators: Bertolt Brecht, Guillaume Apollinaire, Senator George McGovern, Allen Ginsberg, Norman Mailer, R. D. Laing, Bob Dylan, Herbert Marcuse, Eugene Debs, Eldridge Cleaver, as well as to contemporary music and public speeches at the University at Berkeley and elsewhere during the period of Vietnam War protests. The quotes are blended into his own phrasing and attributed at the very end, so that it flows as one pure statement in American speech.

His metaphors are inherent in his approach yet offer a humorous analogy for perspective. He begins with a face-mask metaphor for Nixon. His visage has become an enigma of the face of adult America, the face of television America, and Ferlinghetti warns, "And the mask an actor wears is apt to become his face" (*Tyrannus*, 1). Yet Nixon's face is particularly troubling to the poet who would understand this man's psyche, his alienation and motivation, which are so American. In fact, the direct question is the main motif of the work, questions which reveal as they confront. Nixon's face, however, has not gone slack like those of his "liberal Presidential opponents the slack lips and fallen chins betraying the higher ideals of the fine brow" (*Tyrannus*, 5). Then the poet shifts to a baseball-nation analogy, referring to his work as "this baseball Diamond Sutra from way out here in New Left field in the International League" (*Tyrannus*, 9), which he picks up again and again throughout the statement. There are a host of baseball metaphors which act also as puns for satiric effect—the draft, the new team with new uniforms, the pitcher who wears a mask, and the fact that there is "no relief." It is an effective cohering and comic device. Another such analogy is to *Moby Dick* in which Nixon is compared to Captain Ahab, another "Quaker King" whose obsessions lead him to chase the great white whale.

What surprises the reader who expects an easy personal attack is the writer's sincerity that goes beyond anger or insult. Indeed, the work ends on a vision of embracing love: "The Lotus might yet open and open into the very stoned heart of light The void of serenity might yet prove not too strange for the mind of man We are daily faced with the Miraculous And the air is electric with hate And the air is alive with love and we are charged with loving You too" (*Tyrannus*, 74). Again, it is a mixture of Buddhist and romantic oneness that takes us beyond the mundane details of resignation to a transfixing vision of change. It is a message made all the more poignant by the tragic recognition alluded to in the appended "Watergate Rap: 1969–1973" which acknowledges the corruption "beyond our wildest 'paranoid' fantasy of the depths of your deception."

It should be noted that Ferlinghetti is acutely aware of the limitations of doing political writing which may have an immediate impact yet becomes immediately dated. "But that's what you get into if you write about these boring subjects, and politics *is* boring. . . . I mean it's really deadening. And if you make that kind of thing the main subject of your poetry, then you're condemning yourself to be buried early."[1] Yet this is certainly an overstatement, for such commitment is also the occasion for fine writing such as this strong image of man's misdirected power: "It occurs to me it also sees a minotaur at the heart of that labyrinth which is the Pentagon while outside its eyeless walls citizens without hats wind their whitestring as Buddhists burn And the air is shaken with light" (*Tyrannus*, 31). This fine and unforgettable image which aches at the national conscience testifies to the necessity of such writing and to why Ferlinghetti is still America's most engaged political spokesman-poet. He has provided us with statements for all the recent Presidents: "Assassination Raga" (John Fitzgerald Kennedy), "Where Is Vietnam?" (Lyndon Johnson), "The President Who Was Nothing" (Gerald Ford), as well as such recent pointed political and moral poems as "White on White," "Home Home Home," and "A Nation of Sheep." As he himself declares, it is necessary at times to speak out against the napalm murder by complicity which a government detached from the best values of its people engenders. Such engaged writing is certainly judged by standards beyond the literary or historical.

CRITICISM

DESPITE his avowed disinterest in writing criticism, and despite his chief critical function as a careful and dynamic editor and publisher of City Lights Books, Ferlinghetti has the training, interest, and intuition of a good critic. At times he puts this skill into written practice. His 1947 M.A. thesis at Columbia University was on the critical writing of John Ruskin as it treated the painting of J. M. W. Turner. Steeped in the British Victorian era of craftful and analytical essayists, it examines Ruskin's development of a written criticism to meet the painting form of Turner, thus giving Ferlinghetti a firm foundation in rhetorical and art theory. His 1949 dissertation at the Sorbonne was done in French and took him far and wide into international modern writing. In particular, he examined the development of a modern urban poetry in "The City as a Symbol in Modern Poetry." Not only did he reveal a "metropolitan tradition" in the works of Whitman, Crane, Eliot, Mayokovsky, Francis Thompson, and Verhaeren, but he became a part of it. His comprehensive and original study took him out of the role of student-follower of literature and placed him in the vanguard of exploring this new frontier. His quick and discerning mind combined with his basic and intuitive response as a fellow creator make him ideally suited for criticism. Though he writes little of it, his opinions are strong and clear. He finds Ezra Pound "a greater literary catalyst and editor than a poet" and T. S. Eliot's *Four Quartets* "the greatest modern prose, the most beautiful modern prose there is, I think. It's called poetry, but it's essentially prose."[2] It is not surprising that his critical writing bloomed for a time on the frontier of San Francisco when he worked during 1951 and 1952 as an art critic for *Art Digest* and the *San Francisco Chronicle* (1951–55).

The few times he has ventured into the field of criticism in the 1960s and 1970s have been in the attempt to provide a critical basis for a new Third Stream Theatre in the introductions to his collections of experimental theatre (*Unfair Arguments with Existence* and *Routines*), in his Populist Manifestoes, and, of course, in the editing and scant introductions to *City Lights Journal* and *City Lights Anthology*. However, his long interest in San Francisco as a literary-art-cultural center and his personal collection of photographs led him to launch in 1978 a pictorial history of *Literary San Francisco* (City Lights & Harper and Row, 1980). As the scope and intent of the project expanded to a comprehensive history with photos and text, Nancy Joyce Peters joined Ferlinghetti as a coeditor.

Literary San Francisco: A Pictorial History from Its Beginnings to the Present Day is admittedly "full of our own predilections and prejudices" (p. xi), without being confined by them. It has the same basic drive for a caring comprehension that has characterized Ferlinghetti and City Lights Books from the start. As Ferlinghetti notes, "Writing history is a poetic endeavor, akin to astronomy, or its opposite. Looking through the wrong end of the telescope, scanning the past, we see the gesturing figures disappearing over the horizon, into the great night of time" (p. xi). Rather than champion the provincial, Ferlinghetti and Peters locate and connect the particular character and genius of San Francisco writing. As Nancy Peters explains, "I began at the beginning and moved forward chronologically, while Ferlinghetti set off from the contemporary period back through the twentieth century" (*Literary*, 235). They meet roughly in the book's middle at the turn of the century, and what they write is mutually revealing of Ferlinghetti and his world.

Described as a "galloping cavalcade of personalities, anecdotes, and insights" (cover notes), the book finds in this rebel province at land's end an amazing cast of characters and themes catalogued by Peters as:

> wilderness writers, prophesying bearded bards, humorists in dead earnest, novelists of the road (with their comrades and muses), women writers struggling to be heard. Drug fiends, geographers of inner and outer space; tracers of lost persons and the dark intricacies of the human heart. Visionary mystics and poets of apocalyptic or hermetic illumination. Realists, reformers, feminist enragées, and radicals. Wits and gossips; playful, satiric, and muckraking journalists; populist poets and sentimental favorites; hard-drinking Wild West macho poets, and queens of Bohemia. The scandalous, the invisible, the anguished, the suicides. (*Literary*, 235).

The names and faces to match these labels include an international array of great and near-great writers, those who were born, lived, or died in San Francisco. Peters's early history includes the Costanoan Indians, Richard Henry Dana; a golden rush of journalists and tale tellers—Mark Twain and Bret Harte—during the 1840s to 1860s and championed in the early literary journal *The Golden Era;* the rise of bohemia in the 1860s with such unique characters as George Sterling,

Charles Stoddard, Joaquin Miller, Clark Ashton Smith, and Ina Donna Coolbirth and her *Overland Monthly* magazine. In a characteristic pattern of combatting provincialism, public readings took place at Platt's Hall in which Ralph Waldo Emerson, Oscar Wilde, James Russell Lowell, and even Walt Whitman presented their writing and views. While utopias flourished and faded during the 1860s, the social cynic Ambrose Bierce persisted with his cutting wit and analysis. In particular, Peters brings together a recurring pattern of bohemian lifestyle and personality—gay, tragic, rebellious—in such figures as Mary Austin, Gelette Burgess, Porter Garnett, Gertrude Atherton, Nora May France, and perhaps the strongest writer of the period, Jack London.

Ferlinghetti gathers the pieces at the turn of the century with a panoramic view of such radical free thinkers as Alice B. Toklas, the Indian Nobel Prize winner Rabindranath Tagore, Sadakichi Hartman, and Isadora Duncan. Ferlinghetti's existential attachment to the present moment prompts his method of interjecting parenthetic comment relevant to the contemporary. Thus we learn that though Isadora Duncan regarded herself as "the spiritual daughter of Walt Whitman," in today's San Francisco Whitman's images is that of "the Good Gay Gray Poet. Isadora typified the nineteenth-century heterosexual view of the bard. Her life and her dance were her own 'Song of Myself'" (*Literary*, 130). Rather than detract from the historical reporting, Ferlinghetti's comments most often add understanding, revelation, and color through the personalism of humor as well as through the anecdotal accuracy and poetic prose. Thus in the 1950s, where Ferlinghetti really warms to his task, he can describe with confident familiarity the Beat writer Neal Cassady as "a prototype for a certain kind of great western hero lost among machines, racing his hotrod rather than his horse (not John Wayne but Paul Newman—Cassady, in fact, looked and moved like a young Newman in *The Hustler*). Cassady was a great nonstop talker, and he rapped as he ran. It was only when he sat down silent to write it all out in his autobiography, *The First Third*, that he became a bit tongue-tied" (*Liter-*

ary, 178–79). *Beatitude* magazine is described from the inside as being like "a floating crapgame during the twenty years of its funky existence, edited by whatever resident visionary happened to want to do an issue" (*Literary*, 188). At times the book warms to a kind of photo memoir by a resident chronicler as his photos and prose portraits create a renewed life fusion for such writers as Kenneth Patchen, Jack Kerouac, Philip Whalen, Philip Lamantia, Kenneth Rexroth of the literary-anarchist soiree and the poetry-and-jazz, Bob Kaufman, and Allen Ginsberg. His summary of philosopher Alan Watts rises to the level of poetic elegy: "He was a brilliant speaker, a casuist who could take either side of an argument and win. He was also known for his wild laughter and was a friend of many poets. His Zen spirit still lives on his old houseboat in Sausalito . . . and in the high woods on Mount Tamalpais, where he had a retreat for many years, cloud-ridden" (*Literary*, 203). Describing the "Human Be-In" held at Golden Gate Park in February 1967, Ferlinghetti captures in first-person accuracy the hush that fell over the crowd of flower children as "a parachutist floated down directly into the last rays of the setting sun, and a great 'ah' went up"; he also reveals with rich anecdotal authenticity how Allen Ginsberg turned to him on stage and whispered, "What if we're all wrong?" (*Literary*, 200).

What emerges from Ferlinghetti's chronicle of the modern and contemporary writing of San Francisco is a dense yet moving revelation, as though the intimate photos and portraits had yielded up the unexpressed yet understood life of the literary pathways and streets of San Francisco. He not only catalogues the places—The Vesuvio Bar, Cafe Trieste, The Black Cat, The Eagle Cafe, The Co-Existence Bagel Shop, The Cellar, Cavalli and Company Bookstore, City Lights Bookshop—he also captures their character and function. He weaves the same fabric of understanding for the publications: the early attempt to raise a composite voice in *Continent's End: An Anthology of Contemporary California Poets* (Book Club of California in San Francisco, 1925), George Leite and Bern Porter's *Circle* magazine (1944–48) which acted as a key force in establishing an international perspective and in releasing the antiwar, anarchist spirit of the Berkeley Renaissance, *Ark* magazine's bridging of this same Berkeley Renaissance with the beat rebellion of the mid 1950s, followed by later works such as *Ark II-Moby I, The Evergreen Review, Beatitude,* and the radio programs of KPFA/FM (Pacific Foundation, Berkeley). The list of writers, readings, publications, and relationships is too extensive to detail here, and Ferlinghetti and Peters fall back on a wide bibliography of the chief works of the period. What is remarkable is the editors' comprehensiveness of view and the respect for individuality, perhaps in itself the most lasting quality of the San Francisco perspective.

In assessing present-day San Francisco writing, Ferlinghetti frankly admits a growing isolation by writers and less of a pervasive scene. He explains, "Literary New Yorkers especially turn up here frequently, looking for the literary 'scene,' and often find nothing 'happening.' The writers are holed up on their hills, or blissed-out in their alleys. Or living in hot-tub suburbs like Mill Valley, working on hot books for New York publishers" (*Literary*, 215). Peters's assessment is the complement of Ferlinghetti's as she envisions these writers facing "the land of first and last chance. A pervading sense of impermanence, of mortality, urges renewed awareness of *being*. It not only impels life to overcome literature, but our best writers to make a conscious stab at the impossible, to invent a high existence" (*Literary*, 236). It is extremely right to have this book by these two writers and editors who are so intimate with this cultural world and yet so determined to have it live beyond itself. Ferlinghetti emerges as San Francisco editor-at-large with his values as open and clear as ever.

Fiction

Ferlinghetti's fiction consists chiefly of the experimental novel *Her* (New Directions, 1960), a sequel work-in-progress entitled "Her Too," and an apprentice novel set in America and Paris and written during 1948–50. This earliest work, which Ferlinghetti confesses is frankly derivative of the novels of Thomas Wolfe, exists in various unpublished versions and under various titles, chiefly, "The Way of Dispossession." Almost always classified as a poet, Ferlinghetti, nevertheless, produced one of the most successful American experimental novels of the contemporary period. *Her* is a book demanding great attentiveness, engendering multiple readings, and yet one which is ultimately rewarding for its insight and its bold evolution of form. Vincent McHugh describes it simply as a "great triumph of the narrative, . . . the most important American prose work I've seen in the last 20 years, and decidedly the pleasantest."[3]

It would be tempting to discuss Ferlinghetti's *Her* without ever coming to terms with what it is, to look at what it contains without recognizing it as the radically new novel that it is in form and intent. And this has, in fact, become the standard approach in the more than twenty years since its publication. It is quickly labeled with some vague term and then as readily misunderstood; thus we have the terms "surrealistic novel," "avant-garde writing," "expatriate novel," "anti-novel," even "underivative creation."[4] All the terms fall short of this intrinsically new and complex form. What is surrealistic about it are the forces embodied in it—a breaking down of rational and moralistic limits, a release of the repressed subconscious, the surrealist image of desire and wonder embodied in the figure of woman, and its frequent use of chance creation. What is symbolist is the attention of the artist's life and his act of creation and the basic symbolist method of suggested significance. What is existential about the work is its overriding philosophical basis in man's essential path through an absurdist world to an authentic self realized in a life of humanity with its strikingly human God of blood. Perhaps it is Albert Camus who best expresses the basic motive for such bold and eclectic creation when he confesses, "I sometimes need to write things which I cannot completely control but which therefore prove that what is in me is stronger than I am."[5] Ferlinghetti is writing beyond himself and the limits of art toward a new wholeness in content and form. The book is an act of discovery—an open and authentic quest and creation.

In his after comments and within the heart of the work Ferlinghetti repeatedly drives toward a comprehension of the writing form and content. Calling it "a surreal semi-autobiographical blackbook record of a semi-mad period in my life" (*Her*, cover notes), the author at least opens the door to a fuller consideration of the nature of the writing. Without this questioning and working toward understanding on the part of the author, narrator, and audience—the basic engaged appeal of the work—*Her* cannot be realized. The answers are embedded in the work, just as the radical nature of the work is a large part of its message.

Ferlinghetti is certainly one who heard well the cry of Ezra Pound to "MAKE IT NEW,"[6] and in this extremely inventive and new novel form he is at the forefront of the avant-garde, pushing beyond the established borders of the novel form into new areas of awareness and expression. While it is a contradiction in terms to define an "anti-novel," it is well to recognize that an anti-novel is not a reaction against the novel itself, but a creative act which seeks to demonstrate the inadequacies of the restrictive definitions of form which tradition has sanctified. By its very existence it is a cry for life. As Philip Stevick explains in his *Anti-Story* collection, "Doing away with many of the fictional conventions we have all grown used to, the 'new novelists' leave us with a phenomenal world broader than we might have expected, virtuous in execution, and extraordinarily vital."[7] Stemming from the artist's crucial confrontation with a radically changed world, the new or anti-novel which he creates may be as new and raw as each man's daily sense of life. Though old standards for fiction evaluation must clearly be dropped—character credibility, coherence and unity of plot, syntactic clarity—the lasting and vital standards of truth and applicability to life remain. Rather than seeking a formlessness, Ferlinghetti in *Her* attempts to revise and revive the elements of plot, structure, character, narration, and style. It is best perceived then as a radically "new novel," as a genuine evolution of form-seeking new life in a world made absurd by unassimilated change and institutionalized denial.

Originally conceived and written during Ferlinghetti's years in Paris (1948–50), when he was reading all the most modern writers and studying the work of abstract and non-objective painting, it is an eclectic blend, within the artist, of the many forces of the modern—symbolist, absurd, existential, surrealist, as well as his own autobiographical consciousness. Ferlinghetti explains that he liberally reworked his own notebooks from that period in composing *Her*. The book was revised several times during the beat period of the 1950s and put into final form shortly before its 1960 publication, thus broadening its composite nature. As Ferlinghetti has his artist-narrator-persona declare, it is "the final composite city of himself seen from fourteen angles and fiftythree philosophies" (*Her*, 95). Just as the theme and design of the work are tied to the act of its own creation, so Ferlinghetti exposes the roots of the work. There are direct and favorable allusions, by name mostly, to: Jean-Paul Sartre, Albert Camus, James Joyce, Louis-Ferdinand Celine, Alain Robbe-Grillet, Henry Miller, Rene Char, Samuel Beckett, Pablo Picasso, Fernand Leger, Marc Chagall, and the surrealist film "Un Chien Andalou." There is a direct quoting of H. D.'s *Palimpsest* prose, as well as developed pastiche of Joyce's *Finnegans Wake* (*Her*, 146–47), and T. S. Eliot's *Four Quartets* (*Her*, 140–41). Commenting elsewhere, Ferlinghetti frankly admits an indebtedness to two works, Andre Breton's autobiographical novel *Nadja* and Djuna Barnes's semi-surrealistic novel *Nightwood*.[8] A further parallel exists with Kenneth Patchen's daring anti-novel *The Journal of Albion Moonlight* (1941). And yet, *Her* is an amazingly original and unique work. Built on the best of what had gone before in fiction and thought, *Her* is a visionary and inventive work, integral with the author's life and artistic development. Perhaps the best analogy to the book as a whole is provided in the author's use of the montage of filmmaking to equate the book's sense of life: "I see now, I am just beginning to see, how all these stray things add up and everybody adds up to the same thing and the damn thing's still growing and this movie made-up out of a lot of parts of other people's films all glued together in space only it's all kept in the dark it's all kept coiled away except for one small frame at a time flashed upon the screen of the present and out I come and out everybody comes" (*Her*, 150–51). The book is thus tied in content and form to the evolution of art and life into the immediacy of the present, to the artist's very struggle to understand and express life. Daniel Leary thus describes the sustaining image of the book as that of the "celluloid sequence," the ever present state of consciousness which "seems to be coiling and recoiling both image and existence."[9]

Ferlinghetti has chosen, or rather created, his narrator persona well. He is an artist-writer obsessed with life. By examining his use of this fictive double of himself we can better approach both the life and the underlying art of this novel. It is a narrative innovation fraught with formal and thematic significance.

The French title for *Her* is *La Quatrieme Personne du Singulier* (*The Fourth Person Singular*), which affirms the twin perspective of the creator and creature which he has wrought, the implied author's conscious declaration of the need to create a character to act for him. This twin point of view, more accurately an overlapping Siamese twin perspective, is consciously posed to the reader when he tells us he is "adding a narrative voice which was supposed to be myself but was some kind of fourth-person-singular voice" (*Her*, 23), thereby providing an integral plot-perspective struggle and immediately projecting the book into a multi-leveled reality. As Michael Skau points out, "The relationship between the author, frustrated in his attempt at autobiography, and his created character, prevented from asserting a measure of autonomous independence, symbolizes Ferlinghetti's view of the human predicament. He shows man as the inadvertant operator of the machinery of associations, frustrated in his attempts at 'underivative creation'."[10] The author-narrator and his character persona both fall prey to the forces of illusion, both fail to achieve the ideal of pure creation—art or woman—because of their human nature, the "associational eye," "the old associational turning eye that turns all it sees into its own" (*Her*, 93). Thus the author's life, the book's form, and the philosophical stance of the work are bound to each other. In what Michael Skau terms "the indeterminacy of a chairoscurist world"[11] the double narrators are victim to the confusions of fantasy and reality bound up in the subjective eye. This ontological questioning of the nature of conceptual reality is no less than the book's fundamental motive. Toward the end of Part I, the narrator describes how in both painting and writing he seeks to capture the ideal of the pure abstract yet ends by painting over the non-objective surface with "a continuous concrete city of yellow houses and womblike windows" (*Her*, 54). He finds that the non-objective image made with concrete objects of brush and paint has made life "inescapably an illusion and hallucination" (*Her*, 54). This process is repeated later when the narrator-artist finds that continually his "one nice clean underivative line" (*Her*, 112) becomes enmeshed anew in the thick reality of faces and things. This philosophic yet common struggle with conceptual reality, embodied as it is in the narrative perspective, pervades the process and theme of the book. Stated more dramatically and explicitly: "there is no Orphic explanation of the world and no anthropomorphic and no analogic and no mystic explanation and no historic and no hysteric explanation and no ethnological mythological geological anthropological geopolitical metaphysical . . . phenomenal explanation . . . for the values of life are constantly and perpetually to be re-deduced from the conditions of living" (*Her*, 89). This is the dawning realization which writer, persona, and reader must make; this is the existential and philosophical basis for the world presented as well as for the act of writing.

Elsewhere the fourth-person-singular voice is given fuller definition as the narrator begins to see himself as "all the travelers that had ever travelled merged in myself, . . . a long-playing record of talking existence" (*Her*, 84). It is this oral mind-talk, which Ferlinghetti is so effective at, that projects the ongoing flow of the novel. In more beat terms, he defines "that fourth person singular who is the true final swinger engaged in the final pure digging of everything and everyone and so half-awakening to that first awareness of what it is To Dig" (*Her*, 94). This section, obviously written in the later fifties and part of the section originally published in *Big Table* magazine (Chicago, 1960), testifies to Ferlinghetti's sense of keeping the work contemporaneous with his life. And, indeed, the narrative voice takes many turns in tone and style, at times lyrical, dreamlike, cutting, punning, philosophic, engaged, outraged, passionate, and perplexed. It is a part of the narrative life of the book. Yet, we are repeatedly called back and given aesthetic distance from the process by having our attention drawn to the act of writing. In a sense we are shown the puppet's strings or the flicker of the projector, as in this symbolic image of the persona Andy Raffine, who knows that in this God-man "tale of myself" the creator-projectionist is driven by his own passions and just as likely to rush into the streets "to embrace the first person he met who could laugh and love" (*Her*, 33). Ferlinghetti thus provides the clues to this compound relationship, a sustaining and deepening device for the entire book, one which the reader must also recognize, enter into, and contend with.

While a plot summary of *Her* would be not only impossible but fruitless, an examination of the structural elements and devices which the author uses to replace plot is revealing. There are themes, forces, imagery, voices, and motif composing the book's narrative form. Foremost of the themes and motif is the quest—for self and for completeness through the female. These two goals are bound inextricably, for, as Raffine comes to recognize the male in the female and the female in the male through the sexual act of the drone and queen bee, this Yin-Yang / anima-animus realization is the result of one long and labored climb. Skau explains, "Raffine's quest for 'her' is symbolic of his search for his own completed self,"[12] thus defining the basic motive toward synthesis and wholeness. In more explicit yet equally mythic terms, Raffine explains his sexual search through a succession of Her's as an attempt to find "an anonymous vessel, an anonymous receptacle into which I could pour myself, pour the history of myself without words, the act of love its own eloquence" (*Her*, 36). McHugh describes it as "one of the great quest themes, . . . the young man's search for the young woman who is at once in his head and somewhere outside him, the girl who will be mate, mother, virgin and Holy Virgin, wife, mistress, muse, organic principle and other self."[13] The series of Her's that compose his film of love include the mother with blue breasts and blue bed, the young girl with the hoop running along the street, the Her having sex behind the door, in the close carriage, the farm girl who metamorphoses into a bird, the American girl in Rome who craves her own mythic release, all the women who hold the potential to complete him—in fantasy, fiction, autobiographical memory, or fact. The spokesman confesses, "I arrive in a shambles of childbirth to claim my flippy home in the unconscious . . . in a lack-love sickness for some unmet androgynous angel" (*Her*, 86), and he enigmatically discloses, "I found myself, the one and only girl-in-white curled up, inside of me" (*Her*, 87). In images of doorways, keys, muddy and foggy streets, windows, and mirrors, the combined narrators search for a phallic and philosophic answer. It is a path which leads through the world neurosis—"her door no more than a screen between us in some schizophrenic hospital we are all in" (*Her*, 40)—into a sanity of love—"the true mad hero confronts ever more and more touchingly the world he desires to seize in its entirety, . . . hunting for the one door behind which sits or hides or waits or meditates his true unmad self" (*Her*, 28). He comes finally to strip away most of the delusions as the sexual and compassionate drives merge in the Lawrencian declaration: "Making love was a means of proving that life existed, a means of proving that love existed, spiritual love, was something that existed. Making love with bodies was a kind of speech to prove it, a language of being" (*Her*, 132). The quest is not completed but clarified and accepted as a process of living, in a remarkable parallel to Ferlinghetti's own biographic life.

Sprung from desire, the Her of the quest is as translucent and transforming as the mythic "philosophy stone" of the French surrealists—woman as the symbol of mystical sexual powers "to meditate between man and the marvelous."[14] Thus we have precedence in the great surrealist love poetry—mystical and erotic, mythic and concrete—of Paul Eluard, Hans Arp, Aime Cesaire, and Andre Breton, particularly the figure of the transforming young woman in Breton's *Nadja*. As the embodiment of sexual and loving release and completeness, the Her compels the search and yet is also made whole by the union of female and male. As Ferlinghetti states it, "I myself am the subject of my sentence and she's the object" (*Her*, 147), and both are integral parts of the quest for understanding.

The book spirals forward, non-stop, on this quest, and it does so through a host of motifs and stylistic devices connoting motion. The motif of climbing and falling is used, the phoenix pattern of birth-death-rebirth is rhythmically repeated in the womb symbolism, there is walking and running, sexual ejaculations, and finally the flight of an Icarus. All these motifs help to hold the book together while moving it forward. None, however, can rival the author's use of cinematic analogy as a pervasive pattern and mode. The book begins with this image-explanation: "It was a transaction with myself, and the scene corresponded almost exactly with reality, the negative of it having slipped just a very little while being printed. Like an extra in a grade B movie, I could not walk out of it, trapped in the celluloid sequence" (*Her*, 9–10). This filmic metaphor combining perspective and motion is developed further: "It was a battle with the image, and existence a coiling and recoiling of one's self, with the plot spinning out so smoothly always, although one never could be certain just where one had come in. Added to this was the fact that someone seemed always to be rewinding and restarting the story, each time at a different point" (*Her*, 10). It is an apt description of this novel's inner mechanism as well as of the mode of the French "novel nouveau," with its focus on patterns of consciousness. It is a particularly contemporary metaphor equipped to render the pronounced sense of change and alienation that abound, with "two stories going on in my film at once, and someone's just adjusted the focus" (*Her*, 139). This cosmic-filmic analogy runs throughout the novel, capturing both the God-man vulnerability and the ambiguity of experience in this chiaroscuro flow of light and time.

To heighten the basic quest motif of the book Ferlinghetti provides a series of compulsive spiraling styles. At times it is a liquid movement: "I had come and I have come and I have come almost to the end of that indescribable journey almost into that far place where the blown music hung there where the statues have the look of loving to see a sudden leap of gothic as my umbered face would strike against the arched doortree and burst into that Virgin's place" (*Her*, 140–41). At other times the pace quickens to the frantic: "There had been a light in a window, a white face in it, white as the bleached skull of a cow. She'd turned my bed down, a blue bed, sun went away, a sweet tongue spoke in my sleep, a brass ball shone. Rang. With light. That room did not last long. Gone, with a dingdong bell" (*Her*, 120). Here the phrases gasp and leap with heightened consciousness of impending action as Raffine telegraphs his alarm. And the book closes with neither a bang nor a whimper but with another spiral forward: "I smear my forehead ash my white skin sandals on I see dawn's angels stoned for good I see green lights turn yellow in the mad grain dust the tar roofs bleed I see God grips the genitals to catch illusionary me stunned down in air of death's insanity to kiss me off he plays the deepsea catch he reels me in" (*Her*, 157). Thematically the run-on thought of the ending reinforces Ferlinghetti's premise that each realization simply leads on to the next, that there is no ultimate answer, only process, existence preceding essence. As in Eliot's *Four Quartets*, we are immersed then abandoned to that process—the self-evolving quest of life.

These images become symbols within the writer and

narrator's consciousness, then develop into patterned motifs within the quest and composition of the novel. Yet it is a symbolism which, like Kafka's, is multi-leveled and often transformed from within. Perhaps the most striking example is the image-symbol-motif of the white string. In the beginning it represents a lost innocence, as the pure young girl "exiled me to spend the rest of my life picking up string in the streets of Paris" (*Her*, 19). Then it becomes desire as he pleads, "No one recognized the white string for what it was, no one recognized it as the shriveled armature of that primal nude figure which hid in all the statues, public and private, and in everyone's clothes as they walked down the street" (*Her*, 34–35). In the Metro Station the white string is transformed through the associational eye into neckties and shoelaces as well as into the phallic and emblematic act of free union. When he meets the young American girl and they open sexually to each other, he discovers that the string, which passes from her hand to the floor, has become soiled. And in the book's close he tells us that the strings are the fragments which he has been collecting all through his life, that he might yet break away, "were I not tangled up and trussed in all these ropes of string I stole" (*Her*, 156). The Proustian quest for recovering the past is echoed here in the collection of string, as the narrator asserts, "Memory is what makes existence continuous" (*Her*, 24). Beyond this progressive telescoping symbolism is the composite meaning given to the string which he declares in a description of his broken union with the beautiful farm girl: "and it was the string I was always stealing and where did the string lead then when with a sudden jerk the couplings break and something in the wheels is broken or tangled and all grinds to a halt in time and place way out along the tracks to watch repairs by lantern-lights with brakemen voices underneath the car and the black fields about stand lost in their own eternity" (*Her*, 105). The intricate double entendre of the phallic train images conveys the subconscious energy of the suggestive in the actual. It is carried further as the couple makes love again on a grassy bank while the train is being repaired, then each engine with its giant cyclops eye speeds on, rushing them through the great doors of "the crossfigured city" where he is touched on the forehead with a drop of holy water that is transformed into the blood of humanity. Raffine is thus prepared for his entry into "the crossfigured cave of Rome through jungles of tenements overhead trolleylines owls and madonnas" (*Her*, 106). It is a complex, dreamlike passage through telescoping realities in which significance just outreaches elucidation, yet the key symbols of light, water, blood, the cross, phallic doors, strings, and engines all come together in the transfiguring rite of the quest. Like the novel's sense of reality, the symbols are fragmentary and overlaid, fading as the quest advances.

Two strong and original symbols deserve special attention—the Piblokto madness and the Poetry Police—for integrating a humorous dimension in the book. "A madness of the long, dark winters" (*Her*, 12), Piblokto madness manifests itself in uncontrollable frenzies, a tearing off of clothes, "their own or others" (*Her*, 12), and a running or pacing about attaching fetishes to objects or tossing and kicking things about. Significantly it is succeeded by a complete loss of memory after which "Rational behavior immediately followed" (*Her*, 13). Instead of running toward each other, the victims run away from all others. Andy Raffine thus ponders, "They were all running away from me, in the streets, through which I was always walking. Perhaps I myself had Piblokto" (*Her*, 13). Ferlinghetti has created here an elaborate metaphor for the common neurosis of too much rationality, resulting in bizarre and often violent manifestations of the repressed subconscious. Like the existentialists, he sees the need for a more "sane" balance of the irrational; like the French surrealists, he envisions the release of the marvelous and beautiful through opening the gates of subconscious desire. He is not seeking a derangement of the senses but rather a return to the healthy and reasonable recognition of the irrational. This is foretold in yet another motif, the comic but pointed echoing of the distant flush of a toilet, signalling the need for a fresh start.

The symbolic Poetry Police is a more developed segment of the novel, a barbed and comic statement. When a "wailing wild ragged band of American poets from the Rue Git-le-Coeur" rush into the boulevards singing and shouting of the coming deliverance of the Poetry Police, they are greeted by the descent of their deliverers "in parachutes made from the pages of obscene dictionaries" who arrive in the streets of major cities in order to "clean up the mass mess" (*Her*, 43) and preserve the world's beauty and love. It is a riotous piece of writing, charged as it is with Ferlinghetti's vaudevillian sense of language, in which the poetic saviors climb aboard the backs of fellow citizens and hang from their necks "shouting true profound wiggy formulas for eternal mad salvation" and thus capture "all libraries, newspapers, printing presses, and automats, and force their proprietors at pen's point to print nothing henceforth but headlines of pure poetry and menus of pure love" (*Her*, 43). Andy sees himself in black tights and a headband, like the one of the Statue of Liberty, mounted upon an enormous black thrush blazing about the city writing "great endless mad poems I draped across the streets and boulevards, from streetlamp to streetlamp" (*Her*, 44). It is truly a spirited, though somewhat self-mocking, projection of the optimistic goals of the beat and San Francisco poetry movements put on a grand and imaginative scale in the transforming "Poetry Revolution" for Peace and Love. Yet another of the many voices and identities which the author tries out on his narrator-persona-self Raffine, it exemplifies the author's expansive yet integrated use of symbolism. Thomas Parkinson characterizes the prose of the beat movement as "release, liberation from fixed categories, hilarity—it is an ongoing prose that cannot be concerned with its origins. There are no origins and no end, and the solid page of type without discriminations is the image of life solidly continuous."[15] It is an apt description of this particularly hilarious and beat segment of the novel which projects itself through the imaginative light of reflection.

A stylistic device which deepens the book's ambiance of tone is Ferlinghetti's associational imagery, often irrational with symbolic overtones. Like his narrator-persona, Ferlinghetti uses a surrealistic basis for creation of the images of the associational eye, but directs them into the narrative flow of significance. We are reminded that Ferlinghetti is never the totally automatic surrealist, but rather sees himself as an eyes open surrealist exemplified in his frequent re-working of the manuscript of *Her*. He clarifies his alliance with Surrealism at the time of writing *Her*: "I considered myself a surrealist in Paris in those days, in as much as I considered myself anything. . . . And I was reading some surrealism, but I was a *Nadja* surrealist, rather than a Manifesto surrealist. I mean I followed Andre Breton's book *Nadja*, but not his *Manifestoes*."[16] What we have is writing that is open to subconscious suggestions yet directed toward at least semi-rational discourse within the labyrinthine path. The imagery that results is often startling and revealing, as in this associational image of the rain: "The rain fell down in loose swirling skeins, the kind a child makes with string between the fingers. The string was black and fell tangled like a shadow of itself, dissolving into puddles that covered the Place Montparnasse in front of the station like backless mirrors from which the gray quicksilver of light still drained" (*Her*, 29). In addition to the marvelous drift of the image through an analogical linking, there is a gentle symbolic echoing of the string, shadows, light and finally the desilvered mirrors, which he develops into its own haunting and emblematic image of self-knowing: "In the great place of my sleep where sperm of light still fell. De-silvered mirrors lay about, face up, each a window, and those windows no longer blind. Each was an open eye on myself, each revealed a part of me, each a window in the house of myself" (*Her*, 30). This conscious sense of the narrator's receptivity to the mystery of the irrational and the emblematic is in keeping with Breton's approach in *Nadja* and contrasts with the telescoping irrationality of pure automatic writing. Windows, glasses, mirrors, eyes, broken fragments of a world, all echo the quest for self in a fourth, associational, dimension.

There are also the calmer solipsistic images such as Breton makes in *Nadja* in which everything seems suffused with mystical meaning: "In a little side hotel, its door a dark mouth through which a woman's figure might just have passed" (*Her*, 16). And later the American Her is described as lying on a bed with closed eyes "waiting and not waiting, a photograph that had to be taken before the film got too old to be developed" (*Her*, 119). Qualities of immanence pervade such images, the stilling and deepening of the moment and our approach to it. Our too-conscious mind subdued, an effusion of desire and wonder opens the world, as Raffine exclaims, "the liberated image of desire sprung again upon the canvas-ground" (*Her*, 54). Though the book suffers from its lack of dialogue outside of Raffine's self-talking, when dialogue is introduced it too is given a surreal charge. While making love to his shadow, the early artist Her speaks to him: "It is different in my country. It is too warm there for people to die" (*Her*, 41). The book is a rare combination of thematic insistence within an open-ended reality. It is animated revelation.

In this very openness of the book—its salient characteristic a self-evolution in form and an ontological questioning—Ferlinghetti adopts a rich variety of voices and modes. Like Djuna Barnes's *Nightwood*, which he much admires, it is specific and ambiguous in its dense narrative perspective. Just as Barnes creates Dr. Matthew O'Connor to speak a semi-automatic blend of irrationality and truth, Ferlinghetti, through Andy Raffine, captures the sense of life through the ontological ramblings of a compulsive questing narrator who gathers from the streets of reality, and from his own mind, stunning fragments of truth. Neither in content nor in form will Ferlinghetti falsify the nature of things with affected polish or truthless completeness. *Her* is a free mixture of controlled and uncontrolled creation in which confusion and struggle become part of the work's very color and texture. Creating a whole barrage of structural, stylistic, and narrative devices, he leads an assault on the confining norms of fiction content and form, and produces an expansive questing for reality which produces a broadened expression and a new attentiveness to life. The method of this madness is being put into action again in Ferlinghetti's recent work-in-progress, "Her Too."[17] In what French critic Pierre Lapape extolled as an "incredible verbal virtuosity"[18] Ferlinghetti has created in *Her* a major avant-garde novel. Rich in prose devices and poetic vision, its dynamics are yet to be assimilated.

6

Toward New Conclusions

> The solution is to be, where you are, what you are, with such persistence and courage as can be called to life. The best of the beat writers exemplify precisely that state of secular grace. In this world of shifting conflicts the integrity of the person might not be enough, but without it, all else is lost.
>
> (Thomas Parkinson, "Phenomenon or Generation," in *A Casebook on the Beat*, 290)

IN Thomas Parkinson's carefully wrought conclusion on the beat writer he does what criticism should do—locate and acclaim the salient quality of the art. In the courageous existential "integrity" of the person the work stands. No writer from the period exemplifies that position better than Lawrence Ferlinghetti. During his quarter century of writing, editing, and publishing, his uncompromising independence has proven to be of permanent value to us all. He continues to provide the necessary tension and alternatives that keep us from the stasis of cultural reinforcement. It was Allen Ginsberg who suggested in 1969 that Ferlinghetti be awarded a Nobel Prize for the cultural enrichment embodied in his publishing at City Lights Books, for he is that rare combination of literary catalyst, populist spokesman, and creative craftsman. And, though some of the edge may have worn off his avant-garde thrust over the years, the direction of his work is still relentlessly toward an authentic, engaged, and visionary art.

Grounded in a truly international view of the writer as a dynamic cultural force, he may be recognized in such modern poet-prophets as Whitman, Rimbaud, Apollinaire, Prévert, Cummings, Patchen, and Ginsberg. For he is among the poets who seek to transcend themselves by transforming the world. In the resurrected romanticism of his vision he would make the world his own by the process of naming it—reclaiming and expanding the world through the word. As his own life has been a long quest for the truths of identity and place in the world, so his writings seek to capture that same looming of the universal in the individual. The quest for the essence of self pervades through its consolidation and integration of all reality levels in full consciousness. Thus Ferlinghetti perceives the poet's task as one of comprehension—to gain sympathy with the world by identifying with it. This vision of poetry as the "common carrier" with subjective and subversive levels, "with terrible eyes and buffalo strength," is proclaimed to public and poet alike in his Populist Manifestoes. The sharp realities of life are met with a visionary idealism that encompasses them, as he boldly proclaims, "Poetry still falls from the skies / into our streets still open" (*Who*, 64). The paradoxes of his life and his art resolve themselves in the complexity of the man and in the unity and integrity of his life and work.

His poetics are functional. Directed toward a "resocialization" of art, he creates lasting work that combines realism and revelation in a cry for conscience and change. Exploring the possibilities of the world, he seeks to expand and connect all levels of consciousness—from public surface to subconscious plunging, from mass culture to artistic climates, from socio-political involvements to visions of union and wonder—his is a living and comprehensive art dedicated to making a difference. Committed to life in an absurd time, his work is anti-cool, engaged, and beyond nationalities and political or artistic dogmas. Crale D. Hopkins is profoundly correct in proclaiming Ferlinghetti as a writer of "some of the most sensitive lyrics of the last twenty years."[1] His work is some of the most memorable and engaging of contemporary writing.

In the literary and critical world he commits the cardinal offense of perversity, and the critical response has been the predictable silence of intimidation. What is needed now is a serious reassessment of the work, a productive period of amnesty and assimilation. All of his major books are still in print—the poetry, the theatre, the journals, and the fiction. Neeli Cherkovski's fortuitous *Ferlinghetti: A Biography* offers the critical inroads to a closer tie of the poet's work and life. Bill Morgan has done an exhaustive descriptive bibliography (New York: Garland Publications, 1981) to supplement the checklist provided in David Kherdian's *Six Poets of the San Francisco Renaissance: Portraits and Checklists* and to provide further access to a critical appreciation of the works. Ferlinghetti himself has produced a critical-historical document in *Literary San Francisco: A Pictorial History*, and his Populist Manifestoes have been published together (San Francisco: Grey Fox Press, 1980). His new works continue to appear from New Directions, City Lights, and in small-press pamphlets and broadsides. *Endless Life: Selected Poems* appeared from New Directions in 1981.

It is time to fill the critical gap surrounding his writing. Such an endeavor must, however, be based on the broad foundation of his work, one that goes beyond his associations with movements, writers, or locales and recognizes the poet's originality, diversity, and firm commitment to an international vision of writing as a cultural force, authentically engaged and engaging. Lawrence Ferlinghetti has produced some of the most powerful and popular writing of our time. As one of the great artistic borrowers of our time (Eliot and Pound being others), he has taken his influences from the gamut of world literature, philosophy, art, and affairs, and yet integrated it all into his own personal vision—genuine and aware. Beyond his function as a literary figure or catalyst in the beat movement and San Francisco Renaissance in poetry, he is a truly international artist and publisher, and is a contemporary model of the poet of revolt and affirmation. Exclaiming the injustices and suppression of life and propounding the compassionate unity of all life—earth to man to creature—he is forever that personal and public poet-at-large.

Ferlinghetti's achievement as an artist cannot be separated from his work as a man. Yet, it is essential to recognize both planes of this overlapping development. He has recreated a popular oral poetry, integrated open-form poetics with abstract expressionist theory, created a vital poetry of the streets, molded a rhetorical poetics that embraces the methods of surrealism, filmmaking, satire, and has developed diverse forms and applications of the prose poem. He is a poet of genuine humor and hard-won lyricism. His theatre is provocative and engaging, a contemporary amalgam of expressionist, absurdist, existentialist, and surrealist theatre. In his journal writing he has developed the poet-journalist perspective and brought about a further synthesis of poetry and prose. For some time he has been America's most outspoken and adept poet of political satire, and his anti-novel *Her* stands as a major achievement for its expansion of the fiction techniques of narrative perspective, structural and stylistic devices, deep imagery and symbolism—all directed toward an open exploration of the nature of reality. While his artistic faults are invariably those of daring excess, his most stunning achievements are those of innovation and synthesis within his functional life-art dynamics. Repeatedly he has shown himself to be a craftsman with a broad artistic comprehension, a fine inner ear, and an unfailingly open eye and heart.

If his writing seems at times harsh in its immediate declamations at social injustices, it is equally sublime in its romantic and lyrical affirmation of life's sentient meaning. His long poem-in-progress, "Endless Life," confirms the integrity of his life and work, for he still envisions a reality—vital and full:

> Endless the splendid life of the world
> Endless its lovely living and breathing

its lovely sentient beings
seeing and hearing feeling and thinking
laughing and dancing sighing and crying
through endless afternoons endless nights
of love and ecstasy joy and despair

(*Endless Life*, 210)

Ferlinghetti has tied himself to our mutual humanity, and his writing is that clear call to recognize what we share of each other. As a poet-prophet of the contemporary world, he is unfailingly there watching it "walk by / in its curious shoes" and recording it in an immediate and enduring art. He is the contemporary embodiment of the committed artist. It is time to comprehend the engaged and authentic basis and dynamics of his art, and time to acknowledge it as essential to us all.

Notes
Selected Bibliography
Index

NOTES

Preface

1. Guillaume Apollinaire, "The New Spirit and the Poets," *Selected Writings of Guillaume Apollinaire,* trans. Roger Shattuck (New York: New Directions, 1971), p. 227.

2. Lawrence Ferlinghetti, *Endless Life: Selected Poems* (New York: New Directions, 1981), cover notes.

1. Biographical Portrait

1. Leslie A. Fiedler, *Waiting for the End* (Hammondsworth, England: Penguin, 1964), p. 260.

2. William Everson, *Archetype West: The Pacific Coast as a Literary Region* (Berkeley: Oyez, 1976), p. 119.

3. Karl Malkoff, *Crowell's Handbook of Contemporary Poetry* (New York: Crowell, 1973), p. 122.

4. Lawrence Ferlinghetti, *Landscapes of Living and Dying* (New York: New Directions, 1979), p. 45. All further references to this book, designated as *Landscapes,* will be given parenthetically in the text.

5. Lawrence Ferlinghetti, "15," *A Coney Island of the Mind* 14th printing (New York: New Directions, 1958), p. 30. All further references to this book, designated as *Coney* will be given parenthetically in the text.

6. Lawrence Ferlinghetti, "True Confessional," *Open Eye, Open Heart* (New York: New Directions, 1973), p. 3. All further references to this book, designated as *Open,* will be given parenthetically in the text.

7. Neeli Cherkovski, *Ferlinghetti: A Biography* (Garden City, N.Y.: Doubleday, 1979), pp. 1–3.

8. Ibid., pp. 14–15.

9. Lawrence Ferlinghetti, in ibid., p. 25.

10. Lawrence Ferlinghetti, *Tyrannus Nix?* (New York: New Directions, 1969), pp. 69–71. All further references to this book, designated as *Tyrannus*, will be given parenthetically in the text.

11. Lawrence Ferlinghetti, in Cherkovski, pp. 39–40.

12. Lawrence Ferlinghetti, personal interview with the author at 250 Francisco St., San Francisco, California, 7 and 8 June 1980. Interview to be published in *Pig Iron* magazine in 1983.

13. Ferlinghetti, in Cherkovski, p. 42.

14. Ferlinghetti, personal interview.

15. Lawrence Ferlinghetti, *Her* (New York: New Directions, 1960), p. 25. All further references to this book will be given parenthetically in the text.

16. Lawrence Ferlinghetti, in "Lawrence Ferlinghetti," *The San Francisco Poets*, ed. David Meltzer (New York: Ballantine, 1971), p. 156.

17. Ibid.

18. Ibid.

19. Ferlinghetti, in Cherkovski, p. 62.

20. Kenneth Rexroth, in "Kenneth Rexroth," *The San Francisco Poets*, ed. David Meltzer (New York: Ballantine, 1971), pp. 9–15.

21. Lawrence Ferlinghetti, in Ralph Sipper, "A Cultural Catalyst," (City Lights promotional sheet, 1979), reprinted from *California Living: The Magazine of the San Francisco Sunday Examiner & Chronicle*, 19 Jan. 1975.

22. Ferlinghetti, in "A Cultural Catalyst."

23. Ferlinghetti, *The San Francisco Poets*, p. 166.

24. Lawrence Ferlinghetti, "26," *Pictures of the Gone World* (San Francisco: City Lights, 1955). All further references to this book, designated as *Pictures*, will be given parenthetically in the text.

25. Ferlinghetti, in Cherkovski, p. 99.

26. James Laughlin, in Cherkovski, p. 85.

27. Chester McPhee, in Cherkovski, p. 101.

28. Lawrence Ferlinghetti, "Lawrence Ferlinghetti: Horn on 'HOWL'," *Evergreen Review,* 1, no. 4, (1957):146.

29. Ibid.

30. Ibid., p. 147.

31. Barney Rosset and Donald Allen, quoted in Ferlinghetti, "Horn on 'HOWL'," p. 151.

32. Mark Schorer, quoted in Cherkovski, p. 109.

33. Clayton Horn, quoted in Ferlinghetti, "Horn on 'HOWL'," pp. 156–58.

34. David Kherdian, *Six San Francisco Poets* (Fresno, Calif.: The Giligia Pr., 1969), p. 10.

35. Lawrence Ferlinghetti, quoted in *Poetry Reading in "The Cellar,"* cover notes.

36. Kenneth Rexroth, *Evergreen Review,* 1, no. 2 (1957):7.

37. Some of the chief poetry-and-jazz albums that evolved out of this period are: Kenneth Rexroth and Lawrence Ferlinghetti, *Poetry Reading in "The Cellar"* (Fantasy, 1958); Kenneth Patchen, *Kenneth Patchen Reads His Poems to the Chamber Jazz Sextet* (Cadence, 3004); Kenneth Patchen, *Kenneth Patchen Reads with Jazz in Canada* (Folkways, FL9718); Jack Kerouac, *Jack Kerouac: Blues and Haikus* (Hanover, HM 5906); Philip Whalen and Lawrence Ferlinghetti, *Jazz Canto, Vol. I: An Anthology of Jazz & Poetry* (World Pacific, WP–1244); Jack Kerouac, with Steve Allen, *Poems for the Beat Generation* (1959); Kenneth Rexroth, *At the Blackhawk* (Fantasy, 7008); Leroi Jones, *New York Art Quintet* (ESP–DISK, 10004, 1965).

38. Ferlinghetti, personal interview.

39. Lawrence Ferlinghetti, quoted in Ann Charters, *Kerouac: A Biography* (San Francisco: Straight Arrow Books, 1973), p. 323.

40. Ferlinghetti, *Landscapes,* p. 47.

41. Lawrence Ferlinghetti, "Tentative Description of a Dinner to Promote the Impeachment of President Eisenhower," *Starting from San Francisco* (New York: New Directions, 1967), p. 41. All further references to this book, designated as *Starting,* will be given parenthetically in the text.

42. "Letters from the FBI," *City Lights Journal* no. 4 (San Francisco: City Lights, 1978), pp. 233–40.

43. Lawrence Ferlinghetti, *"Tentative Description of a Dinner Given to Promote the Impeachment of President Eisenhower" and Other Poems* (Berkeley: Fantasy Records, 1959), cover notes.

44. Ferlinghetti, *Her,* cover notes.

45. Ferlinghetti, in Cherkovski, pp. 143–44.

46. Cherkovski, p. 144.

47. Lawrence Ferlinghetti, "Notes on the Plays," *Unfair Arguments with Existence* (New York: New Directions, 1963), p. vii. All further references to this book, designated as *Unfair,* will be given parenthetically in the text.

48. Lawrence Ferlinghetti, "Notes on Routines," *Routines* (New York: New Directions, 1964), p. 1. All further references to this book, designated as *Routines,* will be given parenthetically in the text.

49. Lawrence Ferlinghetti, "Pound at Spoleto," *City Lights Journal* no. 3 (San Francisco: City Lights, 1966), pp. 157–58.

50. Kherdian, p. 16.

51. Lawrence Ferlinghetti, "Genesis of *After the Cries of the Birds,"* in *The Poetics of the New American Poets,* ed. Donald Allen and Warren Tallman (New York: Grove, 1973), p. 445.

52. Ferlinghetti, "Genesis," p. 447.

53. Ibid., p. 448.

54. Ibid., p. 449.

55. Lawrence Ferlinghetti, "After the Cries of the Birds," *The Secret Meaning of Things* (New York: New Directions, 1968), p. 39. All further references to this book, designated as *Secret,* will be given parenthetically in the text.

56. Ferlinghetti, in Cherkovski, p. 186.

57. Lawrence Ferlinghetti, *The Mexican Night* (New York: New Directions, 1970), p. 57. All further references to this book, designated as *Night,* will be given parenthetically in the text.

58. Bruce Cook, *The Beat Generation* (New York: Scribners, 1971), p. 56.

59. J. M. Warner, "Lawrence Ferlinghetti: *Open Eye, Open Heart," Library Journal* 98 (15 Sept. 1973):2556.

60. Ferlinghetti, *The San Francisco Poets*, pp. 138–39.

61. Lawrence Ferlinghetti, *A Political Pamphlet* (San Francisco: The Anarchist Resistance Pr., 1976). All further references to this book, designated as *Political Pamphlet*, will be given parenthetically in the text.

62. Ferlinghetti, personal interview.

63. Lawrence Ferlinghetti, "The Jack of Hearts," *Who Are We Now?* (New York: New Directions, 1976), p. 1. All further references to this book, designated as *Who*, will be given parenthetically in the text.

64. Mutlu Blasing, *The Art of Life* (Austin: Univ. of Texas Pr., 1977), p. xxvii.

A Stance Toward Life and Art

1. Charles Olson, "Projective Verse vs. The NON-Projective," *New American Poetry* ed. Donald Allen (New York: Grove, 1960), p. 394; reprinted from *Poetry New York*, no. 3, 1950.

2. The Ferlinghetti-Prévert comparison is discussed in Kenneth Rexroth, "The New Poetry," *Assays* (New York: New Directions, 1962), p. 193; Samuel Charters, "Lawrence Ferlinghetti," *Some Poems / Poets* (Berkeley: Oyez, 1971), p. 77.

3. Lawrence Ferlinghetti, "Translator's Note," Jacques Prévert, *Paroles* (San Francisco: City Lights, 1958), p. 3; "Translator's Note" was appended in 1964. All further references to this book, designated as *Paroles*, will be given parenthetically in the text.

4. Lawrence Ferlinghetti, "Genesis of *After the Cries of the Birds*," *The Poetics of the New American Poetry* ed. Donald Allen and Warren Tallman (New York: Grove, 1973), p. 445.

5. Karl Malkoff, "Lawrence Ferlinghetti," *Crowell's Handbook of Contemporary Poetry* (New York: Crowell, 1973), p. 122.

6. Lawrence Ferlinghetti, "Note on Poetry in San Francisco," *Chicago Review* 12, no. 1 (Spring 1958), 4.

7. Michael Benedikt, "Jacques Prevert," *The Poetry of Surrealism: An Anthology* (Boston: Little, 1974), p. 315.

8. Paul Schmidt, "Introduction," *Arthur Rimbaud: Com-*

plete Works, trans. Paul Schmidt (New York: Harper, 1976), p. xiv.

9. Samuel Charters, p. 81.

10. Kenneth Patchen, "Patchen Interviewed by Gene Detro," *Outsider* 2, no. 4/5 (Winter, 1968/1969):121.

11. Malkoff, p. 123.

12. Ferlinghetti, *The San Francisco Poets,* p. 154.

13. Ferlinghetti, personal interview.

14. Andre Breton, *Manifestoes of Surrealism,* trans. Richard Seaver and Helen R. Lane (Ann Arbor: Univ. of Michigan, 1972), pp. 4–5.

15. See Herbert Marcuse, *Eros and Civilization* (Boston: Beacon, 1974).

16. Ferlinghetti, *The San Francisco Poets,* p. 154.

17. Roger Shattuck, "Introduction," *Selected Writings of Guillaume Apollinaire,* trans. Roger Shattuck (New York: New Directions, 1971), p. 5.

18. Shattuck, p. 6.

19. Cherkovski, p. 98.

20. Lawrence Ferlinghetti, *Northwest Ecolog* (San Francisco: City Lights, 1978), p. 52. All further references to this book, designated as *Northwest,* will be given parenthetically in the text.

21. Lawrence Ferlinghetti, *"Tentative Description of a Dinner Given to Promote the Impeachment of President Eisenhower" and Other Poems* (Fantasy Records 7004), cover notes.

22. Jean-Paul Sartre, *What Is Literature?* (New York: Harper, 1965), p. 40.

23. Sartre, p. 43.

24. Lawrence Ferlinghetti, "Horn on 'HOWL'," 146.

25. Ferlinghetti, "Note on the Poetry of San Francisco," p. 4.

26. Kenneth Patchen, *Collected Poems* (New York: New Directions, 1968), pp. 160–61.

27. Kenneth Patchen, "Patchen Interviewed," p. 217.

28. Edward-Lucie Smith, "Lawrence Ferlinghetti," *Contemporary Poets* (New York: St. Martin's), p. 359.

29. Ferlinghetti, *The San Francisco Poets,* p. 145.

30. Ibid., p. 146.

31. Kenneth Rexroth, *American Poetry in the Twentieth Century* (New York: Herder & Herder, 1971), p. 166.

32. Lawrence Ferlinghetti, "Modern Poetry Is Prose (But It Is Saying Plenty): Third Populist Manifesto," in *Literature & the Urban Experience* (Rutgers Univ. Pr., 1981), p. 9.

33. David Meltzer, "Golden Gate: Introductory Materials," *The San Francisco Poets* (New York: Ballantine, 1971), pp. 43–47.

34. Cherkovski, p. 205.

3. The Poetry

1. For examples of critical attacks based on personalities see Vernon Young, "Poetry in Review," *Parnassus* (Spring/Summer, 1974), pp. 170–71; Joscha Kessler, "Sentimental Trifles in Frisco Vein," *Los Angeles Times*, 20 July 1969, 49.

2. Crale D. Hopkins, "The Poetry of Lawrence Ferlinghetti: A Reconsideration," *Italian Americana*, ed. Ruth Palbo and Richard Gambino (Autumn 1974), 74; Vincent McHugh, *San Francisco Chronicle*, 5 March 1961, p. 27.

4. Samuel Charters, "Lawrence Ferlinghetti," *Some Poems*, p. 77.

5. Alan Dugan, review of Lawrence Ferlinghetti's *Starting from San Francisco, Poetry*, 100 (Aug. 1962), 314. Note that the first edition of the book was issued with a small recording of the poet reading the major poems of the collection.

6. Lawrence Ferlinghetti, "Note on Poetry in San Francisco," p. 4.

7. Dugan, 315.

8. Ibid.

9. Ibid., p. 316.

10. Kenneth Rexroth, *American Poetry in the Twentieth Century*, p. 166.

11. A. Poulin, Jr., "Lawrence Ferlinghetti," *Contemporary American Poetry*, ed. A. Poulin, Jr. (Boston: Houghton, 1975), p. 430.

12. Ihab Hassan, *Contemporary American Literature* (New York: Ungar, 1973), p. 117.

13. J. M. Warner, 2556.

14. Lawrence Ferlinghetti, "Genesis of *After the Cries of the Birds*," pp. 445–46.

15. Jack Kerouac, "The Origin of Joy in Poetry," *Chicago Review* 12, no. 1 (Spring 1958): 3.

16. Kerouac, "The Origin," p. 3.

17. Norman Mailer, *The White Negro* (San Francisco: City Lights, 1957). My pagination, beginning with first page of text, p. 11.

18. Ferlinghetti, in Cherkovski, p. 43.

19. Lawrence Ferlinghetti, quoted in Ihaab Hassan, *Contemporary American Literature*, pp. 116–17.

20. Ferlinghetti, in Cherkovski, p. 71.

21. Ibid.

22. Ferlinghetti, personal interview.

23. Ibid.,

24. Charles Olson, "Projective Verse vs. The NON-Projective," p. 387.

25. Rexroth, *American Poetry in the Twentieth Century*, p. 142.

26. Olson, pp. 387–88.

27. Olson, p. 395.

28. Ferlinghetti, *The San Francisco Poets*, pp. 158–59.

29. Ibid., p. 152.

30. Ibid., p. 153.

31. Andre Breton, *Manifestoes of Surrealism*, p. 26.

32. Ferlinghetti, *The San Francisco Poets*, p. 154.

33. Pierre Reverdy, quoted in *The Poetry of Surrealism*, ed. Michael Benedikt, p. xix.

34. Andre Breton, quoted in *The Poetry of Surrealism*, ed. Michael Benedikt, p. xx.

35. Paul Eluard, "Donner a voir," quoted in J. H. Matthews, *The Imagery of Surrealism* (Syracuse, New York: Syracuse Univ. Pr., 1977), p. 185.

36. Toyen, quoted in *The Imagery of Surrealism*, p. 154.

37. Paul Eluard, "Coeur a pic," quoted in Mary Ann

Caws, *The Poetry of Dada and Surrealism* (Princeton: Princeton Univ. Pr., 1970), p. 142.

38. Michael Benedikt, "Introduction," *The Prose Poem: An International Anthology* (New York: Dell, 1976), pp. 39–50.

39. Lawrence Ferlinghetti, "Endless Life," in *Endless Life: Selected Poems* (New York: New Directions, 1981), p. 214. All further references to this book, designated as *Endless*, will be given parenthetically in the text.

4. The Theatre

1. Ferlinghetti, "Notes on the Plays," *Unfair Arguments with Existence*, p. vi. Note that in subsequent editions two plays were cut: "The Soldiers of No Country" and "The Nose of Sisyphus." Though not noted as revised editions, the omissions occur in the fifth and subsequent printings.

2. Early productions of Ferlinghetti's plays occurred at the following dates and places: "The Alligation": June 1962 at San Francisco Poetry Festival, directed by Lee Breuer; Nov.–Dec. 1962 Houston, Tex., directed by Ned Bobkoff; "The Customs Collector in Baggy Pants": 1965 in New York by R. G. Davis Mime Troupe; then by Warren Finnerty for Provincetown Theatre, New York; "The Nose of Sisyphus": Sydney Univ., 1965; "Victims of Amnesia": Antioch Univ., 1965; "Soldiers of No Country" and "Victims of Amnesia": Bleeker Street Workshop, 1965. The plays continue to be performed by high school, university, and drama clubs throughout the English-speaking world: by 1981, no fewer than 115 different productions had been made.

3. Ferlinghetti, "Notes on Routines," pp. 2–3.

4. Richard Duerden, review of *Unfair Arguments with Existence*, *Poetry*, (May 1966): pp. 125–26.

5. Clive Barnes, review of "Three by Ferlinghetti," *The New York Times*, 13 Sept. 1970.

6. John Simon, review of "Three by Ferlinghetti," *New York Magazine* (5 Oct. 1970).

7. Lawrence Ferlinghetti, quoted in *City Lights Journal*, no. 3 (1966), p. 5.

8. Antonin Artaud, *The Theatre and Its Double* (New York: Grove Pr., 1958), p. 85.

9. Susan Sontag, "Against Interpretation," *Against Interpretation and Other Essays* (New York: Dell, 1966), p. 17.

10. Artaud, p. 28.

11. Martin Esslin, *The Theatre of the Absurd* (Garden City, N.Y.: Doubleday, 1969), p. 366.

12. Sontag, pp. 143–44.

13. Esslin, pp. 352–53.

5. The Prose

1. Ferlinghetti, personal interview.

2. Ibid.

3. Vincent McHugh, review of Lawrence Ferlinghetti's *Her*, *The San Francisco Chronicle*, 5 Mar. 1961.

4. See Dorothy Nyren, review of Lawrence Ferlinghetti's *Her*, *Library Journal* 85 (15 Nov. 1960): 4162; cover notes of *Her*; Michael Skau, "Toward Underivative Creation: Lawrence Ferlinghetti's *Her*," *Critique: Studies in Modern Fiction* 19, no. 3 (1978): 40–46.

5. Albert Camus, *Notebooks 1935–1942* (New York: Random, 1963), p. 44.

6. Ezra Pound, "Canto LIII," in *Selected Poems* (New York: New Directions, 1957), p. 147.

7. Philip Stevick, "Introduction," *Anti-Story* (New York: Free Pr., 1971), p. xxi.

8. Ferlinghetti, *The San Francisco Poets*, p. 157.

9. Daniel Leary, review of Lawrence Ferlinghetti's *Her*, *Minnesota Review*, (Summer 1961) p. 505.

10. Skau, 45.

11. Skau, 40.

12. Skau, 44.

13. McHugh, p. 27.

14. J. H. Matthews, *An Introduction to Surrealism* (University Park: Pennsylvania State Univ. Pr., 1965), p. 163.

15. Thomas Parkinson, "Phenomenon or Generation," *A Casebook on the Beat* (New York: Crowell, 1961), p. 288.

16. Ferlinghetti, personal interview.

17. An excerpt from "Her Too" entitled "Prose in the Style of *Her*" has appeared; (New York: Nadja Pr., 1980).

18. Pierre Lepape, *Her*, cover notes.

6. Toward New Conclusions

1. Crale D. Hopkins, "The Poetry of Lawrence Ferlinghetti: A Reconsideration," *Italian Americana*, eds. Ruth Palbo and Richard Gambino (Autumn 1974), p. 63.

SELECTED BIBLIOGRAPHY

Lawrence Ferlinghetti— Bibliography of Primary Sources in Chronological Order

1. The Writings

Pictures of the Gone World. San Francisco: City Lights (Pocket Poets Series no. 1), 1955.

A Coney Island of the Mind. Norfolk, Conn.: New Directions, 1958. (Includes *A Coney Island of the Mind*, "Oral Messages," and selections from *Pictures of the Gone World*.)

Tentative Description of a Dinner Given to Promote the Impeachment of President Eisenhower. San Francisco: Golden Mountain Pr., 1958. (Wrappers)

Her. Norfolk, Conn.: New Directions, 1960.

One Thousand Fearful Words for Fidel Castro. San Francisco: City Lights, 1961. (Broadside)

Berlin. San Francisco: Golden Mountain Pr., 1961. (Wrappers)

Starting from San Francisco. Norfolk, Conn.: New Directions, 1961. Revised edition, enlarged, 1967. (First issue included a recording of Ferlinghetti reading.)

Dear Ferlinghetti. San Francisco: White Rabbit Pr., 1962. (With Jack Spicer, wrappers).

Modern Poets 5: Gregory Corso, Lawrence Ferlinghetti, Allen Ginsberg. London: Penguin, 1963.

Thoughts of a Concerto of Telemann. San Francisco: San Francisco Arts Festival Commission, 1963. (Broadside)

Unfair Arguments with Existence. New York: New Directions, 1963.

Routines. New York: New Directions, 1964.

Where Is Vietnam?. San Francisco: City Lights, 1965. (Broadside)

To Fuck Is to Love Again. New York: Fuck You Pr., 1965. (Wrappers)

Lawrence Ferlinghetti. Spoleto, Italy: Spoleto Festival, 1965. (English and Italian mimeograph sheets)

Christ Climbed Down. Syracuse, N.Y.: Syracuse Univ., 1965. (Broadside)

After the Cries of the Birds. San Francisco: Dave Hasselwood Books, 1967. (Wrappers)

Moscow in the Wilderness, Segovia in the Snow. San Francisco: Beach Books, 1967. (Broadside)

An Eye on the World: Selected Poems. London: MacGibbon and Kee, 1967.

Repeat After Me. Boston: Impressions Workshop, ca. 1967. (Broadside)

Fuclock. London: Fire Publications, 1968. (Broadside)

The Secret Meaning of Things. New York: New Directions, 1968.

Tyrannus Nix?. New York: New Directions, 1969. Rev. 1973 with addition of wrap-around band *Watergate Rap 1969–1973*.

The Mexican Night. New York: New Directions, 1970. (Includes illustrations by the author)

Sometime During Eternity. Conshohocken: Poster Prints, ca. 1970. (Broadside)

The World Is a Beautiful Place. Conshohocken: Poster Prints, ca. 1970. (Broadside)

Back Roads to Far Towns After Basho. San Francisco: Privately printed, 1970. (Wrappers)

Back Roads to Far Places. New York: New Directions, 1971. (Includes illustrations by the author)

Love Is No Stone on the Moon. Berkeley: Arif Pr., 1971. (Wrappers)

The Illustrated Wilfred Funk. San Francisco: City Lights, 1971. (Wrappers)

A World Awash with Fascism & Fear. San Francisco: Cranium Pr., 1971. (Broadside)

Open Eye. Melbourne, Australia: Sun Books, 1972. (Wrappers, bound back-to-back with *Open Head* by Allen Ginsberg)

Open Eye. Cambridge, Mass.: Pomegranate Pr., 1973. (Broadside)

Open Eye, Open Heart. New York: New Directions, 1973.

Constantly Risking Absurdity. Brockport, New York: Dept. of English, State Univ. College, 1973. (Wrappers)

Soon It Will Be Night. N.p.: Privately printed, ca. 1975.

Populist Manifesto. San Francisco: Cranium Pr., 1975. Rev. edition by City Lights.

The Jack of Hearts. San Francisco: City Lights, ca. 1975. (Broadside)

Director of Alienation. San Francisco: City Lights, ca. 1975. (Broadside)

Who Are We Now?. New York: New Directions, 1976.

A Political Pamphlet. San Francisco: Anarchist Resistance Pr., 1976. (Wrappers)

White on White. San Francisco: City Lights, 1977. (Broadside)

Northwest Ecolog. San Francisco: City Lights, 1978. (Includes illustrations by the author)

Ferlinghetti: Adieu a Charlot. San Francisco: City Lights, 1978. (Broadside)

Landscapes of Living and Dying. New York: New Directions, 1979.

The Sea & Ourselves at Cape Ann. Madison, Wis.: Red Ozier, 1979. (Wrappers)

Literary San Francisco: A Pictorial History, coedited with text by Lawrence Ferlinghetti and Nancy Joyce Peters. New York: Harper & Row and San Francisco: City Lights, 1980.

A Trip to Italy and France. New York: New Directions, 1980.

Endless Life: Selected Poems. New York: New Directions, 1981.

"Third Populist Manifesto: Modern Poetry is Prose (But It Is Saying Plenty)," in *Literature & the Urban Experience: Essays on the City and Literature* ed. Michael C. Jaye and Ann Chalmers Watts. New Brunswick, N.J.: Rutgers Univ. Pr., 1981, pp. 3–9.

Populist Manifestoes. San Francisco: Grey Fox Pr., 1981.

2. *Editorships*

Beatitude. San Francisco, 1960. Coedited with Bob Kaufman, John Kelley, William J. Margolis, Allen Ginsberg.

Journal for the Protection of All Beings no. 1. San Francisco: City Lights, 1961. Co-edits with David Meltzer and Michael McClure.

City Lights Journal no. 1. San Francisco: City Lights, 1963.

City Lights Journal no. 2. San Francisco: City Lights, 1964.

City Lights Journal no. 3. San Francisco: City Lights, 1965.

Journal for the Protection of All Beings no. 3. San Francisco: City Lights, 1969.

The First Third (Writings by Neal Cassady). San Francisco: City Lights, 1971.

City Lights Anthology. San Francisco: City Lights, 1974.

City Lights Journal no. 4. San Francisco: City Lights, 1978.

3. *Recordings*

San Francisco Poets. Evergreen Records. LP EVR–1, New York, 1957. (Now distributed by Hanover Records, New York)

Poetry Reading in "The Cellar," with Kenneth Rexroth and Lawrence Ferlinghetti LP7002 Berkeley: Fantasy Records, 1958.

Tentative Description of a Dinner to Impeach President Eisenhower & Other Poems LP7004 Berkeley: Fantasy Records, 1959.

Lawrence Ferlinghetti Reading at Better Books. London: Better Books, 1965.

The World's Great Poets, Vol. 1, with Allen Ginsberg and Gregory Corso, Spoleto Festival, 1965, CMS LP617, 1971.

Contemporary American Poets Read Their Works: Lawrence Ferlinghetti C–502, 1972.

Tyrannus Nix? & Assassination Raga LP7014 Berkeley: Fantasy Records, 1971.

4. *Films*

Have You Sold Your Dozen Roses? Filmscript by Lawrence Ferlinghetti, produced by Philip Greene, David Meyers, and Allen Willis at the California School of Fine Arts, 1957. (Black and white, 9 mins.)

U.S.A.Poets: Allen Ginsberg and Lawrence Ferlinghetti. Produced by National Education Television, 1965. (Black and white, 30 mins.)

Tyrannus Nix? Produced by National Education Television, 1969.

Assassination Raga. Produced by Max Crosley, 1973.

The Old Italians Dying. Produced by Herman Berlandt, San Francisco, 1980.

5. *Translations*

Paroles by Jacques Prévert. San Francisco: City Lights (Pocket Poets Series no. 9), 1958.

"Spurt Blood" by Antonin Artaud, in *Evergreen Review* 7, no. 28 (Jan.–Feb., 1963).

Dogalypse by Andrei Voznesensky. San Francisco: City Lights (Pocket Poets Series no. 29), 1972. Translations by Lawrence Ferlinghetti, Maureen Sager, Catherine Leach, Robert Bly, Vera Reck, and Vera Dunham.

Love Poems by Karl Marx. San Francisco: City Lights, 1977. Translations by Richard Lettau and Lawrence Ferlinghetti.

Pathe Baby by Blaise Cendrars. San Francisco: City Lights (Pocket Poets Series no. 39), 1980. Translations by Lawrence Ferlinghetti and Mary Beach.

6. *Foreign Editions*

Foreign editions of Ferlinghetti's works, most commonly, *A Coney Island of the Mind*, *Her*, and a *Selected Poems*, have appeared in the following countries: Italy, Argentina, Denmark, France, Japan, China, Germany, Mexico, Czechoslovakia, Hungary, as well as Australia and England.

Secondary Sources

Allen, Donald M., ed. *The New American Poetry*. New York: Grove, 1960. One of the best collections of contemporary American poetry and one which brought attention to the nonacademic poets of the 1950s. It includes poets' statements on their writing.

———, and Warren Tallman, eds. *The Poetics of the New American Poetry*. New York: Grove, 1973. A thorough collection of statements on modern poetics from the poets. It contains Ferlinghetti's "Genesis of *After the Cries of the Birds*."

Benedikt, Michael, ed. *The Prose Poem: An International Anthology*. New York: Dell, 1976. A rare discussion of the prose poem form in the introduction has applications to Ferlinghetti's work.

Blasing, Mutlu. *The Art of Life: Studies in American Autobiographical Literature*. Austin: Univ. of Texas Pr., 1977. Through an examination of Thoreau, Whitman, Henry James, Henry Adams, William Carlos Williams, and Frank O'Hara, Blasing establishes an excellent context for understanding the personalism and personism of American writing. It has direct application to Ferlinghetti's position as poet-at-large.

Charters, Ann. *Kerouac: A Biography*. San Francisco: Straight Arrow Books, 1973. A carefully detailed biography of Jack Kerouac's life and writing; includes a panorama of the San Francisco Beat scene and biographical details of the Ferlinghetti-Kerouac relationship.

Charters, Samuel. *Some Poems/Poets: Studies in American Underground Poetry Since 1945*. Berkeley: Oyez, 1971. Charters's introduction and section on Ferlinghetti (pp. 77–83) locate Ferlinghetti's writing in the contemporary tradition and focus particularly on an analysis of his oral methods in the poem "One Thousand Fearful Words for Fidel Castro."

Cherkovski, Neeli. *Ferlinghetti: A Biography*. Garden City, N.Y.: Doubleday, 1979. In addition to being a very detailed and accurate biography, this book contains rare quotes from interviews with Ferlinghetti and from his notebooks. Though it lacks direct application to the critical appreciation of the writing, it lays the biographical groundwork for further study.

Chicago Review 12, no. 1 (Spring 1958). This issue includes an important early recognition of the poetry "From San Francisco," including Jack Kerouac's introductory "The Origins of Joy in Poetry," and Ferlinghetti's "Note on Poetry in San Francisco."

Duerden, Richard. Review of *Routines. Poetry*, May 1966, pp. 125–26. Duerden is reviewing the book, rather than the plays, here, and he finds Ferlinghetti a natural and adept playwright.

Dugan, Alan. "Three Books, A Pamphlet, and a Broadside." *Poetry* 100 (Aug. 1962):310–19. An important review of Ferlinghetti's *Starting from San Francisco*, for its insight into the oral form and Ferlinghetti's reading method.

Ehrlich, J. W. *Howl of the Censor*. San Carlos, California: Nourse Books. 1961. This book by the chief attorney for the defense in the trial of *HOWL* presents background and analysis of this important censorship trial.

Ellman, Richard and Robert O'Clair. *The Norton Anthology of Modern Poetry*. New York: Norton, 1973. Contains an introduction on the movements of modern and contemporary poetry (American and British) and an ample selection of Ferlinghetti's work with some biographical-critical analysis.

Everson, William. *Archetype West: The Pacific Coast as a Literary Region*. Berkeley: Oyez, 1976. Chapter 15 in particular places Ferlinghetti in the tradition of the West Coast literary archetype, though it grants his cosmopolitan uniqueness.

Evergreen Review 1, no. 2 (1957) and *Evergreen Review* 1, no. 4 (1957). These two issues contain the earliest writing and appraisal of the Beat-San Francisco writing. No. 4 contains Ferlinghetti's "Horn on 'Howl'" article (145–58).

Fiedler, Leslie A. "Into the Cafes: A Kind of a Solution," in *Waiting for the End*. London: Penguin, 1964. Fiedler provides a general though brief assessment of Ferlinghetti as a populist poet.

Haselmayer, Louis A. "Beat Prophet and Beat Wit," *Iowa English Yearbook 6* (Fall 1961), 9–13. Comparison of Ginsberg and Ferlinghetti as examples of the diversity of Beat writing; recognizes the spirit of irony in Ferlinghetti's work.

Hassan Ihab. "Poetry" in *Contemporary American Literature*.

New York: Ungar, 1973, pp. 116–17. Assesses the importance of the publication of *Howl* and links Ferlinghetti with E. E. Cummings and Kenneth Patchen as comic and populist poets.

Hopkins, Crale D. "The Poetry of Lawrence Ferlinghetti: A Reconsideration," in *Italian Americana*, ed. Ruth Falbo and Richard Gambino. 1974, pp. 59–76. Hopkins provides one of the most thorough and positive analyses of Ferlinghetti's work, form and function, in directing a reconsideration of his literary contribution.

Ianni, L. A. "Lawrence Ferlinghetti's Fourth Person Singular and the Theory of Relativity," *Wisconsin Studies in Contemporary Literature* 8 (Summer 1967): 392–406. An analysis of the theme and form of *Her* based on the philosophy of relativity.

Jouffroy, Alain. "Lawrence Ferlinghetti," *Les Temps Modernes*, No. 223 (Dec. 1964), pp. 990–95. Recognizes convergence of Ferlinghetti's militant pacifism and spirituality as international qualities linking his work with the Beat Movement and the writings of Artaud, Michaud, Prevert, Voznesensky; also analyzes the oral narrative form of his poetry.

Kerouac, Jack. *Big Sir*. London: Granada Publishing, 1980. This 1963 novel records Kerouac's stay at Ferlinghetti's Bixby Canyon cabin. Ferlinghetti is presented as fictional character Lorenzo Monsanto. Ferlinghetti also appears as fictionalized character "Larry O'Hara" in Kerouac's *The Subterraneans* (New York: Grove, 1958) and as "Danny Richman" in *Book of Dreams* (San Francisco: City Lights, 1960) and *Visions of Cody* (New York: New Directions, 1960).

Kherdian, David. *Six Poets of the San Francisco Renaissance: Portraits and Checklists*. Fresno, Calif.: Giligia Pr., 1967. Kherdian provides an introduction to the San Francisco Renaissance and a personal portrait of Ferlinghetti and City Lights Books. His checklist is briefly annotated and somewhat dated.

Krim, Seymour. *The Beats*. Greenwich, Conn.: Fawcett, 1960. One of the earliest critical assessments of the Beat Movement.

Lee, Lawrence and Barry Gifford. *Jack's Book: An Oral Biography of Jack Kerouac*. New York: Penguin, 1979. This excellent collection of various oral portraits of Jack Kerouac also provides a revealing panorama of the Beat scene and interview comments from Ferlinghetti among a host of others.

Leary, Daniel. Review of *Her. Minnesota Review*, Summer 1961, p. 505. Good critical analysis of *Her* for reality theme and cinematic methods.

Leper, Gary M. "Lawrence Ferlinghetti," in *A Bibliographical Introduction to Seventy-Five Modern American Authors*. Berkeley: Serendipity Books, 1976. A limited checklist of Ferlinghetti's publications in book broadside, and pamphlet form.

Lipton, Lawrence. *The Holy Barbarians*. New York: Julian Messner Books, 1959. Chapter 12, in particular, treats the poetry-and-jazz phenomenon, though from a slanted perspective.

Lowenfels, Walter, ed. *Where Is Vietnam?* Garden City, New York: Doubleday, 1967. This provocative anthology contains Ferlinghetti's preface and poem.

Lucie-Smith, Edward. "Lawrence Ferlinghetti," in *Contemporary Poets*, ed. Rosalie Murphy and James Vinson. New York: St. Martin's, 1970. pp. 357–59. An assessment of Ferlinghetti as an essential spokesman of the times.

McClure, Michael. *Meat Science Essays*. San Francisco: City Lights, 1963. Contains Ferlinghetti's introductory "A Note on Meat Science Essays."

McDonald, Gerald D. "Lawrence Ferlinghetti. A Coney Island of the Mind," *Library Journal* 15 (June 1958): 1937–1938. This early review spotlights Ferlinghetti's innovative form and direction; compares it briefly with Eliot's *The Waste Land*.

McHugh, Vincent. Review of *Her. San Francisco Chronicle*, 5 Mar. 1961. Contains high praise for the anti-novel *Her* as a major prose achievement in the contemporary period.

Malkoff, Karl. "Lawrence Ferlinghetti," *Crowell's Handbook to Contemporary American Poetry*. New York: Crowell, 1973, pp. 120–25. Malkoff provides an excellent analysis of

Ferlinghetti's position and his poetic methods as demonstrated in several poems.

Meltzer, David. ed. *The San Francisco Poets.* New York: Ballantine Books, 1971. An excellent source for the San Francisco Renaissance in Poetry; contains the editor's "Golden Gate: Introduction," an excellent interview with Lawrence Ferlinghetti, as well as interviews with West Coast peers—Kenneth Rexroth, Lew Welch, Michael McClure, William Everson, and Richard Brautigan. The book has also appeared in a revised edition as *Golden Gate* (Berkeley: Wingbow, 1976).

Metzger, C. R. "Lawrence Ferlinghetti as Elphin's Bard," *Midwest Quarterly* (Autumn 1974), pp. 25–41. An interesting analysis of the oral basis of Ferlinghetti's work in the Celtic and Druid bards of ancient literature, as well as a comparison with Robert Graves's *White Goddess.*

Morgan, Bill. *Lawrence Ferlinghetti: A Descriptive Bibliography.* New York: Garland Publications, 1981. An exhaustive list of primary and secondary sources with an extensive description of each; an important critical tool for future study of Ferlinghetti.

Nyren, Dorothy. Review of Lawrence Ferlinghetti's *Her, Library Journal* 85 (15 Nov. 1960): 4162. An early review of *Her* which briefly compares it with the writings of James Joyce and Guillaume Apollinaire.

Parkinson, Thomas F. ed. *A Casebook on the Beat.* New York: Crowell, 1961. An early collection of writing by and about the Beat Movement; contains Parkinson's "Phenomenon or Generation" analysis of underlying engagement of the movement and Ferlinghetti's poems and essays, "Horn on *HOWL*" and "Note on Poetry in San Francisco."

Poulin, A., Jr. *Contemporary American Poetry.* Boston: Houghton Mifflin, 1975. Contains work by Ferlinghetti as well as an analysis of his place as an oral poet of the streets.

Rexroth, Kenneth. *American Poetry in the Twentieth Century.* New York: Herder & Herder, 1971. Rexroth attempts to cover the gamut of contemporary writing in America; includes a background on the San Francisco Renaissance

(Chap. 11) and a brief appraisal of Ferlinghetti as poet and publisher.

———. *Assays*. New York: New Directions, 1961. A collection of essays with some focus on Ferlinghetti (p. 193), comparing him with Raymond Queneau, Jacques Prévert, Paul Eluard, and E. E. Cummings.

Rosentahl, M. L. "The Naked and the Clad," *Nation* (11 Oct. 1958), 214–15. A strongly positive view of *A Coney Island of the Mind;* compares Ferlinghetti with William Carlos Williams.

Schevill, James. "The Pulsing Voices of the New Poets," *San Francisco Chronicle: This World*, 25 Mar. 1962. Contains a favorable review of Ferlinghetti's *Starting from San Francisco* examining Ferlinghetti's oral methods.

Shapiro, Harvey. "Five Voices in Verse," *The New York Times Book Review* 63 (7 Sept. 1958):10. An early favorable review of *A Coney Island of the Mind*, though it mistakenly characterizes Ferlinghetti as a "hipster."

Simon, John. Review of *Three by Ferlinghetti. New York Magazine*, 5 Oct. 1970. Simon mixes praise and derision in this review of the off-Broadway production of three of Ferlinghetti's plays.

Skau, Michael. "Toward Underivative Creation: Lawrence Ferlinghetti's *Her*," in *Critique: Studies in Modern Fiction* 19 (1978), no. 3, 40–46. One of the rare and important critiques of Ferlinghetti's *Her*. It locates the themes and forms and demonstrates their relationship through the narrative perspective.

Smith, Larry. *Kenneth Patchen*. Boston: Twayne, 1978. See in particular the engaged and functional poetics of Patchen which parallel Ferlinghetti's and the section on poetry-and-jazz for chronology and formal dynamics.

———. Personal interview with Lawrence Ferlinghetti, June 7 and 8, 1980, at 250 Francisco Street, San Francisco, California. The interviews were taped, transcribed, then approved by Ferlinghetti. They appeared in the special Ferlinghetti issue of *Pig Iron* magazine, 1982.

———. Review of *Northwest Ecolog. Northeast Rising Sun*, Summer 1980. Reviews Ferlinghetti's poetry and prose in this journal book form. Features analysis of "prose/" technique and of Ferlinghetti's mature perspective.

———. "The Poetry-and-Jazz Movement of the United States," *Itinerary* 7 (Fall 1977): 89–104. An overview of the Poetry-and-Jazz Movement with particular attention to the work of Ferlinghetti, Rexroth, and Patchen.

Street, Douglas O. "A Phoenix at Fifty," *Prairie Schooner* (Fall 1974): 275–76. A review of *Open Eye, Open Heart* as socio-political statement and as functional poetics.

Stevick, Philip. "Introduction" to *Anti-Story*. New York: Free Pr., 1971. Excellent discussion of anti-story and anti-novel forms; offers indirect insight into Ferlinghetti's *Her*.

Tytell, John. *Naked Angels: The Lives & Literature of the Beat Generation*. New York: McGraw-Hill, 1976. Analysis of Ginsberg, Kerouac, and Burroughs as key figures in the Beat Movement; contains some analysis of the role of City Lights in the whole counter-cultural movement.

Vane, Thaddeua. "Lawrence Ferlinghetti: A Candid Conversation with the Man Who Founded the Beat Generation," *Penthouse: The Magazine for Men* 1, no. 4 (Aug. 1965): 24, 26, 71–73. Though somewhat off focus in its title, Ferlinghetti discusses his relationship with the Beat Movement and San Francisco.

Warner, J. M. Review of *Open Eye, Open Heart*. *Library Journal* 98 (15 Sept. 1973): 2559. A favorable review of this collection of Ferlinghetti's poems, seen as a landmark in his career.

Young, Vernon. "Lawrence Ferlinghetti. *Open Eye, Open Heart*." *Parnassus: Poetry in Review* (Spring/Summer 1974) pp. 170–71. A good example of the irresponsible criticism based on personal attack which Ferlinghetti has been subjected to from established and avant-garde circles alike.

INDEX

Index

LAWRENCE FERLINGHETTI

Designed by Guy Fleming

Composed by G & S Typesetters
in Linotron Palatino

Printed by Thomson-Shore
on Glatfelter B-31, Cream Smooth

Bound by John H. Dekker & Sons
in Holliston Roxite Vellum